LYNN POVICH

· · · · ·

How the Women
of *Newsweek*
Sued their Bosses
and Changed
the Workplace

· · · · ·

THE
GOOD
GIRLS

The inspiration
for the online
television
series

REVOLT

"As compelling as
any novel.... Povich turns this
epic revolt into a lesson on how and
why we've just begun." —Gloria Steinem

Praise for *The Good Girls Revolt*:

"Povich's account of the case unspools with a cinematic energy. . . . But *The Good Girls Revolt* is powerful in part because it doesn't seek to tie up the messy, imperfect, real-life events with a neat bow of made-for-TV, proto-you-go-girl closure. . . . In delving into a piece of women's history and exploring its legacy for women today, *The Good Girls Revolt* is both a compelling case study and a reminder that we shouldn't be too quick to append the prefix 'post' to the word 'feminism.'"
   —*Los Angeles Review of Books*

"A powerful chronicle of how—in the context of wider social ferment—institutions can be forced to evolve. . . . [Povich] does not shy away from the emotional and political complexity of feminist struggle."   —*Ms. Magazine*

"*The Good Girls Revolt* is as compelling as any novel, and also an accurate, intimate history of new women journalists invading the male journalistic world of the 1970s. Lynn Povich turns this epic revolt into a lesson on why and how we've just begun."
   —Gloria Steinem

"The personal and the political are deftly interwoven in the fast-moving narrative. . . . *The Good Girls Revolt* has many timely lessons for working women who are concerned about discrimination today. . . . [T]his sparkling, informative book may help move these goals a tiny bit closer."
   —*New York Times*

"A meticulously reported and highly readable account of a pivotal time in the women's movement."   —Jeannette Walls

"Feminist history at its best. Povich evokes, with clear-eyed affection and a keen sense of history the heady atmosphere of 'Swinging Sixties'-era *Newsweek*: a real-life Mad Men with a social

conscience and sense of mission. . . . The transformation of Povich—who subsequently became *Newsweek*'s first female senior editor—and her colleagues from polite, deferential girls to women of courage forms the heart of this lively, engaging book."
    —Publishers Weekly

"Solidly researched and should interest readers who care about feminist history and how gender issues play out in the culture."
    —Boston Globe

"Povich's memoir of the tortuous, landmark battle that paved the way for a generation of female writers and editors is illuminating in its details [and] casts valuable perspective on a trailblazing case that shouldn't be forgotten."   **—Macleans**

"[Povich] strikes a fair tone, neither naïve nor sanctimonious. . . . Among her achievements is a complex portrait of *Newsweek* editor Osborn Elliott and his path from defensive adversary to understanding ally."   **—American Journalism Review**

"Crisp, revealing. . . . [A] taut, firsthand account of how a group of razor-sharp, courageous women successfully fought back against institutional sexism at one of the country's most esteemed publications."   **—Washingtonian**

"Women still have a long way to go, the journalist Lynn Povich rousingly reminds readers in *The Good Girls Revolt*, her fascinating (and long overdue) history of the class-action lawsuit undertaken by four dozen female researchers and underlings at *Newsweek* magazine four decades ago. . . . If ever a book could remind women to keep their white gloves off and to keep fighting the good fight, this is the one."
    —Liesl Schillinger, *New York Times*

"Povich's in-depth research, narrative skills, and eyewitness observations provide an entertaining and edifying look at a pivotal event in women's history."   —*Kirkus Reviews*

"With vivid recollections of the author and major and minor participants, Povich, a party to the suit, succeeds in making recent history enraging, poignant, and even sexy."
—*Philadelphia Inquirer*

"[H]er storytelling is compelling and she ably makes the case for the debt still owed to all forty-six *Newsweek* women for their willingness to 'take off the white gloves.' Quickly-paced social history for media, feminism, and history buffs."
—*Library Journal*

"A painstakingly researched story of one of the seminal events affecting the rights of women in the American work place in the early years of the women's movement. . . . I would recommend this volume especially to young women who were born long after the struggles fought by their mothers and grandmothers."
—Rabbi John Rosove, JewishJournal.com

"*The Good Girls Revolt* . . . is a book that needed to be written. Those of us who came of age during those years can relate to the courage it took to fight for equality. . . . This story is not just a Who's Who of feminist achievement, but an honest portrayal of the battles of a few meant to benefit not only themselves but those who came after them. Young women of today will benefit from being reminded about what it took to secure their places in today's workplace and far beyond."
—*New York Journal of Books*

THE
GOOD GIRLS
REVOLT

How the Women of *Newsweek*
Sued their Bosses and Changed the Workplace

Lynn Povich

PUBLICAFFAIRS
New York

Published in the United States by PublicAffairs™, an imprint of Perseus Books, a division of PBG Publishing, LLC, a subsidiary of Hachette Book Group, Inc. First paperback edition published in 2016 by PublicAffairs

Printed in the United States of America.

PublicAffairs books are available at special discounts for bulk purchases in the U.S. by corporations, institutions, and other organizations. For more information, please contact the Special Markets Department at Perseus Books, 2300 Chestnut Street, Suite 200, Philadelphia, PA 19103, call (800) 810-4145, ext. 5000, or e-mail special.markets@perseusbooks.com.

Book Design by Pauline Brown
Typeset in 11.75 point Adobe Garamond Pro by the Perseus Books Group

The Library of Congress has cataloged the printed edition as follows:
Library of Congress Cataloging-in-Publication Data

Povich, Lynn.
     The good girls revolt : how the women of Newsweek sued their bosses and changed the workplace / Lynn Povich.—1st ed.
          p.   cm.
     Includes bibliographical references and index.
     ISBN 978-1-61039-173-3 (hardcover)—ISBN 978-1-61039-326-3 (paperback)—ISBN 978-1-61039-174-0 (electronic)
     1. Sex role in the work environment—United States. 2. Sex discrimination in employment—United States. 3. Women journalists—United States. 4. Newsweek. I. Title.
     HD6060.5.U5P65   2012
     331.4'81070572—dc23

ISBN 978-1-61039-746-9 (2016 paperback)

10 9 8 7 6 5 4 3 2

For Steve, Sarah, and Ned
and for the *Newsweek* women

CONTENTS

PROLOGUE   What Was the Problem?   xi

CHAPTER 1   "Editors File Story; Girls File Complaint"   1

CHAPTER 2   "A Newsmagazine Tradition"   15

CHAPTER 3   The "Hot Book"   33

CHAPTER 4   Ring Leaders   51

CHAPTER 5   "You Gotta Take Off Your   71
             White Gloves, Ladies"

CHAPTER 6   Round One   93

CHAPTER 7   Mad Men: The Boys Fight Back   111

CHAPTER 8   The Steel Magnolia   125

CHAPTER 9   "Joe—Surrender"   139

CHAPTER 10   The Barricades Fell   161

CHAPTER 11   Passing the Torch   181

EPILOGUE   Where They Are Now   201

             The Good Girls Who Signed On   223
             Acknowledgments   225
             Note on Sources   227
             Bibliography   237
             Reader's Guide   239
             Index   253

Photo insert between pages 124–125

PROLOGUE

WHAT WAS THE PROBLEM?

J ESSICA BENNETT GREW UP in the era of Girl Power. It was the 1980s, when young women were told there was no limit to what they could accomplish. The daughter of a Seattle attorney, Jessica regularly attended Take Your Daughter to Work Day with her dad and was the academic star in her family, excelling over her younger brothers and male peers. In high school, she was a member of Junior Statesmen of America, a principal in the school orchestra, and a varsity soccer player. Jessica was accepted to the University of Southern California, her first choice, but transferred after freshman year to Boston University because it had a stronger journalism program. When the *Boston Globe* offered a single internship to a BU student, she was the recipient.

Then Jessica got a job at *Newsweek* and suddenly encountered obstacles she couldn't explain. She had started as an intern on the magazine in January 2006 and was about to be hired when three guys showed up for summer internships. At the end of the summer, the men were offered jobs but Jessica wasn't, even though she was given one of their stories to rewrite. Despite the fact that she was writing three times a week on *Newsweek*'s website, her internship kept getting extended. Even after she was hired in January 2007, Jessica had to battle to get her articles published, while guys with the same or less experience were getting better assignments and faster promotions. "Initially I didn't identify it as a gender issue," she recalled. "But several of us women had been feeling like we weren't doing a good job or accomplishing what we wanted to. We didn't feel like we were being heard."

Being female was not something that ever held Jessica back. "I was used to getting everything I wanted and working hard for it," said the twenty-eight-year-old writer at Newsweek.com, "so my feeling was, why do I need feminism? Why do I need to take a women's studies course? And, of course, there was the stereotype of the feminist—the angry, man-hating, granola-crunching, combat-boot-wearing woman. I don't know that I consciously thought that, but I think a lot of young women do. I went to public school in the inner city, so issues of racial justice were more interesting to me than gender because, frankly, gender wasn't really an issue."

Her best friend at *Newsweek*, Jesse Ellison, was also frustrated. She had recently discovered that the guy who replaced her in her previous job was given a significantly higher salary. She was doing well as the number two to the editor of Scope, the opening section of the magazine that featured inside scoops and breaking news. But that summer, a half-dozen college-age "dudes" had come in as summer interns and suddenly the department turned into a frat house. Guys were high-fiving, turning the TV from CNN to ESPN, constantly invading her cubicle, and asking her, as if she were their mother, whether they should microwave their lunches. They were also getting assigned stories while she had to pitch all her ideas. Since a new boss had taken over, Jesse felt as if she had been demoted. She didn't know what to do.

Jesse, thirty, sought the advice of a trusted editor who had been a mentor to her. He told her, "You're senior to them—shame them." Then he said, "The problem is that you're so pretty you need to figure out a way to use your sexuality to your advantage," she recalled, still incredulous about the remark. "Even though I think he was just being an idiot for saying this—because he had really fought for me—hearing that changed my perception of the previous six months. I was like, 'Wait a minute! Were you being an advocate for me because you think I'm pretty and you want me in your office? And, more important, is this what other people in the office think? Not that I'm actually talented, but this is about something else?' It really screwed with my head."

Jesse had grown up in a conservative town outside Portland, Maine. Her mother, a former hippie who was divorced, had started a small baby-accessories business. During the Clarence Thomas Supreme Court hearings, Jesse was the only one in her eighth-grade class to support Anita Hill. She went to a coed boarding school, where she was valedictorian of her class, and then to Barnard, an all-women's college, where she graduated cum laude. She, too, never took a women's studies course. "I just felt like I didn't need it," she said. "Feminism was a given—it was Barnard!" After a brief job at a nonprofit, she enrolled part-time in Columbia University's Graduate School of Journalism. She also got an internship on the foreign language editions of *Newsweek* and was hired full-time when she graduated with her master's degree in June 2008. But now, a year later, she, too, was struggling to move ahead at *Newsweek*. What was the problem?

"It wasn't like I believed that sexism *didn't* exist," said Jesse. "It was just that it didn't occur to me that what was happening at work was sexism. Maybe it's because we are a highly individualized culture now and I had always done really well. So I just assumed that everything that was happening was on the basis of merit. I grew up reading *Newsweek* and I had tremendous respect for it. I felt like, I'm in this world of real thinkers and writers and I have to prove myself. The fact that I wasn't being given assignments was simply an indication that they didn't think I was good enough yet. It didn't occur to me that it was about anything else. For the first time in my life, I was feeling inadequate and insecure."

Jessica Bennett felt the same way. "Maybe it's a female tendency to turn inward and blame yourself, but I never thought about sexism," she said. "We had gotten to the workforce and then something suddenly changed and we didn't know what it was. After all, we had always accomplished everything we had set out to do, so naturally we would think *we* were doing something wrong—not that there *was* something wrong. It was us, not it."

What *was* the problem? After all, women composed nearly 40 percent of the *Newsweek* masthead in 2009. It wasn't like the old days, when there was a ghetto of women in the research department from which they couldn't get promoted. In fact, there were no longer researchers on the magazine, except in the library. Young editorial employees now started as researcher-reporters. There were women writers at *Newsweek,* several female columnists and senior editors, and at least two women in top management. Ann McDaniel, a former *Newsweek* reporter and top editor, was now the managing director of the magazine in charge of both the business and editorial sides—a first. So it couldn't be that old thing called discrimination that was inhibiting their progress. The fight for equality had been won. Women could do anything now at *Newsweek* and elsewhere. Hadn't Maria Shriver's report on American women just come out in October 2009, declaring, "The battle of the sexes is over"?

Jesse and Jessica stewed about the situation, discussing it with other *Newsweek* women and friends outside the magazine, who, it turned out, were also feeling discouraged in their careers. "It felt so good just talking to each other," recalled Jesse. "It was like, 'Oh my God, I'm so sick of feeling silent and scared. It's not fair and we should say something.' That impulse was great; knowing that 'I'm not alone' was empowering."

One day Jen Molina, a *Newsweek* video producer, was talking about the magazine's "old boys club" to Tony Skaggs, a veteran researcher in the library. Tony informed her that many years before, the women at *Newsweek* had sued the magazine's management on the grounds of sex discrimination. Jen was shocked. She had no idea this had happened—and at her own magazine. She told Jessica, who told Jesse, and the two friends began investigating. Jessica immediately Googled "*Newsweek* lawsuit" and "women sue *Newsweek*" but she couldn't find any reference online. "Funny," she remarked, "we're trained in digital journalism, so we think if it's not on Google, it doesn't exist."

A few weeks later, Tony walked into Jessica's office with a worn copy of Susan Brownmiller's vivid chronicle of the women's movement, *In Our Time: Memoir of a Revolution*. A crumpled Post-it note marked the chapter mentioning a lawsuit at *Newsweek* in 1970, almost forty years earlier. "I just remember sitting at my desk reading it," she said, "and every two sentences saying, 'Holy shit,' because I couldn't believe this had happened and I didn't know about it! So I instant-messaged Jesse and said, 'You have to get over here and read this.' Why didn't we know this? Why has this died? And why was there only one person in the research department who had to get this book for us to let us know about it?"

When they read about the case, it all seemed so familiar. "We realized we were far from the first to feel discrimination," said Jesse. "So much of the language and culture was still the same. It helped drive home the fact that it was still the same place, the same institutional knowledge, the same *Newsweek*."

This happened in the fall of 2009, just as a scandal at CBS's *Late Show with David Letterman* was making headlines. Joe

Halderman, a CBS News producer who was living with one of Letterman's assistants, had found her diary revealing her ongoing affair with her boss. Halderman threatened to expose the relationship if Letterman didn't give him $2 million. On October 1, Letterman confessed—on air—that yes, "I have had sex with women who work for me on this show." That same month, ESPN analyst Steve Phillips, a former general manager for the New York Mets baseball team, was fired from the sports network after admitting that he had an affair with a twenty-two-year-old production assistant. In November, editor Sandra Guzman, who was fired from the *New York Post*, filed a complaint against the newspaper and its editor-in-chief alleging "unlawful employment practices and retaliation" as well as sexual harassment and a hostile work environment. (The case is pending in Manhattan federal court.)

The Letterman scandal infuriated Sarah Ball, a twenty-three-year-old Culture reporter at *Newsweek*, particularly after she read an article by a former Letterman writer. "I was galvanized by Nell Scovell's story on VanityFair.com," recalled Sarah, who cited the beginning of the piece by heart: "At this moment, there are more females serving on the United States Supreme Court than there are writing for *Late Show with David Letterman, The Jay Leno Show*, and *The Tonight Show with Conan O'Brien* combined. Out of the fifty or so comedy writers working on these programs, exactly zero are women. It would be funny if it weren't true." Sarah told her editor, Marc Peyser, about the piece and in the course of the conversation, Peyser suggested a story on young women in the workforce, pegged to the scandals. "He was really into it," Sarah recalled. "He kept saying, 'This could be a cover, this could be a cover.'" Sarah, who had seen the Brownmiller book, immediately told Jessica and Jesse about Peyser's interest. The three women went back into his office and pitched a story combining the old and new elements. "It was perfect," said Jesse. "It was bigger than us, we had our own narrative that we felt was important, and there was the forthcoming fortieth anniversary of the lawsuit in March."

Peyser had heard about the lawsuit and told them that it had gone all the way to the US Supreme Court. That night, Jesse started searching online through all the 1970 Supreme Court cases but found nothing mentioning *Newsweek*. "We knew there was something about a lawsuit," she said, "but we didn't know what it meant." Jessica finally paid to search the *New York Times* archives, where several articles on the lawsuit turned up. "I was bouncing out of my chair I was so excited," she said. "We knew we had to do something but it still wasn't clear from those clips whether the suit had been settled or whether it actually went to court."

The three women spent the next few weeks digging deeper and calling various sources, including Susan Brownmiller and some former *Newsweek* women whose names were mentioned in the book. I was one of the women. Jessica and Jesse contacted me when they learned that I was writing about the case. They wanted to find out what had happened and why. They were determined to write a piece for *Newsweek* questioning how much had actually changed for women at the magazine, in the media, and in the workplace in general.

When I met the two young women for lunch, they reminded me so much of my friends and myself forty years earlier. We, too, had been bright young things, full of energy and expectations. We also had been thrilled to be working at an important magazine and we, too, had begun to realize that something wasn't right at *Newsweek*. But if they were post-feminists, we were pre-feminists. Unlike these young women, many of us were far more conflicted about our ambitions and clueless about having a career. My only desire after college was to go to Paris, and I was lucky enough to get a job there as a secretary in the *Newsweek* bureau. I never imagined that five years later, I would be suing the magazine for sex discrimination.

As I listened to Jessica and Jesse struggle to understand what they were feeling—their marginalization, the sexual banter and innuendo, the career cakewalk for men their age—it reminded me of "the problem that had no name" that Betty Friedan had defined in her 1963 groundbreaking book, *The Feminine Mystique*: that "strange stirring, a sense of dissatisfaction" of the American housewife who, "as she made the beds, shopped for groceries, matched slipcover material, ate peanut butter sandwiches with her children, chauffeured Cub Scouts and Brownies, lay beside her husband at night—she was afraid to ask even of herself the silent question—'Is this all?'"

Friedan's "problem" did not apply to working-class women, who had to earn a living but were confined mainly to low-paying jobs. It described the condition of the postwar suburban house-wife. Although many middle-class women had been recruited to work during World War II, they were forced to go home when the soldiers returned. For educated women, whose husbands could support them, *not* having to work was seen as a status symbol until, as Betty Friedan pointed out, many of them realized they wanted—needed—something more than a husband and children.

Finding meaningful work, however, was not easy. In just about every industry, "office work" for women meant secretarial jobs and typing pools. Even in creative fields, such as book publishing, advertising, and journalism, where there was a pool of educated females, women were given menial jobs. In the 1950s, full-time working women earned on average between fifty-nine and sixty-four cents for every dollar men earned in the same job. (It wasn't until the passage of the Equal Pay Act in June 1963 that it became illegal to pay women a lower rate for the same job.) And there were very few professional women. Until around 1970, women comprised fewer than 10 percent of students in medical school, 4 percent of law school students, and only 3 percent of business school students.

At *Newsweek,* our "problem that had no name" in the mid-1960s was sexism, pure and simple. At both *Time* and *Newsweek,* only men were hired as writers. Women were almost always hired on the mail desk or as fact checkers and rarely promoted to reporter or writer. Even with similar credentials, women ended up in lesser positions than men. One year, two Columbia Journalism School graduates were hired—

Paul Zimmerman as a writer and Ann Ray Martin as a researcher/reporter. That's just the way it was, and we all accepted it.

Until we didn't. Just as young women today are discovering that post-feminism isn't really "post," we were discovering that civil rights didn't include women's rights. Just like Jesse, Jessica, and Sarah, we began to realize that something was very wrong with the *Newsweek* system. With great trepidation, we decided to take on what we saw as a massive injustice: a segregated system of journalism that divided research, reporting, writing, and editing roles solely on the basis of gender. We began organizing in secret, terrified that we would be found out—and fired—at any moment. For most of us middle-class ladies, standing up for our rights marked the first time we had done anything political or feminist. It would be the radicalizing act that gave us the confidence and the courage to find ourselves and stake our claim.

***

THIS BOOK IS THE FIRST full account of that landmark *Newsweek* case, the story of how and why we became the first women in the media to sue for sex discrimination. Like *Mad Men,* the popular TV series on life at an advertising agency in the 1960s, not only does our tale reflect the legal and cultural limits for women at the time, but it also is a coming-of-age story about a generation of "good girls" who found ourselves in the revolutionary '60s. But if our pioneering lawsuit has been forgotten by many people, even at *Newsweek,* our fight for women's rights still reverberates with the younger generation.

There have been many victories. Women today have more opportunities and solid legal support. They are more confident, more career-oriented, and more aggressive in getting what they want than most of us were. But many of the injustices that young women face today are the same ones we fought against forty years ago. The discrimination may be subtler, but sexist attitudes still exist.

Jessica, Jesse, and Sarah, and many young women like them, are beginning to understand that legal principles are not the only impediment to power. They see that the rhetoric they were taught—and believed—does not fully exist in the real world; that women still don't have equal rights and equal opportunities; that cultural transformation is harder than legal reform; and that feminism isn't finished. The struggle for social change is still evolving, and now they realize that they are part of it, too.

Here is our story.

CHAPTER 1

"Editors File Story;
Girls File Complaint"

O N MARCH 16, 1970, *Newsweek* magazine hit the newsstands with a cover story on the fledgling feminist
movement titled "Women in Revolt." The bright yellow cover
pictured a naked woman in red silhouette, her head thrown
back, provocatively thrusting her fist through a broken blue
female-sex symbol. As the first copies went on sale that Monday
morning, forty-six female employees of *Newsweek* announced
that we, too, were in revolt. We had just filed a complaint with
the Equal Employment Opportunity Commission charging that
we had been "systematically discriminated against in both hiring and promotion and forced to assume a subsidiary role"
simply because we were women. It was the first time women
in the media had sued on the grounds of sex discrimination

and the story, irresistibly timed to the *Newsweek* cover, was picked up around the world.

"'Discriminate,' le redattrici di *Newsweek?*" (*La Stampa*)
"Newsweek's Sex Revolt" (*London Times*)
"Editors File Story; Girls File Complaint" (*Newsday*)
"Women Get Set for Battle" (*London Daily Express*)
"As Newsweek Says, Women Are in Revolt, Even on Newsweek" (*New York Times*)

The story in the *New York Daily News,* titled "Newshens Sue Newsweek for 'Equal Rights,'" began, "Forty-six women on the staff of *Newsweek* magazine, most of them young and most of them pretty, announced today they were suing the magazine."

The UPI photograph capturing the announcement shows three young white women sitting alongside our attorney, a serious black woman with an imposing Afro. Behind them are pictured several rows of women in their twenties; I am shown standing in the corner with long dark hair. At 10 A.M. our lawyer, Eleanor Holmes Norton, the assistant legal director of the American Civil Liberties Union, began reading a statement to a packed press conference at the ACLU's office at 156 Fifth Avenue. "It is ironic," she said, waving a copy of the magazine, "that while *Newsweek* considers women's grievances newsworthy enough for such major coverage, it continues to maintain a policy of discrimination against the women on its own staff. . . . The statistics speak for themselves—there are more than fifty men writing at *Newsweek,* but only one woman." She pointed out that although the women were graduates of top colleges, held advanced degrees, and had published in major news journals, "*Newsweek*'s caste system relegates women with such credentials to research jobs almost exclusively and interminably."

Eleanor noted that a copy of the complaint had gone to Katharine Graham, publisher of the *Washington Post* and president of the Washington Post Company, which owned *Newsweek*. "The *Newsweek* women believe that as a woman, Mrs. Graham has a particular responsibility to end discrimination against women at her magazine," she said. She called on Mrs. Graham and the editors to negotiate and asked for "the immediate integration of the research staff and the opening of correspondence, writing, and editing positions to women."

Then she opened the floor to questions for the three *Newsweek* women at the table. One reporter asked who was the top woman at the magazine. Lucy Howard, a researcher in the National Affairs department, replied that it was Olga Barbi, who was head of the researchers and had been at *Newsweek* for forty years—which got a big laugh. Then Gabe Pressman, the veteran investigative reporter for local WNBC-TV, pushed his microphone in front of Mary Pleshette, the Movies researcher, and asked whether the discrimination was overt. "Yes," she answered. "There seems to be a gentleman's agreement at *Newsweek* that men are writers and women are researchers and the exceptions are few and far between."

It was an exhilarating moment for us, and a shocking one for *Newsweek*'s editors, who couldn't have been more surprised if their own daughters had risen up in revolt. We had been secretly strategizing for months, whispering behind closed doors, congregating in the *Newsweek* ladies' room, and meeting in our apartments at night. As our numbers increased, we had hired a lawyer and were just reviewing our options when we were suddenly presented with a truly lucky break. In early 1970, *Newsweek*'s editors decided that the new women's liberation movement deserved a cover story. There was one problem, however: there were no women to write the piece.

I was the only female writer on the magazine at the time, but I was very junior. As a researcher at *Newsweek*, I had also done a lot of reporting, and my editor in the Life & Leisure department, Harry Waters, had liked my work and encouraged me. He recommended to our senior editor that I be promoted to a junior writer, and in March 1969, I was. In addition to fashion, I wrote about social trends, including the gay-rights and women's movements. But things weren't going well. The senior editor who promoted me had moved to another department and the new editor thought my stories were too sympathetic to the activists. My copy was often rewritten.

When the idea of doing a women's lib cover was proposed in early 1970, the editors were savvy enough to realize they couldn't have a man write the story. Though I was not experienced enough to tackle a cover story, another woman on the magazine could have written it: Liz Peer, a gifted reporter in *Newsweek*'s Washington bureau. But the editors never reached out to her. (When I asked my editor why they hadn't asked Liz, he told me that although she had been a writer in New York and a foreign correspondent for five years, he "wasn't sure" she could write a *Newsweek* cover.)

Instead, for the first time in the history of the magazine, the editors went outside the staff and hired Helen Dudar, a star writer at the *New York Post,* to do the piece. (Helen's husband, Peter Goldman, was a top writer for *Newsweek.*) That galvanized us. Our case might take years to wind its way through the EEOC backlog, but announcing our lawsuit the morning the "Women in Revolt" cover came out would get us prominent press coverage. We knew that worse than being sued, the publicity would mortify the magazine's editors, who prided themselves on the progressive views and pro–civil rights coverage that put *Newsweek* on the map in the 1960s.

The Sunday night before the press conference, we gathered at Holly Camp's West Eighty-Third Street apartment to prepare for the historic day ahead. We were nervous, excited, and resolute. I felt especially happy for my close friend Judy Gingold, the conscience of our collective. Judy had been the first one to see our situation at *Newsweek* as a moral issue, and against the grain of her good-girl up-bringing, she had pushed us to file a lawsuit. First on our agenda was deciding who would speak at the press conference. Silence. No one wanted to do it. Pat Lynden, a reporter in the New York bureau who never shied from confrontation, finally said, "I'll do it with someone else." Lucy Howard, a good friend of Pat's, stepped up. "I thought if I don't do this, the whole lawsuit will go down the drain," she recalled. "It never occurred to me that I would have to answer a question. I just assumed I would be a warm body and that Eleanor would speak." Then Mary Pleshette proposed that I join them, but I demurred. "As someone who has become a writer, I don't think I should represent the class," I said, throwing it back to her. "Mary, why don't you do it?" Mary, always the first to raise her hand in class, said she would be willing to do it as long as everyone agreed, which they did.

The three spokeswomen moved to a corner to practice answers and to discuss what they would wear (Lucy decided on a pink John Kloss dress, Pat a rose-colored T Jones dress, and Mary a burnt-orange shift). Another group formed to write a release about the Monday press conference, which Susan Agrest's husband would drop off later that night at various news organizations to get the event on their daybooks. The rest of us, with our lawyer's help, drafted a letter to Katharine Graham informing her that we were about to file the suit. "We are writing to you," the letter said, "because we cannot believe that you are fully aware of the extent to which we are discriminated against at *Newsweek*." Then we all chipped in to fly Sunde Smith, a twenty-three-year-old Business researcher, to Washington the next day because she still qualified for the $17 student fare on the Eastern Airlines shuttle. Sunde, who had to get back to work Monday morning, was to hand the letter to a friend of Lucy's, who would deliver it to Kay Graham at her stately Georgetown home.

The top editors were off on Mondays, having put the magazine to bed Saturday night, so we had to find someone to deliver a similar notice to *Newsweek*'s editor-in-chief, Osborn "Oz" Elliott. None of us wanted to confront our fearsome leader at the door of his East Seventy-Second Street town house. I volunteered my husband, who relished the task. As we carefully choreographed our insurrection, several women were still arguing that we should first go to management with our grievances. Others were filled with dread. "When I got home that night," recalled Lucy Howard, "I sat sobbing in the bathtub and thinking my eyes were going to be all puffy tomorrow. I was feeling I have to do this—but I can't."

We were hardly radical women. Nine days earlier, on March 6, five members of the Weatherman Underground had accidentally blown up a town house on West Eleventh Street as they were assembling bombs in the basement, killing two men and a woman—all in their twenties. Even in the media, there were far more outrageous actions than ours. Several weeks before our suit, freelance writer Susan Brownmiller convinced the newly formed Women's Media Group to hold a sit-in at one of the major women's magazines. Except for Helen Gurley Brown's *Cosmopolitan,* which promoted sexual liberation (mostly to please men), the other leading women's publications, all edited by men, were still preaching *Kinder, Küche, Kirche*, the German maxim for "children, kitchen, and church." The protestors decided to target the *Ladies' Home Journal,* whose slogan, "Never underestimate the power of a woman," took on new meaning two days after we filed our complaint. On March 18, more than one hundred members of various women's lib groups gathered at the *Journal* building at 9:15 A.M. and filed up to the fifth-floor corner office of John Mack Carter.

In his career, Carter had edited the big three women's magazines: *Good Housekeeping, McCall's,* and *Ladies' Home Journal.* A small, Southern, courtly gentleman, Carter was stunned as the brigade of women barged into his office. The protestors immediately began reading a list of demands, including hiring only female staffers—and a female editor-in-chief—providing free on-site day care, ceasing to publish advertisements that degraded women, and turning over the editorial content of one issue to the women, to be named the *Women's Liberated Journal.* Cornered at his desk for more than eleven hours, Carter was silent while various women spoke to him about their lives, their aspirations, and their frustrations. Elsewhere on the floor, protestors engaged secretaries and editorial assistants in earnest conversations. Only Lenore Hershey, Carter's deputy editor, spoke up. "She was a tiger at the gate, a bear guarding her cub, a magpie passing judgment on our clothes, our hair, our extremely rude manners," wrote Brownmiller in her memoir. "Sisterhood failed us badly with Lenore Hershey. I got the feeling that even Carter wished she'd just shut up and listen."

At one point, Shulamith Firestone, leader of the New York Radical Feminists, jumped onto Carter's desk screaming, "I've had enough of this," and lunged at him. One of the radicals who had taken judo grabbed Firestone's arm and flipped her into the crowd. After that, according to Brownmiller, Carter started negotiating with the women. In the end, the *Journal* agreed "to explore" opening a day-care center and to turn over eight pages in the August issue to the protestors, paying them $10,000.

Compared to that kind of guerrilla action, we were models of propriety. We didn't want to overthrow the system. We were proud to be part of a powerful and liberal institution like *Newsweek*; we just wanted to transform it to make it better for women. In the 1960s, feminists had scored several important legal victories, including the 1963 Equal Pay Act, the 1964 Civil Rights Act, and in 1967, an executive order that prohibited sex discrimination in hiring and promotion by federal contractors. In the 1970s, female journalists would declare war on their newsrooms and protest how women were covered in the media—and we were the first to challenge the industry's sexist policies. "The *Newsweek* case was pathbreaking in terms of impact on the law and on society," Eleanor Holmes Norton told me. "It encouraged other women to come forward, it had an effect on journalism, and it had a wide-ranging effect on women. Journalists had to write about it, and because the women were so extraordinary, because the case was so clearly one of blatant, unmitigated discrimination, it made people understand discrimination against women in an important way."

Two months after we filed our complaint, ninety-six women at Time Inc. would file a sex discrimination complaint against *Time, Life, Fortune,* and *Sports Illustrated.* In the next few years, women sued their employers at the *Reader's Digest, Newsday,* the *Washington Post,* the *Detroit News,* the *Baltimore Sun,* the *New Haven Register,* and the Associated Press. In 1974, six women at the *New York Times*—represented by one of our lawyers—filed sex discrimination charges on behalf of 550 women and in 1975, sixteen women at NBC initiated a class action lawsuit covering 2,600 present and past employees. "When women with staff jobs in the media began to rise up, feminism moved into another dimension," said Brownmiller. "Their courageous actions were to change the face of journalism forever."

In the end, it turned out that our extraordinary efforts to reach Katharine Graham that Monday in March were for naught. She was on vacation in the Bahamas. When Oz Elliott and *Newsweek* chairman Frederick "Fritz" Beebe telephoned her later that morning to tell her about the women's lawsuit, she was flummoxed. "Which side am I supposed to be on?" she asked them.

***

LIKE KATHARINE GRAHAM, we all were confused. We were women in transition, raised in one era and coming of age in another, very different time. It is hard for people today, even many women, to comprehend the social order that prevailed in the roughly two decades after World War II. The 1940s and 1950s were a period of growing prosperity, incipient suburban sprawl, and a baby boom that kept our mothers fully occupied. Jim Crow was nearly everywhere, gays were strictly closeted, and a woman's place was in the home, at least after marriage and children. In those rare instances when women were hired for jobs usually held by men, they generally earned a lot less and often were treated as sexual fodder.

"We were the tail end of the old generation," explained personal finance columnist Jane Bryant Quinn, who worked briefly at *Newsweek* in the early 1960s. "We wore hats and gloves. We couldn't go to proms and parties without dates—and the men had to do the asking. We also didn't have many role models in the working world." Most of us had graduated from college in the '60s, when half of our classmates earned their "M-R-S" and got married when they graduated in June. "Our generation was raised to be attractive and smart—but not too smart," said Pat Lynden. "We were to be deferential to men, to get married, raise children, and be ornamental wives dedicated to our husbands' careers."

Yet here we were, entering the workplace in the 1960s questioning—and often rejecting—many of the values we had been taught. We were the polite, perfectionist "good girls," who never showed our drive or our desires around men. Now we were becoming mad women, discovering and confronting our own ambitions, a quality praised in men but stigmatized—still—in women. In her insightful book, *Necessary Dreams: Ambition in Women's Changing Lives,* psychiatrist Anna Fels described the two emotional engines of ambition: the mastery of specific skills and the necessary recognition of that mastery by others. Even today, she told me, as women have developed skills and expertise, they are "subtly discouraged from pursuing their goals by a pervasive lack of recognition for their accomplishments." Women fear that seeking recognition will expose them to attacks on everything from their popularity to their femininity. But recognition in all its forms—admiration from peers, mentoring, institutional rewards, and societal approval—is something that makes us better at what we do,

Fels explained, and without it "people get demoralized and ambitions erode."

In January 2012, Sheryl Sandberg, chief operating officer of Facebook, spoke about an "ambition gap" at the World Economic Forum in Davos, Switzerland. She noted that ever since the 1980s, women have progressed at every level except at the top, where, in the past ten years, they've leveled off at 15 percent to 16 percent of executive jobs and board representation. "We don't raise our daughters to be as ambitious as our sons," she said. One reason, she noted, was that "success and likeability are positively correlated for men and negatively correlated for women. As a man gets more powerful and successful, he is better liked. As a woman gets more powerful and successful, she is less liked."

What led to our revolt? Why did our generation suddenly realize that our place in society was changing—and had to change? In part, we were carried by the social and political currents of our time. The civil rights movement was forcing a national conversation about equality and providing a model for all the protest movements of the 1960s. The music revolution was empowering a new "youth generation," which in turn was creating a "youthquake" in art and fashion. And over it all, like an ominous shadow, the war in Vietnam was fostering a deep skepticism—and cynicism—toward authority.

For women, especially young, white, middle-class, college-educated women, the booming postwar economy provided new opportunities and jobs far more interesting than the tedious suburban lives of our mothers. The birth-control pill, which went on sale in 1960, allowed us to control our destinies while the sexual revolution gave us permission to explore our desires. All that fueled a women's movement that questioned how we wanted to live our lives. As Gail Collins wrote in *When Everything Changed,* her 2009 history of American women from 1960 to the present, "It was, all in all, a benevolent version of the perfect storm."

But even with the social winds in our sails and the women's movement behind us, each of us had to overcome deeply held values and traditional social strictures. The struggle was personally painful and professionally scary. What would happen to us? Would we win our case? Would we change the magazine? Or would we be punished? Who would succeed and who would not? And if our revolt failed, were our careers over—or were they over anyway? We knew that filing the suit legally protected us from being fired, but we didn't trust the editors not to find some way to do us in.

Whatever happened, the immediate result is that it put us all on the line. "The night after the press conference I realized there was no turning back," said Lucy Howard. "Once I stepped up and said I wanted to be a writer, it was over. I wanted to change *Newsweek,* but *everything* was going to change."

CHAPTER 2

"A Newsmagazine Tradition"

W HEN *NEWSWEEK'S* EDITOR-IN-CHIEF, Osborn "Oz" Elliott, responded to our lawsuit that Monday in March, he released a statement that served only to confirm the institutional sexism of the magazine. "The fact that most researchers at *Newsweek* are women and that virtually all writers are men," it said, "stems from a newsmagazine tradition going back almost fifty years."

That was true—and most of us never questioned it. Although we held impressive degrees from top colleges, we were just happy to land a job—even a menial one—at an interesting place. Saying you worked at *Newsweek* was glamorous compared to most jobs available to college-educated women. Classified ads were still segregated by gender and the listings under "Help Wanted—Female" were mainly for secretaries, nurses, and teachers or for training programs at banks and department stores such as Bloomingdale's (that wouldn't change until 1973, when the US Supreme Court ruled sex-segregated ads were illegal). But compared to jobs at newspapers, where women were reporters and editors—even if they were ghettoized in the "women's pages"—the situation for women at the newsmagazines was uniquely injurious. We were confined to a category created especially for us and from which we rarely got promoted. Not only was research and fact-checking considered women's work, but it was assumed that we didn't have the talent or capability to go beyond it.

That infamous "tradition" began in 1923, when Henry Luce and Brit Hadden founded *Time, The Weekly News-Magazine*. Positioning their publication between the daily newspapers, which printed everything, and the weekly reviews, which were filled with lengthy commentary, these two young Yalies decided to create a conservative, compartmentalized digest of the week's news that could be consumed in less than an hour. But although *Time* would give both sides of the issues, it would, they said in their prospective, clearly indicate "which side it believes to have the stronger position." In the beginning, the magazine was written by a small group of their Ivy League friends, who distilled stories from newspapers and wrote them, echoing Hadden's beloved *Iliad,* in a hyphenated news-speak ("fleet-footed Achilles") and a backward-running sentence structure ("Up to the White House portico rolled a borrowed automobile"). *Time* didn't hire "stringer correspondents" until the 1930s, when the magazine decided to add original reporting.

But from the very beginning, the editorial staff included "girls" known as "checkers," who verified names, dates, and facts. Thus was created a unique group-journalism model, which, unlike newspapers, separated all the editorial functions: the reporters sent in long, colorful files from the field; the writers compiled the information and wrote the story in the omniscient, Lucean Voice of God; and the researchers checked the facts. Only "lady assistants" were hired as fact checkers, which, according to Oz Elliott, who worked at *Time* for six and a half years, was a "liberating thing for young fledgling women out of college because they could get into publishing without being stenographers or secretaries."

Years later, the honorific of "checker" was upgraded to "researcher." At *Time*'s twentieth anniversary dinner in 1943, Luce explained that although "the word 'researcher' is now a nation-wide symbol of serious endeavor," the title was originally conceived when he and Hadden were doing some "research" for a drinking club called the Yale Professors. "Little did we realize," he said, "that in our private jest we were inaugurating a modern female priesthood, the veritable vestal virgins whom levitous writers cajole in vain, and managing editors learn humbly to appease."

When *News-Week* began in 1933, it copied *Time*'s "tradition" of separating editorial functions. But at *Newsweek* (which joined its name in 1937 when it merged with the weekly journal *Today*), women didn't even start as researchers; we were hired two rungs below that—on the mail desk. At *Time,* office boys delivered the mail and relevant newspaper clippings. But at *Newsweek* only girls with college degrees—and we were called "girls" then—were hired to sort and deliver the mail, humbly pushing our carts from door to door in our ladylike frocks and proper high-heeled shoes. If we could manage that, we graduated to "clippers," another female ghetto. Dressed in drab khaki smocks so that ink wouldn't smudge our clothes, we sat at the clip desk, marked up newspapers, tore out relevant articles with razor-edged "rip sticks," and routed the clips to the appropriate departments. "Being a clipper was a horrible job," said writer and director Nora Ephron, who got a job at *Newsweek* after she graduated from Wellesley in 1962, "and to make matters worse, I was good at it."

We were all good at it—that was our mind-set. We were willing to start at the bottom if it led to something better, and in most cases, it did: to the glorified position of researcher. Working side by side with the writers, we were now part of the news process, patrolling the AP and UPI telexes for breaking news, researching background material in the library, chatting with the guys about their stories, and on closing nights, fact-checking the articles. The wires were clacking, the phones were ringing, and we were engaged in lively conversations about *things that mattered.* It was thrilling to feel the pulse of the news and to have that special pipeline to the truth that civilians couldn't possibly have. "It was everything you wouldn't think of growing up in Merion, Pennsylvania," said Franny Heller Zorn, who still remembered the thrill of finding the first wire report about a breaking news event, in her case when Adlai Stevenson collapsed on a sidewalk in London and died later that day. "The guys were great, the women were terrific, and everyone was smart. It was a privilege to be part of the *Newsweek* culture and to have that job, even with all the crap we had to do."

Our primary job was to fact-check the stories and that meant checking nearly every word in a sentence except "and" and "the." We underlined what we confirmed and in the margin, we noted the source—the reporter's file, a newspaper story, or a reference book. All proper names had to be checked against telephone books or directories. If the only source was the reporter, we grilled him on the correct name, title, and spelling. If we had any questions about the accuracy, we would underline the suspicious word or sentence with a red pencil. A fact was not to be checked against a newspaper story unless it was the only source we had. The *New York Times* was considered the best newspaper, but even that wasn't to be relied on for spellings or history unless it was a last resort. "If there was a difference of opinion between your research and the reporter, you had to call him up and gingerly say something like, 'I'm really sorry and I'm sure you're right, but the *New York Times* said it happened on Monday and you said Tuesday in your file,'" recalled Lucy Howard. "And the reporter would inevitably say, 'Goddamn it, what is the point of sending me out here if you're using the *New York Times*?'"

Unlike our counterparts at *Time,* we also ran interference between the bureau correspondents and the writers and editors. If a *Time* researcher had a problem or question on a story, she wasn't allowed to call the reporter in the field; she could only tell the editor. We were constantly on the phone with the correspondents. "I saw myself as an advocate for the reporter, to keep them out of trouble," said Lucy. "I wanted to make sure the writer didn't screw up and spell anything wrong. But I thought it was more important for the reporters to file what they saw and heard rather than worrying that they got the name wrong." Even Peter Goldman, who had the reputation of being an accurate writer, said, "I don't think I wrote anything longer than eighty lines where one of the researchers didn't catch something."

The modern, green-glassed Time-Life tower on Sixth Avenue and Forty-Ninth Street was only two blocks away from our modest, Art Deco building on Madison Avenue and Forty-Ninth, but the *Newsweek* culture was a world away from Henry Luce's empire. *Time* was WASPier, classier, and better resourced than us younger, scrappier upstarts at *Newsweek*. At *Newsweek*, we spent hours in the thirteenth-floor library, rummaging for relevant information in the "morgue," which housed valuable old (hence, "dead") newspaper and magazine clippings and reporter's files. At *Time,* the researchers would call up the library for sources, and carts would appear at their doors filled with files and books carrying the appropriate place marks.

On Friday nights at *Newsweek,* the writers and researchers went out to the local bars or ordered greasy food from Harman's or Beefburger on Forty-Ninth Street. At *Time,* the editorial staffers were treated to a buffet dinner of lobster or filet mignon on a table set with silver and china, all catered by the ritzy Tower Suite restaurant on the forty-eighth floor of the Time-Life building. While the men at *Newsweek* drank their Scotch and bourbon from bottles hidden in their bottom desk drawers on Friday nights (and many other nights as well), the senior editors at *Time* set up a full bar for their staffers in their offices or antechambers.

Still, working at *Newsweek* was a dream job and I felt lucky to have landed there. Like many of my colleagues, I was a graduate of one of the Seven Sisters schools, which in the early '60s were still mired in the '50s. Vassar College, when I arrived in 1961, was politically apathetic and boy-obsessed. Student clubs had been abolished and even the campus newspaper, the *Misc.* (short for *Miscellaneous*), had ceased publication my freshman year. Every weekend the campus emptied out as girls boarded buses to Yale, Princeton, Columbia, and other nearby men's schools. Other than having female professors and a safe environment where women could be the first to raise their hands— and be heard—there was little left of the founder's feminist legacy when I got there. Women were praised for their intelligence and commended for their capabilities but certainly not encouraged to have careers.

I majored in modern European history but became enthralled by my French professor, Olga Bernal. She would invite her favorite students to her apartment, where we would drink white wine and talk about life, love, and French literature (I was taking her course on avant-garde French writers). It was what I had pictured life at a small college would be like and by junior year, I had a passion if not yet an ambition: I would go to Paris. Since my history degree wouldn't get me a job, my only hope for employment was to be hired as a secretary. I was a fast typist, earning extra money by typing college papers, but I didn't know shorthand. I scoured the local ads and found a course at a nearby high school. My last semester at Vassar, as I was writing my thesis on France between the wars, I spent my evenings walking to Dutchess County Community College to learn Stenoscript.

Although I had taken French through high school and college, I applied only to US companies in Paris, including Pan Am, TWA, the USIA (the government information agency), *Time,* and *Newsweek.* At *Newsweek,* the chief of correspondents offered me a job in New York but I turned it down, determined to go abroad. At his suggestion, I wrote to *Newsweek*'s Paris bureau chief, Joel Blocker, who, unfortunately, had no vacancies. So I planned to go to Paris anyway and find a job when, just before my final exams in May, Blocker sent a telegram to my father, a celebrated sports columnist at the *Washington Post*: UNFORESEEN OPENING STAFF, NOW ALMOST CERTAIN JOB POSSIBILITY FOR LYNN IN PARIS BUREAU. . . . PLEASE ONPASS TO LYNN AND ADVISE SOONEST WHEN SHE ARRIVING AND ABLE BEGIN WORK. It turned out that Blocker's secretary had suddenly quit. Thank God for Stenoscript.

In June 1965, I packed two suitcases and left for Paris. For over a year, I worked in the *Newsweek* bureau as a secretary, photo researcher, occasional reporter, and telex operator. After the correspondents had written their stories, I would stay at night to type them—on a French keyboard—into the telex machine, which transmitted them to New York. Typing the files was a good lesson on how to report and write, even if it was a lonely one. Each night as he was leaving the bureau, the staff photographer would look at me, alone in the office, and say with a smile, "Good luck in your chosen profession."

Newsweek's Paris bureau was on the third floor of the *International Herald Tribune* building at 21 Rue de Berri, just off the Champs-Elysée. In addition to the bureau chief and his French secretary, Jacqueline Duhau, who befriended me, the office housed three correspondents and the magazine's senior foreign correspondent, Arnaud de Borchgrave, a perennially tan Belgian nobleman known around *Newsweek* as "the short count." I was closest to Liz Peer, the only female correspondent. A tall, sharp-featured woman with piercing brown eyes accentuated by layers of mascara, the twenty-nine-year-old Liz was *Newsweek*'s Brenda Starr. She could match the toughest foreign correspondent with her cigarettes, her swagger, and her fluent French. She was also a gifted writer and versatile reporter who covered everything from politics and the arts to fashion and food. (She loved tromping after the boars on the annual truffle hunts.) As I typed Liz's files into the telex, I admired her ability to find just the right anecdote or quote and weave it into a lively, compelling report.

The daughter of a prominent surgeon who was a pioneer of plastic surgery, Liz had graduated from Connecticut College and joined *Newsweek* on the mail desk in 1958. She showed so much talent that in 1962, she was the only woman on staff to be promoted to writer. Two years later, she was assigned to the Paris bureau. But as recounted by Oz in his memoir, *The World of Oz,* Liz later told him, with some bitter-ness, that she never felt she was treated fairly. After Oz an-nounced her posting, proudly telling her that *Newsweek* had never sent a woman abroad, Liz hesitantly asked whether the job would mean a raise—it was after all, a promotion. Accord-ing to Liz, Oz responded indignantly, "What do you mean? Think of the honor we are paying you!"

As a single woman in a highly visible job, Liz led a busy so-cial life in Paris and flaunted it. Returning to the office at night to type her files, she would often end her telexes to New York with "You guys are ruining my sex life." From time to time, she would bring me along on assignments, including a memorable Balenciaga fashion show, or ask me to report a "Newsmaker," the gossipy items about international celebrities that New York regularly requested. But Liz was also status conscious and didn't want to diminish her star in any way. She once asked me to join her one evening because her date was bringing along a male friend. I was surprised at this bit of camaraderie but I was flattered and quickly agreed. Before we left the office, she turned to me and said, "Just say you are a reporter in the bu-reau, not the secretary."

In Paris, I began to have glimmerings of ambition, of finding something to do for the rest of my life. Surrounded by reporters and writers, I naturally began to think about journalism. But that was complicated for me. My father, Shirley Povich, was a famous sports journalist and a very stylish writer. Afraid of measuring up to him—or with what his success represented—I had purposely avoided anything having to do with journalism in school. Then there was the terror of just putting oneself out in the world, to be judged by others. As I wrote to my best friend back home, becoming a writer would be "my first exposure to a real challenge, something which will prove whether I'm really intelligent and disciplined and eager to do something. This is it, baby, either you start to do something good now or forget it—kinda scary, huh?"

After more than a year in Paris, I returned to the States to be with my boyfriend. I had met Jeffrey Young on Christmas vacation during my senior year at Vassar. He was a first-year student at Harvard Law School and also a Washingtonian (his father owned the famous Paul Young's restaurant). With his dark brown hair and dreamy brown eyes, Jeff was bright, handsome, and charismatic, charming everyone in his path, including me. We got serious quite quickly, but with Jeff having two more years in law school, I decided that I would not give up my plan to go to Paris. After a year and a half abroad, I returned to New York in November 1966 to plan for our wedding the following June, when Jeff graduated. But in the spring of 1967, he suffered a serious depression and took to his bed. He managed to go to classes and finish his degree, but the depression lasted several months. I was very worried about him and visited him every weekend in Cambridge. But I wasn't willing—or able—to look deeper into what this might tell me about him or mean for our marriage. At twenty-three, I was in love.

When I returned to *Newsweek* in New York, I requested a position in the back of the book since Liz Peer told me there was more reporting in those sections. The magazine was informally divided into two parts: the front of the book, which comprised three sections—National Affairs (which we called Nation), International (referred to as Foreign), and Business—and the back of the book, which included Life & Leisure, Press, TV-Radio, Sports, Religion, Education, Medicine, Science & Space, and the Arts. I was put in the Life & Leisure section, which appealed to me. A Vassar course on Victorian England had gotten me interested in social behavior after studying the hypocrisy of the Victorians' strict moral code with the prevalence of prostitution. Life & Leisure covered social trends as well as fashion, which in the '60s was a vivid reflection of how men and women were changing and why. I loved reporting on *Newsweek*'s many fashion covers and interviewed every designer from Betsey Johnson and Mary Quant to Yves Saint Laurent and Halston.

The tedium of fact-checking on Fridays was the price I paid for spending the early part of the week doing interviews. Most of the researchers in the back of the book reported for their sections. But unlike many of my colleagues, my boss in Life & Leisure, Harry Waters, encouraged and mentored me. A graduate of Columbia Journalism School (on scholarship), Harry was a gifted writer who was raised in a working-class Catholic family by two older sisters and a strong mother. His politics were to the right of most of us, and he bristled at the Ivy League snobbery on the magazine, but he wasn't afraid of smart women. In fact, he admired them. He gave me opportunities to report and tutored me on getting good quotes. When he sent me to cover the funeral of Robert F. Kennedy at St. Patrick's

Cathedral, across the street from *Newsweek,* I nervously asked him whom I should interview. "Anyone who's crying," he said. He also edited my files so that I could sharpen my writing.

Since we had to provide colorful commentary, quotes, and background material, our files were often very long compared to what ended up in the magazine. When Harry assigned me to cover a traditional singles weekend at Grossinger's, the famous Jewish resort in the Catskills, my report started on an upbeat note: "They came 1600 strong in search of 'the One' or just a good telephone number." For pages, I described the typical Catskill "get acquainted" activities ("Simon says all the single fellows stand up—Simon says all the girls look them over quickly"), the compulsive mingling at the skating rink and on the ski slopes, and the false identities that everyone used to find a partner. "No one tells the truth," said one woman. "We say we're stewardesses one minute and the next minute we're in television." I ended with the scene at the buses back to the city on Sunday—"the last judgment" when everyone desperately exchanged information. "The girls practically have their phone numbers pasted on their foreheads," one guy said. But as a woman bitterly told me, "The boys are up here to have fun and accumulate phone numbers while we're here to get a husband." And with that, my thirty-one-page file was boiled down to a two-page Life & Leisure feature titled "The Last Resort," written by Harry.

The Business researchers also did a lot of reporting, since New York was the financial capital of the world. Because most of the material for Nation and Foreign stories came from the bureaus, the Nation researchers were sent out of the office mainly during political campaigns and crises, such as the riots. Those in Foreign spent their time in the library or on the phone, providing historical context for their stories and cultivating important sources in academia or foreign affairs. Some women, such as Fay Willey, the chief researcher in Foreign, loved that work. With a master's degree in international relations and American constitutional law, Fay had more depth of knowledge of her subjects than most of the writers she was checking. She was promoted three times before she was twenty-four, and found the work intellectually challenging.

Fact-checking might be a decent entry-level job in journalism, but many of us chafed at the work once we realized it was a dead end. Occasionally a researcher was promoted to reporter. Pat Lynden had started on the magazine as a researcher in Nation, took a leave to do reporting, and came back as a reporter in the New York bureau. But most of the eleven female correspondents working in the bureaus in 1970 had been hired from outside. *Newsweek* never hired women as writers and only one or two female staffers were promoted to that rank no matter how talented they were. During and after World War II, there had been several women writers on the magazine, but they had all mysteriously disappeared by the early 1960s. Any aspiring journalist who was interviewed for a job was told, "If you want to be a writer, go somewhere else—women don't write at *Newsweek*."

Some of the more ambitious young women saw the lay of the land right away. Nora Ephron, Ellen Goodman, Jane

Bryant Quinn, and Susan Brownmiller all started at *Newsweek* in the early 1960s, but left fairly quickly and developed very successful writing careers elsewhere. "I thought I'd work my way up—to the clip desk, to research, and eventually to writer—once I proved my worth," said Jane Bryant Quinn. "But I discovered that I'd never become a writer, just an older and older researcher, making my younger and younger male writers look good."

Ellen Goodman, the Pulitzer Prize–winning columnist for the *Boston Globe*, said that for researchers, "the turnover was expected to be great because women didn't stay in these jobs, either because they got married or because they left, but never because they were promoted. We're talking 1963, before the Civil Rights Act of 1964, so sex discrimination was legal." When an opening came up for a researcher in the Television department, Goodman, who graduated from Radcliffe (and never had a woman teacher), ended up working for her Harvard classmate Peter Benchley. "The only difference between Peter and me was gender," she said. "I mean, there were other differences. His grandfather was Robert Benchley. But, you know, it wouldn't have mattered if my grandfather had been Robert Benchley."

Some young women knew they wanted to be writers from the get-go. At fourteen, Jane Bryant Quinn discovered the comic strip *Brenda Starr, Reporter.* "She had glorious hair, impossible eyelashes, mysterious boyfriends—remember the patch?—and an internationally glamorous life," she recalled. "I don't remember that she reported on much, but wherever she was, something thrilling was going on. I wanted to be a reporter, too."

Nora Ephron's father *and* mother worked in Hollywood and Nora had written for both her high school and college newspapers. "My mother was a screenwriter, so of course we were all going to work and we were all going to be writers," she said. "And all four of her daughters are writers—that's a sign of her terrifying strength." When Nora was a researcher in Nation, *Newsweek* did a cover story on McGeorge Bundy, President John F. Kennedy's top advisor on national security. Ambitious and a self-starter, Nora volunteered to report on Bundy's early years at Yale, where he went to college. "Her file was absolutely spectacular," recalled Peter Goldman. "Everyone was passing it around like samizdat, it was so brilliant." But within a year Nora left *Newsweek* for the *New York Post.* "I knew I was going to be a writer and if they weren't going to make me one, I was going to a place that would," she explained. "Had they said to me when I said I was leaving, 'How would you like to be a writer?' I don't think I would have been any good at it. It's a kind of formulaic writing that requires quite a lot of craft and quite the opposite of the kind of writing I was doing."

Even now, I don't know why the rest of us didn't "get it," why we just didn't leave and try our luck elsewhere. Maybe because we were simply happy to have jobs in a comfortable, civilized workplace that dealt with the important issues of the day. Maybe it was because we, too, were elitists, thrilled to be at least a minor part of the media establishment. "Nora was eager to be a writer, so she was quite disgusted by the place," noted Trish Reilly, a researcher in the Arts sections. "I was thrilled to be a handmaiden to the writer gods and thought it was all quite wonderful." Or maybe we just weren't ambitious enough—or angry enough—at that point in our lives to buck an inherently sexist system. "I certainly saw what was going on," Ellen Goodman later said, "but I don't think I was angry about it for years."

For many of us, *Newsweek* was just a way to earn pin money before getting hitched. "At Radcliffe, the expectations were that you would leave college, work for a couple of years, get married, and then write the great American novel while your children were napping," said Ellen Goodman. At least working at a place like *Newsweek* might increase your chances of meeting a more interesting Mr. Right—or even a Mr. Rich and Famous. That fantasy was fueled by Karen Gunderson, a reporter in *Newsweek's* Arts sections. In 1965, Karen was sent out to interview Alan Jay Lerner, the lyricist and librettist of *My Fair Lady* and *Camelot,* among many other musicals. They fell in love and the following year, Karen left *Newsweek* to become the fifth Mrs. Alan Jay Lerner (he married eight times).

Whatever our destinies, *Newsweek* was an exciting place to work. It mattered what the newsmagazines put on their covers in those days. Every Monday morning, *Time* and *Newsweek* set the news agenda for the week and in the 1960s, that agenda was filled with cataclysmic events. In the beginning of the decade, *Newsweek* was a pale also-ran to *Brand X*, which is what we called *Time* magazine. But that would change rather spectacularly under the brilliant hand of Osborn Elliott.

CHAPTER 3

The "Hot Book"

O N THE SURFACE, it seemed unlikely that Oz would be a transformative editor. A balding man with a beak nose, Oz was the quintessential WASP: his Dutch ancestor, Stephen Coerte van Voorhees, had come to New Amsterdam early in the seventeenth century; he was raised on the posh East Side; he graduated from St. Paul's prep school and Harvard; and like everyone in his family except his mother, he was a Republican (he switched to Independent when he became a journalist). But Oz had a rebellious streak that he credited, ironically, to the strong women in his life. His mother's mother, Josefa Neilson Osborn, started a successful dress-designing business in 1898, after her wine-merchant husband lost his money. She held salons at the Waldorf, supplied costumes to the fashionable ladies on Park Avenue, and wrote a monthly column for the *Delineator*, the *Vogue* of its day. When Oz's father lost his money and his partnership at Kidder, Peabody in the Crash of 1929, his mother went to work in real estate, where she became a top broker and the first female vice president of her firm.

During the Depression, Oz's father had to arrange for scholarships to Harvard for Oz and his older brother, Jock, who later became chairman of the Ogilvy & Mather advertising agency. (When Oz's father finally got a job as an investment advisor, he paid Harvard back in full.) After college, which he finished on an accelerated program, Oz served with the navy in the Pacific in World War II. When he returned, he landed a job as a cub reporter on the *New York Journal of Commerce* and two years later went to *Time* magazine, where he became a business writer (he also met his first wife, Deirdre, there). In 1955, Oz moved to *Newsweek* as Business editor and became friends with Ben Bradlee, then a reporter in the magazine's Washington bureau. Five years later, when rumors started that the Vincent Astor Foundation was putting *Newsweek* up for sale, Bradlee called Oz, then the magazine's managing editor, and said, "Ozzie baby, I know where the smart money is. It's in Phil Graham's pocket."

Philip L. Graham was the publisher of the *Washington Post*. His father-in-law, Eugene Meyer, had bought the *Post* in a bankruptcy auction in 1933. His wife, Katharine Meyer, had worked as a newspaper reporter before they married but had retreated home to raise their four children. In 1954, Graham bought the rival morning paper, the *Washington Times-Herald,* and merged it with the *Post,* propelling the *Post* into first place over the afternoon *Washington Star* and doubling its circulation. Phil Graham was a dazzling figure around Washington. A former president of the Harvard Law Review and law clerk to Justice Felix Frankfurter, he was a friend of both John F. Kennedy's and Lyndon B. Johnson's (he helped persuade Kennedy to offer the vice presidency to LBJ) and he was high on Ben Bradlee's radar.

To get Phil Graham interested in *Newsweek,* Bradlee called him at eleven one night and said he wanted to talk. "Why don't you come over?" Graham said. "Now." According to Bradlee, "It was the best telephone call I ever made—the luckiest, most productive, most exciting, most rewarding, totally rewarding." Bradlee enlisted Oz in his crusade and together they convinced Graham to buy *Newsweek* in 1961 for $15 million. In a fifty-page memo to the new owner, Bradlee recommended that the thirty-six-year-old Oz become the new editor.

It was the magazine's salvation. Phil Graham immersed himself in *Newsweek,* setting up shop in New York, visiting reporters in the bureaus and traveling abroad to wave the flag. With his financial support, the magazine grew to sixteen bureaus and some forty correspondents by 1963. When Phil Graham visited *Newsweek's* London correspondents in April 1963, he forever set the mission of the magazine with these now famous words: "So let us today drudge on about our inescapably impossible task of providing every week a first rough draft of history that will never really be completed about a world we can never really understand."

But it was Oz who invigorated the magazine with late-breaking covers, national polling, well-known columnists

(Walter Lippmann and Stewart Alsop), and big "acts" (*Newsweek's* twenty-five pages on JFK's assassination versus *Time's* thirteen). He also instituted in-depth coverage of the incendiary social issues of the 1960s: from student unrest (at Berkeley, Columbia, and Harvard) to sex (Jane Fonda in *Barbarella*), drugs (LSD), and rock 'n' roll. Although the magazine was the first to feature the Beatles on the cover in 1964, it hilariously missed the point. "Visually they are a nightmare: tight, dandified, Edwardian-Beatnik suits and great pudding bowls of hair," *Newsweek* said. "Musically they are a near-disaster: guitars and drums slamming out a merciless beat that does away with secondary rhythms, harmony, and melody. Their lyrics (punctuated by nutty shouts of 'yeah, yeah, yeah!') are a catastrophe, a preposterous farrago of Valentine-card romantic sentiments."

Oz also hired talented deputies in Gordon Manning, a former editor at *Collier's*, and Kermit Lansner from *Art News*, and together they built a staff of better writers and stronger editors. "With Kermit, we had a Jewish intellectual from New York," Oz told the *New York Times*, "and with Gordon, an Irish Catholic sportswriter from Boston, and in my case, a WASP from the Upper East Side. It made for a wonderful balance." Perhaps it was because Oz was so good balancing competing interests and ideas that the top editors of *Newsweek* were called the Wallendas, after the famous circus family and their "death-defying" aerial stunts; their executive offices were dubbed "the Wallendatorium."

It was Oz's commitment to covering the paramount issues of race, poverty, and the war in Vietnam that not only distinguished *Newsweek* in the '60s and '70s, but made it, finally, the equal of *Time*. In 1963, Oz assigned Lou Harris to do a poll of black Americans, which resulted in a July cover story titled "The Negro in America: The first definitive national survey— who he is, what he wants, what he fears, what he hates, how he votes, why he is fighting . . . and why now?" The eighteen-page report found that the black revolution extended to every community and aimed to establish equality in every field. Suddenly everyone was talking about *Newsweek* and the magazine became the place to turn to for full and fair coverage of the civil rights movement. Three months later, the magazine published a cover on "What the White Man Thinks of the Negro Revolt." In 1967, Oz decided that the time for advocacy had come. Departing from the newsmagazine tradition of never editorializing, *Newsweek* appeared on the stands in November 1967 with a special issue titled "The Negro in America: What Must Be Done," a landmark cover that offered a twelve-point program on how to accelerate progress for black Americans.

"Oz was the godfather of our civil rights coverage," explained Peter Goldman, who was the chief writer on civil rights and author of the book *The Death and Life of Malcolm X*. "I don't think he knew very many black people, damn few. But he had a profound WASP social conscience, which led us to jump on the civil rights story and become the voice of the movement in a way. And it also helped on our coverage of Vietnam and our advocacy issues on both race and the war. We were a moderate voice for progressive America and that was Oz's conscience setting the compass." Oz was simply following in the tradition of his WASP forebears, Teddy Roosevelt and his cousin Franklin, those upper-class Episcopalians who, noted Goldman, "starting in the late nineteenth century and early twentieth century, thought, 'Oh my God, our system is broken. It's our duty to intervene and fix it. We have to get political even though we don't want to, because politics has fallen into the wrong hands.'"

In early 1968, Oz decided the magazine should again take a stand, this time against the war in Vietnam. *Newsweek*'s first cover on Vietnam appeared in 1961, when the magazine took a skeptical view of America's strategy even though, as Oz later wrote, "we—I—rarely questioned the basic wisdom of America's commitment to 'holding Southeast Asia.'" But after the Tet Offensive in March 1968, when the North Vietnamese forces surprised the US and South Vietnamese armies, Oz ordered up a special section titled "More of the Same Won't Do," which argued in favor of de-escalation and ultimate withdrawal. "The war cannot be won by military means without tearing apart the whole fabric of national life and international relations," *Newsweek* said. "Unless it is prepared to indulge in the ultimate, horrifying escalation—the use of nuclear weapons—it now appears that the U.S. must accept the fact that it will never be able to achieve decisive military superiority in Vietnam."

We were proud of our leader and of our magazine. Even though we were professional observers, many of us were sympathetic to the antiwar movement. During one antiwar march on Madison Avenue, a group of editorial staffers stood in a silent vigil outside the *Newsweek* building. In 1970, we held an open forum on the war in the *Newsweek* offices, much to the dismay of the reporters in the field as well as a few writers and editors. "No doubt the war has become a tremendously emotional issue in the United States," cabled Saigon bureau chief Maynard Parker, "but if the *Newsweek* staff cannot keep some objectivity and coolness on the subject, then who can?" The Tokyo bureau chief, Bernie Krisher, worried that "once identified with a cause, those who oppose that cause will hesitate to confide in us."

That concerned Oz as well, but as he wrote to the correspondents, "the divisions and passions among the *Newsweek* employees would have been exacerbated had we denied the turf for this purpose." Oz felt better about the staff's ability to keep their feelings in check when Dick Boeth, one of the senior writers and moderator of the mass meeting, wrote to him privately. Boeth said that although a poll of the editorial employees showed that a majority of the staff opposed the war, it also showed that "a majority of them hold exactly the same opinion about company activism as Parker and Krisher do." In other words, they were journalists first.

Under Oz, *Newsweek* became the "hot book" in the media and on Madison Avenue. Coinciding with the 1960s, life at the magazine not only was fascinating, it was a fun and even wild place to be. Since most of the writers were in their thirties and nearly all the researchers in their twenties, the culture inside the office mirrored the "Swinging Sixties" on the street. Everyone, including Oz, was on a first-name basis, which gave a feeling of equality even to us utterly powerless. After work we went out drinking either to the Berkshire Bar, a front-of-the-book favorite, or to The Cowboy, where Pete Axthelm, the Sports department's wunderkind writer and champion drinker, held forth every night.

Waiting for the files to roll in at the beginning of the week, or for the edits on Friday nights and Saturdays, we spent hours joking around in the office. "I loved the intense but nutty, free-wheeling atmosphere on Saturday afternoons," recalled Pat Lynden, "drinking wine, strumming guitars, playing baseball in the hallways." Peter Goldman and Ed Kosner used their downtime in Nation to cowrite a never-finished parody of a dirty novel. Dwight Martin, a senior editor in the back of the book, moved an old Steinway upright into his office so he could practice piano in the afternoons; at cocktail time he poured sherry for his staff.

One Friday night, Betsy Carter, the media researcher, was so bored waiting for her story to be edited that at 2 A.M., she decided to make a copy of herself. "I just lay on the Xerox machine and copied my body piece by piece," she recalled. "I stapled them all together and mailed it to my parents with a note that said, 'Here I am at work and I thought you would like to know.' I think my mother said something like, 'Do you think you're working too hard?'"

The back-of-the-book researchers had a classic "office wife" relationship with their bosses. While the front-of-the-book researchers sat in an open bullpen and checked stories by different writers every week, each of us sat in a twenty-five-foot-by-twenty-five-foot office with our section writer. The men's desks were by the window, of course; we perched by the door. To add some personality to our steel-gray work spaces, we pinned up pictures of our idols or celebrities we had interviewed. I put up photographs of nearly naked models Veruschka and Marisa Berenson from *Vogue,* prompting several writers to ask me if I was a lesbian. Sitting only six feet from our writers, we were on intimate terms with them, sharing more than we ever wanted to know about their personal grooming habits, their intimate medical issues, and their heated arguments with the ex-wife or girlfriend.

The back-of-the-book and the Business sections worked Monday through Friday, but the official week didn't begin until Tuesday morning, when Oz held a 10 A.M. story conference in his eleventh-floor office. After the story line-up was set, the writers sent queries to the bureaus asking for on-the-ground reporting. The color-coded files arrived on Thursday and Friday: blue from the international bureaus, green from Washington, and pink from the domestic correspondents. Then the creative rituals and angst would kick in. Pacing the halls in their socks or rocking in their chairs, the writers would cull the information from our reports and the rainbow-colored files and weave it all into a smart, colorful analysis or description of the week's events. Harry Waters, my boss, would pepper me for the right word or phrase, nervously asking, "How does this sound?" or "Listen to this." Paul Zimmerman, a movie critic,

THE GOOD GIRLS REVOLT

was called "the talking blue" because he proudly read aloud to any passerby the blue-inked mimeographs of his latest review. The entire magazine was written and edited in forty-eight hours, culminating in Friday nights that lasted until one or two in the morning because the Wallendas would take a two-hour, martini-soaked dinner break at Giambelli's across the street.

Describing the weekly routine, Carole Wicker, a researcher at *Time*, wrote a typically sexualized, over-the-top piece for *Cosmopolitan* magazine titled "Limousine to Nowhere . . . if You're a Girl at a News Magazine." In it she quoted an unnamed *Newsweek* staffer on what it was like to be a researcher: "It's a mini-marriage, between researcher and writer, with the orgasm coming at the end of the week. Monday, Tuesday and Wednesday, everything goes easy. By Thursday, the pitch is higher. Friday afternoon you're flying, and by Friday midnight you go over the top." "What she's saying," explained Wicker in the piece, "is that the researcher is drawn into the writer's pattern, inch by inch, pressure by pressure, until she's lost her own being and becomes an extension of her boss."

That didn't describe most of us but there was definitely a caste system at *Newsweek*. "For every man there was an inferior woman, for every writer there was a checker," said Nora Ephron. "They were the artists and we were the drones. But what is interesting is how institutionally sexist it was without necessarily being personally sexist. To me, it wasn't oppressive. They were just going to try to sleep with you—and if you wanted to, you could. But no one was going to fire you for not sleeping with them."

By the mid-'60s when the sexual revolution was in full swing, the magazine was a cauldron of hormonal activity. Protected by the Pill, women felt as sexually entitled as the men, and our short skirts and sometimes braless tops only added to the boil. Mix in a schedule culminating in long days and nights, and it ignited countless affairs between the writers and editors and the researchers. For the most part, the office flings were friendly and consensual, and a few turned into marriages. "The way we related to men was through sexual bantering," recalled Trish Reilly, a former researcher in the back of the book. "It was the way a compliment was made at *Newsweek*." "Flirting was part of the game," said Lucy Howard, "and you knew how to handle it. You had to be charming and witty and not cringe at their dirty jokes. It was a *Mad Men* kind of atmosphere."

There were elements of *Mad Men* at *Newsweek,* except that unlike the natty advertising types, journalists were notorious slobs and our two- and three-martini lunches were out of the office, not in. When she was visiting one time in New York, Liz Peer sat in on a story meeting. "The dialogue was eighth grade boys' locker room," she told a reporter at the *Village Voice.* "To see the powerful decision-makers of a national magazine talking about tits and asses and farts! I thought, *I'm working for these clowns.*" Kevin Buckley, who was hired in 1963, described the *Newsweek* of the early 1960s as similar to an old movie, with the wisecracking private eye and his Girl Friday. "The 'hubba-hubba' climate was tolerated," he recalled. "I was told the editors would ask girls to do handstands on their desk. Was there rancor? Yes. But in this climate, a laugh would follow."

Many guys looked at us as people they wanted to cheat on their wives with—and many women were happy to accommodate them. It was easy with suburban-based writers who stayed at hotels in the city on late Friday nights, but there was also sex in the office, literally. The infirmary, two tiny rooms with single beds, was the assignation of choice. Often a writer would go there to "take a nap" for an hour or two, albeit with a female staffer. The offices in the back of the book also served as action central. "You would open the door sometimes and there were these two heavy bodies against the door," recalled Betsy Carter, "and they would both be on the floor drinking Jack Daniel's or having sex under the desk." The outrageous behavior often spilled out into the corridors. Pete A. and Pete B. (Axthelm and Bonventre), the bawdy Sports writers, would stand outside their twelfth-floor office and audibly rate the women on their physical attributes as they walked by. "It was loose and fraternizing and I thought it was a lot of fun," remembered Maureen Orth, a former back-of-the-book writer, who hung out with the Sports guys. "But women were clearly subordinate."

I, too, was caught up in the sexual energy of the place. In January 1968, Jeff and I married and moved to Greenwich Village to be closer to New York University, where he had enrolled in film school. After graduation, Jeff won an internship with Arthur Penn on *Alice's Restaurant* and lived in Stockbridge, Massachusetts, for several months; I visited on weekends. It looked as if his career was taking off. He made a short film with Viveca Lindfors and in 1969 was hired by Paramount—in the post-*Easy Rider* days—to make a movie based on

Richard Fariña's popular counterculture novel, *Been Down So Long It Looks Like Up to Me.*

But there was something missing in our marriage and I felt emotionally abandoned. I didn't realize just how unhappy I was until I found myself getting involved with a colleague at work. I wasn't the only married researcher who was having an affair, but it scared me. One night I told Jeff about it because I knew the affair had more to do with problems in our marriage than with the guy. Jeff was furious, but then confessed that he, too, had been sleeping with someone. Maybe I had sensed it, I'm not sure. But I certainly wasn't feeling loved. After several long, tearful conversations, we decided to stay together and each of us began psychotherapy.

Looking back, there was a lot of inappropriate behavior at *Newsweek,* the kind of "sexual favoritism" and "hostile work environment" that today might be considered illegal. The Nation researchers were referred to condescendingly as "the Dollies." When a back-of-the-book researcher handed her senior editor some copy, he told her she had "perfectly pointed breasts." One Saturday afternoon, as Betsy Carter was fitting her story into the allotted space at the makeup desk, a writer she barely knew walked by, leaned over, and planted a soft kiss on her neck. Jane Bryant Quinn remembered that when she was on the mail desk, "randy writers and editors would cruise the newcomers, letting them know that their so-called careers would be helped if they joined the guy for drinks."

The short, gray-haired sixty-year-old man who ran the mail room was particularly sleazy. "After a while he would say, 'I want to take you out for a soda at the ice cream parlor around the corner,'" recalled Lucy Howard. "I went with him once. He would tell you his life story, including his war stories and that he had a war wound on his back. Then he would say, 'You have lovely hands,' and would ask you to go to his apartment to massage his back. Nobody did, but nobody said anything and no one turned him in. We just tried to avoid him. Finally somebody thought it was revolting and reported him and he was fired. He was just a creepy little guy."

One Monday my senior editor, Shew Hagerty, assigned me a story on a trendy new club in New York. It was a lascivious lounge where everyone disrobed, tied sheet-like togas around their bodies, and reposed on mattresses floating on pools of water as they were served cocktails. Shew was a gentleman and a good boss, but I was stunned when later that week he asked if he could come along with me. What could I say? To assure me that he was on the up-and-up, he invited Elisabeth Coleman, another of his researchers and a good friend of mine, to join us. I was never more humiliated than when I was lying on a large white cushion in a toga, with nothing underneath, across from my mustached, pipe-smoking boss, who sat there smiling, so pleased to be taking in the scene.

Nation researcher Kate Coleman (not related to Elisabeth), a proud member of Berkeley's Free Speech Movement, described reporting a *Newsweek* cover story in 1967 on the rising use of marijuana. Her senior editor, Ed Diamond, asked if he could come to her apartment and smoke some pot—to better understand the phenomenon. Not wanting her to think he meant just the two of them, he asked her to invite some of her friends as well so he could witness the whole experience. Then, at the last minute, Ed asked Kate if she would mind if he brought along his wife, Adelina. According to Kate, who left *Newsweek* in 1968, both Ed and Adelina came to her pot party and they both took more than a few tokes. Ed later claimed that he never got high; he said he only got a "slight buzz."

A few guys had a habit of hitting on women in ways that would qualify today as sexual harassment. One Thursday afternoon in Nation, Dick Boeth, a talented but temperamental writer, kept harassing Margaret Montagno, who tried to ignore him. He hovered over her desk, speaking quietly but clearly hammering at her. When she didn't respond, he said, very audibly, "Well, if you want to continue playing the thirty-year-old virgin from Columbus, Ohio, you go right ahead and do that." Everyone in the bullpen heard it and Margaret, in tears, fled into Peter Goldman's office. She closed the door and pleaded, "Can't you do anything about him?" "I didn't know what to do," Peter later confessed. "When Dick was in one of his crazies you couldn't deal with him. All the women were kind of scared of him. I should have nonviolently punched him out but I couldn't. After Meg calmed down, she went back to work. I had work to do and I couldn't do it in the eye of that storm, so I packed up and went home."

Several editors and writers were known for having affairs with women who reported to them directly, most likely a firing offense—or at least a reassignment—today. One writer told me that his editor was sleeping with his researcher, putting him in an awkward position, to say the least. A married senior editor, who regularly used the infirmary for his trysts, had a liaison with a researcher in his section and then lobbied for her promotion, which she received. Several editors and writers, married and single, had flings with their researchers. One writer dated both his researcher and his reporter at the same time.

Jack Kroll, the Arts senior editor, was a notorious flirt and played favorites with his young researchers. When Mary Pleshette first started working as the Movies researcher, Jack, who was divorced, asked her out to dinner and then a second time. It was collegial at first, talking about movies and actors and Zero Mostel, a friend of Mary's family. But when Jack asked her to dinner the third time, she told him she didn't feel comfortable accepting his invitation. "In those days," she recalled, "everyone knew that the third date meant you had to put out."

Jack was a Falstaffian character. His belly seemed to inflate and deflate with the seasons. Hidden behind a desk stacked with books in an office piled high with dirty shirts (he couldn't be bothered with sending them to the laundry), Jack was a polymath who could write brilliantly on just about anything. When Lee Harvey Oswald was gunned down by Jack Ruby in a Dallas police station basement, the editors called him in to write the story. The lead was classic Kroll: "It was," he wrote, "as if Damon Runyon had written the last line of a tragedy by Sophocles."

But Jack could also be volatile and vindictive. One evening after a cultural event, a good friend of mine who was one of his researchers asked me to come home with her because Jack was following her. She said he had been stalking her for weeks, sometimes waiting outside her building until two in the morning. When we got into her apartment, we doused the lights and looked out the window. There was Jack, walking up and down the sidewalk looking up at her window. She was terrified and didn't know what to do.

When she started dating the guy she would eventually marry, Jack became crazed. He asked her to lunch one day at a nearby Irish pub. "We started talking and he took out a box," she recalled. "He opened it up and there was a diamond ring. Then he took out an envelope with two tickets to the Iranian film festival, which was to be our honeymoon. I almost threw up. Thank God I was in therapy and had a man in my life. I said, 'You know, Jack, I love you but I'm not in love with you. This is overwhelming, this is incredible, you're such a close friend.' And he said, 'If you don't marry me, you'll have to leave *Newsweek*.'"

She refused his offer and he turned nasty. In the weeks that followed, she told me, "He would walk up and down the hall and yell, 'Where's that c—?' No one said anything, no one did anything." Finally, one of the male writers offered to help her find another job. She left shortly thereafter.

My boss, Harry Waters, told me that when he came to the magazine in 1962, "it was a discreet orgy. When I interviewed for the job, my editor said to me, 'The best part of the job is that you get to screw the researchers.' That," he went on, "reflected the position of women at the newsmagazines, both literally and figuratively. It reinforced in young women that that's their position—it's underneath. That's as far as they can get."

CHAPTER 4

Ring Leaders

J UDY GINGOLD WAS SITTING at her weekly consciousness-raising meeting in Judy Levin's tiny Greenwich Village apartment when it struck her. Levin, a friend from Judy's college days, was working at Ogilvy & Mather and heavily involved in the downtown political scene. The group consisted of eight women, among them a married architect, a social worker, and a woman who worked for the Clergy Consultation Service, a network of twenty-six Christian and Jewish clergy that helped women find safe abortion services.

A precocious New Yorker with a hearty laugh, Judy was intrigued by the new sense of power that women were exploring in their CR groups. Developed by the New York Radical Women, consciousness-raising was a process of using women's feelings and experiences to analyze their lives and society's assumptions about women. A member of that group, Kathie Amatniek Sarachild, who had changed her last name to reflect her mother's lineage—a common move for radical women in those days—had popularized the practice of consciousness-raising in a paper in 1968, which was widely disseminated. Judy's group followed the rules of the Redstockings, another group of radical feminists, which took its name from the seventeenth-century term for intellectual women, "Blue Stockings," and substituted "Red" for revolution. The rules required going around the room so that each woman was forced to contribute to the conversation. By airing their intimate feelings, women were to discover that what seemed like isolated, individual problems actually reflected common conditions all women faced. In other words, the personal was political.

The consciousness-raising session at Levin's Waverly Street apartment was a particularly memorable one for Judy. "Betsy Steuart, who was an assistant at NBC and very beautiful and capable, was saying, 'If I were Barbara Walters I would get ahead,'" she recalled, "and everyone was saying the same thing—'if I were better I would get ahead.' All of us in that room felt inadequate. And that's when I thought, wait a minute, that's not right. It's not because we're undeserving or not talented enough that we aren't getting ahead, it's how the world is run. It made me see that the problem wasn't our fault—it was systemic. That was my first 'click!' moment."

The famous "click!"—that moment of recognizing the sexual politics of a situation. Jane O'Reilly would later coin the term in the 1971 preview issue of *Ms.* magazine. O'Reilly was writing on "The Housewife's Moment of Truth," such as watching one's husband step over a pile of toys that needed to be put away. But in fact, she was writing about every woman's moment of truth. "The click! of recognition," she wrote, "that parenthesis of truth around a little thing that completes the puzzle of reality in women's minds—the moment that brings a gleam to our eyes and means the revolution has begun."

***

JUDY'S "CLICK!" MOMENT was the spark of our rebellion. It might have happened eventually but in the fall of 1969, that moment of insight at her consciousness-raising group got Judy thinking—and Judy was a thinker. Raised on the liberal Upper West Side of New York City, Judy was from a smart but humble family. Her father owned an electrical supply company and doted on his daughter, but from the beginning her parents' marriage was troubled and the household was tense. "I don't recall very many pleasant moments with them," recalled Judy. "They either fought or there was silence." Judy's younger brother Alfred, who became an actor and humor writer, filled the void at the dinner table with jokes and funny stories. Judy agonized. "My mother's favorite color was red and my father's favorite color was green, and when people would ask me, 'What's your favorite color?' I would chose orange," she said. "To me, orange looked like red but tasted like green. I saw myself as someone who couldn't take sides. I loved my parents equally but if I sided with my father, my mother would call me disloyal."

In seventh grade, Judy was admitted to Hunter High School, the elite public school for intellectually gifted girls, but four years later she transferred to Dalton, a top private school. She was attracted by Dalton's progressive curriculum and by its superior record of college acceptances. Judy chose to go to Smith College, where she graduated summa cum laude and Phi Beta Kappa, but she was still filled with insecurities and self-doubt. Her senior thesis at Smith, "Some Metaphysical Views of Logical Necessity," was submitted for a prize that came with the honor of publishing it as a book. Judy won the prize but wouldn't let Smith publish her thesis because she didn't think it was good enough.

After graduation, Judy went to Oxford University in England on a prestigious Marshall Scholarship. At that time, the Marshall was awarded to only twenty-four students and, unlike the Rhodes Scholarships, accepted women as well as men (the Rhodes wasn't extended to women until 1977). At Oxford, she did the typical three-year course in PPE (philosophy, politics, and economics) and wrote her thesis, "Freud's Use of the Concept of 'Meaning' in the Theory of Dreams." She was planning to stay in England, where she was happy and away from family strife, when she received a phone call from her mother in 1967. After twenty-seven years, her father had finally walked out. Her mother was so hysterical that Judy, ever the "good girl," came home.

Back in New York, this brilliant Marshall Scholar couldn't find a job for six months. She thought about going to graduate school in psychology, but "I didn't have a real goal," Judy said.

"I didn't have a goal of getting married, but I didn't have a career goal either. I thought about law school but I needed money." She also needed a home. While living with her mother, Judy continued to see her father, which infuriated her mother even more. Judy finally left, sleeping on friends' couches until, with the help of her father, she rented an apartment at 14 East Ninety-Second Street.

Later that year, Judy got an interview at *Newsweek* with Rod Gander, the chief of correspondents, who told her up front, "If you want to write, go someplace else." Short of money, she took a job as the "Elliott girl," the young woman—always a woman—who ran copy from Oz Elliott to the editors on Thursday and Friday nights until two in the morning, and all day Saturday. It was a terrifying job because when Oz would call "copy," he would eye you like a cop waiting to nab a perp, sternly looking over his glasses to make sure you took the story from the correct wooden out-box. But it was a good schedule for Judy because it allowed her to continue to search for a job where she wouldn't have to type. After six months of looking for work, Judy reluctantly took a research position in early 1968 in the Nation department. The other Marshall Scholar at *Newsweek* was her boss, Nation editor John Jay Iselin, a direct descendant of one of the founding fathers, John Jay.

In the fall of 1969, Judy got a call from Gladys Kessler, a friend of a friend who had just moved to New York. Over lunch Gladys, a lawyer, asked Judy about her job at *Newsweek*. When Judy explained what she did at the magazine and how all the women were researchers, Gladys said, "You know that's illegal?"

Judy was incredulous. Gladys explained that Title VII of the Civil Rights Act of 1964 prohibited employment discrimination based on sex, among other things, and told her to call the Equal Employment Opportunity Commission, which had been set up in 1965 to handle such cases. The next day, Judy went to work and, on the magazine's free tie-line to Washington, dialed the EEOC office. Hesitantly, she explained the situation to the woman on the other end of the line. "I don't think these men know that it's illegal," she said. "They're very liberal and they have daughters and I think we should talk to them." The gruff-voiced woman barked back, "Don't be a naive little girl. People who have power don't like to give up that power. What's so wonderful about your case is that it couldn't be more clear-cut and that's going to change if you let on. You have to organize and keep it secret and file a complaint. If you ask them about it, they will hire two token women and that will be the end of it."

Click!

Judy was shaken by the call. Now there was a moral issue. "I thought if this is illegal and it's going on here, then I should do something to correct it," she later explained. "That was really hard." She also knew that what she was going to do would change her life. "I saw myself as a nice person but I was starting to behave in a way that I never had before," she said. It was tearing her apart. As she weighed her thoughts, Judy struggled, with great inner courage, to overcome a deep-seated code of conduct. "Part of what is involved in participating in cultural change is violating what you were raised to believe was sacrosanct," she said. "It is getting yourself to accept a different set of values and relinquish old ones. That is one of the hardest things I've ever done, but I felt I had to sue." She scheduled a lunch with her two pals in the Nation department, Margaret Montagno and Lucy Howard.

Margaret and Lucy were close friends and later shared a weekend house in the Hamptons, but they were from different worlds. Margaret had grown up in Columbus, Ohio, the daughter of an engineer and a housewife—"standard issue 1950s Republican conservatives," as she described them. More liberal than her parents, she had always been interested in history and avidly read the newspapers. After public school, Margaret went to St. Mary's College, the sister school of Notre Dame, and earned a master's in medieval history from Fordham University. She was working on her PhD in Russian history at New York University when she landed a job at *Newsweek,* which she found far more interesting than a previous teaching job.

A petite brunette with a sardonic sense of humor, Margaret became a Nation researcher just as the 1968 campaign season was heating up. "I loved being plugged into the political scene," she said. She was sent out on the Eugene McCarthy campaign and covered the assassinations of Martin Luther King and Bobby Kennedy. Margaret quickly gave up the idea of teaching and became a political junkie, keeping meticulous track of the ever-changing convention delegate counts on a giant chart in Nation. "We were all obsessed with politics," she recalled. "That's all we talked about, especially in the early part of the week before the files came in. I think that's what brought us all together."

Lucy Anne Calhoun Howard was descended from John Eager Howard, a member of the Continental Congress, a senator from Maryland and former governor for whom Howard County, Maryland, is named. On her mother's side, she was related to the famous American painter Charles Willson Peale. Her father's family had lost everything in the Civil War and, at the age of fourteen, her grandfather went into the investment banking/brokerage business and bought a seat on the stock exchange. After he lost money in the Depression, he wanted his son to become a minister. Instead, Lucy's father became a doctor at Johns Hopkins Hospital.

Lucy's mother, also named Lucy, didn't work outside the home but she was very competitive. She excelled in fox hunting, and after she had children, continued to play tennis— "club tennis," her husband disparagingly called it. She hated to lose and she also hated to give up her maiden name. "Everyone knew her as Lucy Iglehart," said Lucy. "Late in life she said things like, 'If I had been a young woman in the 1980s and 1990s, I would have been a jockey and ridden in the Hunt Cup.' She was a very good rider but women weren't allowed to do that."

Lucy grew up on a small farm outside Baltimore, Maryland. She had a horse, which she showed in competitions and rode to hounds. She was far more competitive in school and sports than her two older brothers. At Garrison Forest, a boarding school, Lucy played field hockey and was a member of the riding team. "I was conditioned to want to do well in school— and I did," she said. "But I didn't do it to get into college. I did it to get more points for my [intramural] team. I was a very competitive person, that's why I wanted to be at the top of the class—you got more points for that. Part of me didn't want to lose that status. But part of me hated it and wanted to disappear from it because it put so much pressure on me and I was always anxious."

A pretty girl who hid her strong opinions beneath a pleasing demeanor, Lucy was also a debutante like her mother. "All my friends were debutantes," she explained. "That's what we were thinking about—parties, dancing, boys, and martinis." Although her parents didn't care whether she went to college, Lucy chose to go to Radcliffe because a cousin went there. "Something was driving me to get out of how I grew up," she said, and indeed, she found life on campus liberating. "I had a good time at Radcliffe. You could goof off. I got contact lenses—I wasn't 'froggy four-eyes' anymore—and I got honors. I didn't take advantage of all the academic things, but I became much more adventuresome in terms of meeting all kinds of people, which is why I came to New York."

In New York, Lucy found herself totally unprepared for the work world. "The word 'résumé' was completely foreign to me," she recalled. "I didn't have a goal. I thought I was going to get married." Determined not to be a secretary—"at Radcliffe, they fill your head with the 'best and brightest,'" she said—she scoured the "Help Wanted—Female" ads for something other than menial jobs and two weeks later, ended up at the Career Blazers employment agency. "They told me there was a training program at *Newsweek*," she recalled. "Did I ask what was involved? Did I have any idea what it was?" In her best dress and gloves, she went off to the interview at *Newsweek,* where an editor asked her if she knew George Trow, another Harvard graduate who later became a writer for the *New Yorker.* Worried that she might say the wrong thing, Lucy cautiously answered that she knew George had written the Hasty Pudding show at Harvard. The editor said, "His father's my best friend—when can you come to work?"

Lucy joined *Newsweek* on the mail desk in September 1963. She got hooked on news when, in November, the first wires came across that President Kennedy had just been shot and *Newsweek* scrambled to cover the story. In March, she moved to Nation as a researcher. During the 1968 primary, when Hubert Humphrey, Eugene McCarthy, and later, Bobby Kennedy were running for the Democratic nomination, Lucy and Margaret did a fair share of reporting. "Jay [Iselin] sent us all out because there were so many candidates in 1968 and not enough guys to cover them," said Lucy, "and we suddenly realized we could be reporters."

In the fall of 1969, Judy Gingold invited Margaret and Lucy to lunch at the New York Women's Exchange, a cheery consignment shop and restaurant on Madison Avenue whose aim was to help "gentlewomen in reduced circumstances"—the perfect description for our little group. Founded in 1878 so that Civil War widows could earn a living by selling their wares, the Women's Exchange was overflowing with knitted baby clothes, hand-made rag dolls, and beautifully embroidered linens hanging on the walls. In the back, down a few stairs, was a small restaurant filled with wooden tables and chairs. Over the next six months, the Women's Exchange became "Command Central" for the *Newsweek* crew as we plotted our homegrown revolution over home-baked crab cakes and claret lemonade.

When Judy approached her, Lucy had just returned from a month in San Francisco, California, where women's lib was in the air. She had brought back tie-dye shirts from the Haight-Ashbury district and buttons that read UPPITY WOMEN UNITE. Over lunch with Lucy and Margaret, Judy explained about Title VII and they discussed writing an anonymous letter to the EEOC describing the *Newsweek* situation and asking the commission to investigate. After endless meetings, they gathered one night at Margaret's apartment on Eighty-Ninth and York, where the three women finally drafted the letter. "Judy was the philosopher and theoretician—super smart and could talk every angle," explained Lucy. "Margaret could cut right to the heart of the matter and say this was wrong, this is what it should be. My role, as I saw it, was to make sure everything was nailed down, that there were no holes or openings for mistakes. On the way home I was supposed to drop the letter in the mailbox but like a good researcher, I wanted to reread it once more, so I didn't mail it after all."

Lucy was particularly offended by the treatment of her friend Pat Lynden, a fellow researcher in the Nation section. Pat had been reporting on New York Mayor John Lindsay, who was hoping for a slot on the Republican presidential ticket in 1968. But just before the Republican convention in Miami that summer, Pat was told that she wasn't going. Instead, a young male reporter would take her place—and by the way, would she please turn over her notes to him? "That made me really angry," said Lucy. "The summer in Berkeley had really changed my view of *Newsweek*. I don't think I was capable of initiating the suit, but when I saw what happened to Pat, that galvanized me." Margaret also felt aggrieved on behalf of both Judy and Pat. "For Judy to come back from a Marshall and be offered a job running copy—that was mind-boggling," she recalled. "Judy was very angry at that point. Pat was someone who did want to be a journalist and had done a lot of reporting work in New York, and then to have to turn over everything to a guy—that was unfair."

Lucy and Margaret suggested that they bring in Pat, who was everything they weren't—ambitious and combative. Pat had graduated from the University of California at Berkeley, where she had worked on the *Daily Cal* and won awards for her reporting. In January 1962, on her way to Europe, she fell in love with New York and landed a job on the *Newsweek* mail desk. After she became a Nation researcher, she wrote several freelance pieces, including cover stories for the *New York Times Magazine* and for the *Atlantic*.

A fearless reporter—the kind who was assigned to cover the riots in Newark—Pat had an unusual background. She was a "red-diaper baby," the epithet given to children of American Communists or Communist sympathizers. Her uncle was Archie Brown, the trade union director of the Communist Party in California. Her father, an official of the International

Longshoreman's and Warehouseman's Union, had been called before the House Un-American Activities Committee, where he invoked his Fifth Amendment protection against self-incrimination. There was a profile relief, in hammered copper, of Joseph Stalin over her grandmother's china cabinet. "I wasn't sure whether it portrayed the Soviet leader or my Russian-born Jewish grandfather as a young man," Pat wrote in an article for *New York Woman* magazine. "I never asked, I suppose, because to me my grandfather and the USSR were one and the same." During the 1950s, Pat and her family became untouchables, she wrote, "partly through our own choice—we had been raised to reject much that capitalism had wrought—but in large measure it was because during the depressing postwar decade of the blacklists . . . doors were closed to us as well as our parents."

That left a powerful impression on Pat. "On the positive side of this Leftist heritage," she wrote in *New York Woman*, "is the pride in a political tradition that stands for egalitarianism, the rights of minorities, economic justice . . . and civil liberties. But ours is also a subculture that will always feel vulnerable to the powers that be; we will always believe that we are irrevocably outsiders. We often wonder when the government will, once again, need political scapegoats and choose us. As a consequence, we have very little faith in, or regard for, duly constituted authority. We also know that friends are often friends only to a point." Still, Pat was no fan of the Communist Party either—giving her a healthy skepticism about everything. "I was aware of a lot of the bullshit on the Left—the hypocrisy and the philandering and the mistreatment of wives," she later told me. "I kept myself on the sidelines."

In 1965, Pat met Allen Gore, a lieutenant of detectives in the police department's Pickpocket and Confidence Division (they would later marry). Two years later, Allen got Pat entrée to the Gypsy subculture for a cover story in *The Atlantic*. But when she showed a draft of the story to Ed Kosner, a friend in Nation, he said, "'You're a good reporter but you're not such a good writer,'" she recalled. "I was devastated." After the Lindsay assignment was taken away from her in the summer of 1968, she said, "my confidence began to flag and I left." She worked for a columnist for a while and went back to San Francisco to do some reporting. She returned in late 1969 when *Newsweek* offered her a job in the New York bureau. Shortly after that, Lucy and Margaret approached Pat in the *Newsweek* ladies' room. "I thought about it for two hours and said, 'Yes, I'll join you,'" Pat recalled. "Then a week or two went by and we didn't know what to do. Who else do we know? Who can we trust? Women just didn't trust each other. We didn't talk about our salaries. We fought over the bones like crazy. We competed with each other instead of saying, 'We're not the enemy.'"

It was around that time, in October 1969, that Judy suggested I join the group. She had transferred from Nation to the Education section the year before and had just been promoted to head researcher in the back of the book. We were sharing a small inside office on the twelfth floor and had become best friends, but approaching me was tricky. My father was a good friend of Kay Graham's and he was working at the *Post* when her father, Eugene Meyer, bought the paper in 1933. In the spring of 1965, as I was finishing up at Vassar, he had asked Kay Graham to set up a job interview for me at *Newsweek,* which she had graciously arranged. But there were no job openings in Paris at the time.

My father was a well-known journalist in Washington and the sports world, widely admired for his integrity, his fairness, and his graceful writing. He was also an Orthodox Jew from Bar Harbor, Maine, the summer playground of the wealthy "rusticators"—the Astors, the Rockefellers, the Vanderbilts, the Carnegies. Every June, they journeyed to Mt. Desert Island on their private railroad cars to spend three months at their "cottages," more often fifty-room mansions with stables and servants' quarters. Dad's father had come from Lithuania to Boston in 1878 at age twelve with his father. They had peddled north, with packs on their back, to Bar Harbor, where they opened a furniture shop on Main Street and lived above the store. The seventh of nine children, Dad caddied at the tony Kebo Valley Golf Club, where one of his clients was Edward B. McLean, owner of the *Washington Post* (his wife, Evalyn, was the owner of the Hope Diamond). Mr. McLean offered Dad a job at his paper if he would continue to caddy for him at his private golf course off Wisconsin Avenue in Washington. So in 1922, at seventeen, Shirley (not an unusual male name in Maine) started as a police reporter at the *Washington Post* before he went to cover sports for $5 more a week.

My mother, Ethyl Friedman Povich, was born in Radom, Poland. Her father, a tailor, had emigrated to Washington with fellow landsmen in the early twentieth century. In 1912, he brought his wife and children—my three-year-old mother and her six brothers and sisters—to live with him (another son would be born in the United States). After meeting on a blind date and marrying two years later, my parents lived the high life, traveling to New York and Florida and clubbing with the other sportswriters and their wives (their honeymoon was at the Washington Senators' spring training camp in Biloxi, Mississippi). But after they had children, and with Dad constantly on the road, Mom became our anchor at home, providing a sweet, warm presence for us.

Sports was the lingua franca at home, especially with two older brothers. Every February, we moved to Orlando, Florida, where the Washington Senators held spring training and where we went to school when we were young. While my brothers were living out their dreams as batboys, I rooted from the bleachers. Since girls weren't allowed in the clubhouse, Dad always arranged for Mickey Vernon or Eddie Yost to play catch with me after the game. Needless to say, I became a big sports fan and understood the finer points of baseball. One of my proudest achievements was when my father used my scorecard at a Senators game to write his column.

Although I played team sports, I didn't want to compete in that arena, so I chose to become a dancer. I was a serious ballet student until, at thirteen, my teacher recommended that I go to the School of American Ballet in New York City. The idea of moving to New York, and not going to college, was out of the question for my family and me—a bridge too far. I switched to modern dance and became part of a performance troupe founded by Erika Thimey, a German émigré who, along with Ruth St. Denis, brought a spiritual dimension to modern dance.

Given the strong personalities of my father and brothers, our house was infused with testosterone. The good part was that I felt comfortable around men and sports, something that helped me later in my career. But at the same time, our house revolved around the guys. I know it bothered my mother (she used to call us "motherless children," since everyone referred to us as "Shirley's kids"), and she took out her frustrations on me, often by being critical. I chafed under her, but I, too, was annoyed that many people didn't even know that Shirley Povich also had a daughter.

At home, the boys ruled. My parents sent my brothers to summer camp each year and, after elementary school, to Landon, an all-boys private school. I went to camp just one summer and continued in public school. Three years after the 1954 US Supreme Court decision in *Brown v. Board of Education,* which declared that separate but equal schools for whites and blacks was unconstitutional, my all-white junior high school suddenly had an influx of black students. The problem was not the kids, as I remember it. In fact, the gangs in my school were mostly white and my best friend was black. The administration just couldn't deal with the racial tensions or the influx of new students. After graduating from the ninth grade at Paul Junior High School in 1958, I went to Sidwell Friends, a private, coed Quaker school across town.

At Friends, I was one of three new students in a class of fifty-three, most of whom had been there since kindergarten. Friends wasn't a fancy school then—the most famous students were children of diplomats, not media stars—and it instilled in us the Quaker values of peace, simplicity, and social justice. I appreciated the silent contemplation of the weekly meetings for worship as well as Friends' first-class education, which helped me get into Vassar.

Still, I shied away from writing. I admired my father's talent and read his column eagerly (he wrote six days a week), but how could I measure up? I once gave an eighth-grade paper to my father to look over. He was a witty and elegant writer and cared deeply about his craft. With the best intentions and wanting me to be a good writer, he criticized my story in what he thought was a constructive way. But to me, it was devastating. I had failed the test; I couldn't play in his league. I never again showed him anything I had written.

I was expected to do well in school, but it was never explained to me that I might have to earn a living. Nor did I realize that I would have to develop my own professional skills and talents. My family's expectation—and mine—was that I would work until I married and had children, like my mother had. But seeing my father out in the world and meeting interesting people certainly appealed to me more than being a housewife. And although it hadn't occurred to me to follow in his footsteps, here I was doing just that.

When Judy confided in me in the fall of 1969, it was complicated for another reason: I was no longer a researcher. My boss, Harry Waters, had suggested that I be promoted to junior writer, and I was in March 1969. "You never voiced much ambition and I don't remember your pushing to get ahead," Harry recalled. "But I thought from your files that you should be a reporter and writer." Still, Judy knew I would be sympathetic to the idea of a lawsuit. In 1969, I had begun covering the gay-rights and the women's lib movements, which was expanding my worldview. I interviewed the radical Redstockings, who insisted on talking only to female reporters, and covered the first Congress to Unite Women, where the Daughters of Bilitis were dropped as a sponsor because Betty Friedan feared that lesbian associations would threaten the new women's movement. I would return to the office fired up by these encounters and Judy and I would talk excitedly about them. That fall, I had suggested a six-column story on women's lib. I was sent to Chicago and Boston to do the reporting because there were no women in the bureaus. My senior editor had moved to another department and Dwight Martin, the fill-in editor, thought I was "too close to the material." He asked a guy to rewrite the piece but the story kept getting delayed and never ran. Then Judy told me about the EEOC.

I must admit I wasn't the first woman to "get it," nor was I particularly angry, although I came to value those who were.

People like Judy and Pat who were angry pushed the rest of us to make it happen. But my consciousness was getting raised and the blinders were beginning to fall. We *were* competing against one another and now I, too, began to question why there was just one slot for a woman and, more important, why we were willing to go along with the system. I had been lucky enough to break through the ranks, but even if I hadn't personally been held back, I knew too many women who had. I signed on.

CHAPTER 5

"You Gotta Take Off
Your White Gloves, Ladies"

For the next few weeks, we were skulking around the office like spies, waiting for the right opportunity to pounce on our next recruit. Our strategy was to bring in women one by one, keeping things as secret as possible until we knew what we were going to do. The *Newsweek* ladies' room was a favorite ambush spot. Peering under the stalls to make sure no one else was there, we would start a casual conversation at the sink about how bad things were. "I would say, 'Oh God, I have to research a story by some male writer and I'm sure I could write it better myself,'" recalled Lucy Howard. "If the woman agreed, then I would tell her some of us had been thinking about what we could do to change this—and slowly bring her in."

Lucy, Margaret, and Pat approached the researchers in the Nation, Foreign, and Business sections while Judy and I took those in the back of the book. "To get into the inner circle you had to be vouched for," explained Lucy. "Given how we were raised, we didn't trust women, we didn't want to talk to women, we didn't even want to sit next to women. It was all about catering to men. You really had to trust someone to make sure she wouldn't see it as an advantage to rat you out. Judy knew Lynn and Lynn knew Mary."

Mary Pleshette and I were becoming good friends. Mary was the Movies researcher and we often double-dated. I first met her boyfriend, Jack Willis, in the fall of 1969, when we went to see *Bob & Carol & Ted & Alice* at the Lincoln Center Film Festival. To me, Mary was the consummate New Yorker. The daughter of a prominent East Side ob/gyn, she had grown up on Madison Avenue, graduated from Sarah Lawrence, and was an aficionado of art, theater, food, and French, which she spoke fluently. Mary was a wonderful storyteller and wanted to be a writer. She had begun to freelance for the counterculture *Village Voice* and other publications when I invited her into our office one evening and closed the door. Explaining that the situation for researchers at *Newsweek* was illegal, I said, "We're beginning to organize—would you be interested in joining us?" "Absolutely," Mary said without hesitation. We ended the conversation by swearing her to secrecy.

Judy and I then approached Phyllis Malamud, who had the office next to ours. Phyllis, whose father was the cantor at the Actors Temple in Times Square, was hired at *Newsweek* in 1960, after graduating from the City College of New York, and had worked her way up to a reporter position in the New York bureau. "Like most women those days, I thought I would meet a guy and get married," she later said, "but I never met the guy, and after working at *Newsweek,* all of a sudden I had a career." Judy and I stood in her doorway, not wanting to look too conspiratorial, and made our usual pitch: "We're thinking about doing something—do you want to join?" Phyllis was surprised by our proposal but readily accepted. "It was the first time I even thought about the injustice," she recalled.

I also enlisted Elisabeth Coleman, the Press researcher, whose nickname was Lala. With long golden-red hair and green eyes, Lala was, hands down, the most beautiful woman at the magazine. Guys lusted after her and many at the magazine tried to date her. After graduating from Vassar, she had come to New York City wanting to work in journalism "as an assistant to a smart man," she recalled. "My parents asked, 'Have you ever thought about being a journalist yourself?' and I replied, 'Oh my gosh, no—I couldn't do that. That's for men.'" Luckily Lala's boss, Bruce Porter, was a generous mentor, taking her along on assignments and training her to become a good reporter. When Bruce was away one day, I walked into the Press office and closed the door. In a hushed voice, I told Lala about our plans and asked if she would be interested in joining our group. She was so excited by the offer she immediately said yes. "I had this tightly wound feeling that we were changing history," she recalled, "that something was going to explode!"

What we didn't know was that for the past year Lala had been asking Rod Gander if she could go to a bureau for a summer internship. Rod, the chief of correspondents, reminded her that the summer positions were reserved as a training program for young black men. When Lala pointed out that white guys from the *Harvard Crimson* and the *Columbia Spectator* were also being recruited for summer internships, Rod told her it was simply too expensive to send her as well. One day over drinks, Lala said, "Rod, there's something you're not telling me. What is it?" After a few more drinks, Rod confessed, "I don't want to say this but—men don't want to work with women."

I also talked to my friend Mimi Sheils (now Merrill McLoughlin), who worked across the hall in the Religion department. Tall, curly-haired, and super smart, Mimi was a proper girl on the outside, but a wild child underneath. She had majored in religion at Smith College, a decision her father, an advertising salesman at *Time,* ridiculed, saying it would get her a job as a telephone operator at Dial-A-Prayer. Instead, it got her a job as the Religion researcher at *Newsweek.* At her 1966 interview, the chief of research, Olga Barbi, asked Mimi what she was interested in. When she told her she had majored in religion, "Olga jumped out of her chair and said, 'No one has ever said they were interested in Religion,'" Mimi recalled, laughing. Mimi wanted to be a doctor and finished her premed requirements in college, but she spent the summer after graduation at Radcliffe taking secretarial courses—just in case. "I got married in '68 and I thought I was going to med school," she recalled, "which is why I never expected to be a journalist or magazine person."

When I approached Mimi, "I wasn't offended that my path was being cut off," she recalled, "because I didn't think my path was there." But she was angry about other talented women being blocked. "I'd always been a little rebellious—I was a bad teenager," she said. "So to some extent rebelling wasn't all that new to me. I was always running afoul of my father, who set very strict rules, and I set my life to break them." As the Religion researcher, Mimi did a lot of reporting and was upset that her work wasn't recognized. "I did a lot of reporting, which was heavily used in stories, and I rarely got credit or mention in Top of the Week [where staffers were acknowledged before there were bylines]. That annoyed me no end."

Another early recruit was Trish Reilly, a tall, impeccably dressed researcher in the Arts sections. Trish's seeming sophistication belied the fact that she was the first in her family to go to college, at UC Berkeley. Born in Alameda, California, Trish was raised with the expectations of becoming a schoolteacher, getting married, and having kids, and she never aspired to rise beyond that. "I knew what was being done to women at *Newsweek* was as wrong as slavery and I was happy to be part of the lawsuit," she recalled. "But I saw myself as someone whose own life wouldn't be changed by it." Trish had qualms about joining the women and talked it over with Mary Pleshette. "I don't know about this whole business of women being in men's jobs," she confessed to Mary. "I like the differences between men and women and I think we should keep them." Mary asked her which differences she was afraid of losing. Trish didn't answer for a long time. "Oh well," she finally said, "we'll still be women—we'll just have better jobs."

As the circle widened in the winter of 1970, we asked the five black researchers on the staff to join us. "I had divided emotions," recalled Leandra Hennemann Abbott, a researcher in the back of the book. "Here was the women's lib movement and while I certainly could identify with that, it seemed to me that women's liberation wasn't out front in support of black liberation and never reached out to black women. I believed the difficulties we felt were because of being black and that a lot of the issues for white women didn't apply to us because we didn't have a choice. They were talking about work and we were working all the time. Our issues were larger than the work world. We had to be strong for the family, too."

Diane Camper, a Syracuse graduate who was a Nation researcher, said that although the black women never caucused, they informally discussed what to do. "There was a feeling that there had been all these conversations going on among the white women about agitating for more women to be reporters and we were an afterthought," she later explained. "At the time, there was more identity with race than gender. People just didn't see the strategic advantage of joining in." In the end, much to our disappointment, the black women decided not to join us.

There were several women we didn't approach. One was Rita Goldstein, the Newsmakers researcher, who was dating a Wallenda, *Newsweek*'s executive editor, Bob Christopher (they would marry in May 1970). We were so paranoid about being discovered that we felt we couldn't risk any pillow talk. We also were worried about approaching Madlyn Millimet, who had married Angus Deming, a writer in Foreign, in January 1970, two months before we filed the lawsuit. But in the end Maddy signed the complaint.

A critical convert to our cause was Fay Willey, the head researcher in the Foreign section. Almost a decade older than most of us, Fay had joined *Newsweek* in 1955, when Vincent Astor and other wealthy stockholders owned the magazine. On election nights, the Astors would invite British nobility in to watch the proceedings, as if the staff were animals in a zoo. Fay was well respected by the top editors, who appreciated her maturity and experience. She had established a solid reputation in the world of foreign affairs and provided important context to *Newsweek* stories with authoritative commentary from "the domes," the scholars and government sources she carefully cultivated. We weren't sure she would join us but we knew our position would be greatly enhanced if she did.

Judy and Pat nervously paid a visit to Fay at her immaculate Upper East Side apartment, the parlor floor of a brownstone filled with antique furniture. Little did they know that Fay had been seething for years about the condescending way research was regarded at the newsmagazines. In October 1964, Otto Friedrich, a *Time* editor, wrote a famous piece in *Harper's* magazine titled "There are 00 Trees in Russia: The Function of Facts in Newsmagazines," which infuriated Fay. Friedrich's article argued that the newsmagazine fetish for "the facts" did not necessarily represent the truth. He explained that *Time* and *Newsweek* had evolved "a unique system which makes it theoretically possible to write an entire news story without any facts at all." By putting in "TK" for "to kum" ("kum" being a deliberate misspelling of "come" to warn copy editors and proofreaders not to let the word get into print)—or, in the case of statistics, "00," to be filled in later—it enabled the writer, he said, "to ignore all the facts and concentrate on the drama."

To guard this fact "fetish" at newsmagazines, Friedrich wrote,

> There came into existence an institution unknown to newspapers: the checker. The checker is usually a girl in her twenties, usually from some Eastern college, pleasant-looking but not a femme fatale. She came from college unqualified for anything but looking for an "interesting" job. After a few years, she usually feels, bitterly and rightly, that nobody appreciates her work. The beginning of the week is lackadaisical and so is the research, but toward the end, when typewriters clack behind closed doors and editors snap at intruders, there are midnight hamburgers and tears in the ladies' room. For the checker gets no credit if the story is right, but she gets the blame if it is wrong. It doesn't matter if the story is slanted or meretricious, if it misinterprets or misses the point of the week's news. That is the responsibility of the editors. What matters—and what seems to attract most of the hostile letters to the editors—is whether a championship poodle stands thirty-six or forty inches high, whether the eyes of Prince Juan

Carlos of Spain are blue or brown, whether the population of some city in Kansas is 15,000 or 18,000.

Fay wrote a scathing letter to the editor of *Harper's* that was published in the December 1964 issue. "As the researcher (not checker, please) who arrived at the number of trees in Russia, permit me to say that Otto Friedrich's article is enough to send any researcher to the ladies' room for a few tears," it read. "Aside from his insulting remarks about what we do to earn a living and how we do it, Mr. Friedrich says we are not *femmes fatales,* which is most ungallant, and 'unqualified for anything,' which is untrue. We can be quite *fatale* in circumstances other than telling a writer that his story is all wrong (perhaps none of us ever trained her guns on Mr. Friedrich), and as for our training, researchers by and large have the same education as the writers they are working for, if not a better one." She ended the letter by citing four facts in Friedrich's article in need of correcting. At the bottom of her letter was his reply: "I am mortified at the accusation of ungallantry and, if guilty, deeply apologetic. As for the rest of Miss Willey's 'corrections,' I say, '*Qui s'excuse, s'accuse.*'" (He who excuses himself accuses himself.)

When Judy and Pat discussed our plans with Fay, she was cool to the idea of taking legal action. She herself didn't want to become a writer, but she did feel women should be allowed to write. What she wanted was for research to be more valued and for researchers to be considered as important to the magazine as the correspondents in the field. She was particularly unhappy that the editors entertained her sources at *Newsweek* lunches and didn't include her. Fay had been horribly embarrassed when a China scholar she had cultivated was asked to *Newsweek* one day and she hadn't been invited. The next time someone asked her to call the man for a quote, she was overheard saying, "Call him up your bloody self—you just had him to lunch!" Fay felt strongly that we should first air our grievances with the editors. She wanted to make sure we had given them a fair chance. The more she thought about the lack of respect given the researchers and their work, however, the more upset she got. She decided to join our band of sisters.

Meanwhile, we had been shopping for a lawyer of the female persuasion. The first attorney we approached was Harriet Pilpel, a senior partner in the law firm of Greenbaum, Wolff & Ernst, which specialized in First Amendment issues. With no experience in the new field of employment rights law, she declined to represent us. Even so, recalled Margaret, "she was thrilled we weren't lesbians. I don't know if she used those words, but she was delighted that we were nice, soft-spoken, decently dressed young women and not part of the lunatic fringe." We then approached the lunatic fringe—Florynce Kennedy, the flamboyant black civil rights lawyer and fiery feminist who had defended Valerie Solanas, the woman who shot Andy Warhol in 1968. Greeting us in her apartment in the East Forties wearing her signature cowboy hat, Flo had lots of ideas of what we could do, including sit-ins and guerrilla theater, but most of them were too outrageous for us. She also discussed how much money she would need, which made us realize we should think about a pro bono lawyer.

That led us to the American Civil Liberties Union, where we met with the assistant legal director, Eleanor Holmes Norton. Five feet, seven inches and five months pregnant, Eleanor was an impressive figure with an Afro to match. As we sat in her office explaining our case, she grabbed a copy of *Newsweek* and opened it to the masthead. She looked at it—then looked at us—and said, "The fact that there are all men from the top category to the second from the bottom and virtually all women in the last category proves *prima facie* that there's a pattern of discrimination at *Newsweek*. I'll take your case." (There was one male researcher on the masthead, a political refugee from Greece whom the editors had hired as a favor.)

Eleanor was perfect for us. A veteran civil rights activist and self-avowed feminist, she was smart, shrewd, and sharp-tongued—"indignant" was her middle name. The great-granddaughter of a slave who walked off a Virginia plantation, Eleanor was from an aspiring and ambitious family. Her grand-father Richard Holmes was one of Washington, D.C.'s few black firefighters and successfully petitioned the department to create the first all-black company in 1921. Her father, Coleman Holmes, a charming and dapper man, went to Syracuse University on a scholarship. In Syracuse, he met Vela Lynch, a shy woman who had grown up on a farm in North Carolina but was sent north after her mother died. They married in 1935 and came back to Washington, where Coleman worked as a public health inspector and Vela took a job in the Bureau of Engraving and Printing. More industrious—and more practical—than her husband, Vela went back to school to earn a teaching degree. In the late 1940s, she also joined the National Association for the Advancement of Colored People and paid $1 annual dues toward its "Struggle for Full Emancipation for the American Negro."

As the oldest of three girls, Eleanor easily assumed the role of the first-born, scoring top grades and leading school organizations from elementary through high school. Washington was still a Southern, segregated city, where white-owned stores in black neighborhoods wouldn't even hire "colored people" to work for them. In 1951, at age twelve, Eleanor had what she describes as her first consciousness-raising moment. The educator Mary Church Terrell threw up a picket line around Hecht's department store, creating one of the biggest civil rights campaigns at the time (even entertainer Josephine Baker dropped by). "You could go in there and use your charge-a-plate [a predecessor to credit cards], but you couldn't use the bathrooms," Eleanor explained in her biography, *Fire in My Soul* by Joan Steinau Lester. Terrell sued the store, citing the District's 1872 and 1873 open accommodation laws, which made segregation in public accommodations illegal. In January 1952, after six months of protests, Hecht's opened its cafeteria to blacks but without stools, forcing people to eat standing up. On June 8, 1953, the US Supreme Court affirmed the District's laws and Hecht's was forced to integrate.

A proud member of Washington's black bourgeoisie—and a debutante—Eleanor went to Antioch College in Yellow Springs, Ohio, where she could earn money in a work-study program. In December 1955, just months after Eleanor arrived on campus, Rosa Parks refused to move to the back of a bus in Montgomery, Alabama, sparking a city boycott led by the twenty-six-year-old Reverend Martin Luther King Jr. Only a freshman but already head of Antioch's NAACP chapter, Eleanor raised money and conducted local sit-ins for nearly a year. In November 1956, the Supreme Court upheld the Fifth Circuit Court ruling that Montgomery's segregated-bus law violated the Fourteenth Amendment's due process and equal protection clauses. "It was," Eleanor later said, "the defining experience of my life."

After Antioch, Eleanor went to Yale University, where she earned two degrees: a master's degree in American studies in 1963 and a law degree in 1964. The only other black student at the law school was Marian Wright (Edelman). Mentored by Pauli Murray, a black feminist lawyer who was getting an advanced legal degree, Eleanor started a New Haven chapter of CORE (Congress on Racial Equality). In the summer of 1963, she joined the Student Nonviolent Coordinating Committee's voter registration drive in Mississippi, where Medgar Evers drove her to meet key civil rights workers, and later helped organize the 1963 March on Washington. "I grew up black and female at the moment in time in America when barriers would fall if you'd push them," she told Lester. "I pushed . . . and then just walked on through."

When we met her, Eleanor was only thirty-two years old but she was already an extraordinarily accomplished lawyer. After clerking for Judge A. Leon Higginbotham Jr., the first black judge on the US District Court for Pennsylvania's eastern district, she joined the ACLU in 1965, where she made her mark. She wrote amicus briefs for Julian Bond (who was refused his elected seat in Georgia's House of Representatives), Muhammad Ali (who refused military conscription based on his Muslim faith), and Adam Clayton Powell (who was expelled from Congress for alleged abuses). Eleanor also represented some prominent racists. In 1968, she successfully defended presidential candidate George Wallace when New York City Mayor John Lindsay initially barred him from speaking at Shea Stadium. But her most famous case was in October 1969, when she represented the National States' Rights Party before the US Supreme Court. A white supremacist group, the States' Rights Party had been kept from rallying in Maryland on a prior restraint ruling. "I jumped at the opportunity," she recalled, "because if there is a constitutional or civil liberties point to be made, you make it most convincingly when you stand up for the right of somebody who disagrees with you. You must obviously be serving a higher cause—and I love that idea." She won that case.

Next to those high-profile clients, we felt inconsequential, but according to Eleanor, "no case I handled was more important than *Newsweek*. Defending George Wallace was an old-fashion First Amendment case. Same with the white supremacists, who were kept from speaking because of their use of defamatory language against blacks and others." *Newsweek* intrigued her for two reasons. She was one of the few prominent black women who, along with Dorothy Height and Shirley Chisholm, declared herself a feminist. "I said to black women,

'Yes, you must be part of the women's movement,'" she later said. "I remember being so frustrated that when we had one of those feminist parades down Fifth Avenue, I—who never wore dashiki-type garb—put a beautiful African turban around my Afro to make the point that if you're black, you should be marching here." But she understood why black women were hesitant to join. "There was great confusion in the black movement at that time," she said. "We were in the throes of the civil rights movement. For black women to make that transition— to make a partnership with white women, who were among the most privileged in society—was uncomfortable for them."

Another reason Eleanor took our case was that we were the first women in the media to sue and the first professional women to file a class action suit. "At that time, there were almost no classes involving women—certainly none involving white women," she recalled. "If there had been a women's class action suit, I hadn't heard of it." Most of the cases, she said, had involved black factory workers discriminated against via seniority systems or biased testing. We were professional women in a field where advancement depended on subjective judgments. "You essentially had to make a case of deliberate discrimination on where women were placed in the corporation," she explained. "I thought this was so clear that it was an offer that couldn't be refused."

Eleanor believed our case was a perfect fit for the new Civil Rights Act of 1964. The most controversial section of the act was Title VII, which in its original form prohibited only racial discrimination in employment. The provision protecting women was added only at the last minute, as a joke to scuttle the bill. The chairman of the powerful Rules Committee, Howard Smith (D-VA), was a staunch segregationist and opposed to granting federal civil rights to anybody. "Congressman Smith would joyfully disembowel the Civil Rights Bill if he could," said a 1964 article in the *New York Times Magazine*. "Lacking the votes to do so, he will obstruct it as long as the situation allows." That February, Smith laughingly moved to add "sex" to the Title VII protections, thinking it would make the bill impossible to pass. But with lobbying from the National Women's Party and Representative Martha Griffiths (D-MI), who had been laboring to get votes, the amendment passed by a vote of 290–130. In the Senate, Everett Dirksen (R-IL), whose support was key to getting it passed, wanted to remove the amendment. But Senator Margaret Chase Smith (R-ME) persuaded the Republican Conference to vote against him. On June 19, the legislation passed the Senate by a vote of 73–27. President Lyndon Johnson signed the Civil Rights Act of 1964 into law on July 2.

When we approached Eleanor in the winter of 1970, the regulations were new and the precedents few. "To me, as a discrimination lawyer, this was an easy case," Eleanor recalled. "Most cases have much of the discrimination hidden. Usually you got cases where all the women are in one place and all the men are on top—that's the way it is throughout the workplace. But women don't always have the same background as men. You all had the same background! Here you had women who were not only well educated, you had women who excelled at some of the best schools. What more could *Newsweek* want?"

Eleanor agreed to take our case in the winter of 1970, and shortly thereafter *Newsweek* decided to run the women's lib cover. Since I had been reporting on the movement, they thought that asking me to work on Helen Dudar's story would be offensive—and they were right. I was relieved not to be involved. Instead, however, they asked Judy Gingold to be the magazine's liaison to Helen on the story—needless to say, an uncomfortable position for the mastermind of *Newsweek's* own women's movement. "I felt like Mata Hari," recalled Judy. "I felt I was betraying Helen, whom I respected and admired—and that was hard."

When we heard that the editors went outside the magazine to hire a woman writer, we were furious and exhilarated. Now we had a deadline and, more important, a news peg; we could see the headlines already. We quickly stepped up our recruiting, bringing in concentric circles of five, ten, and twenty women. One beloved addition was Ruth Werthman, the respected head of the copy desk, who was in her sixties and delighted to be part of the gang. We also invited the women in the Letters department, since they were often promoted into research jobs. That provided us with our one black signatory, Karla Spurlock, who was working part-time in the Letters department. Karla's Barnard roommate, Alison Kilgour, also worked in Letters and had gotten her the job. "Madeleine [Edmonson, the head of Letters] just rounded all of us up one day and told us we were to sign this, so I did," recalled Karla. We did not approach the female reporters in the bureaus since most of them had been hired from outside the magazine. Nor did we include the editorial secretaries whose skills were different from those of the researchers.

One of the strong points of our suit was that most of the researchers had the same or very similar qualifications as the men who held higher positions. To prove it, we came up with a list of nineteen men who had been hired at *Newsweek* as reporters and writers with no prior professional journalistic experience, including several—such as Rod Gander and Kevin Buckley—who had started as researchers in the early 1960s. (The practice of hiring male researchers ended shortly after that.) The editors always insisted they recruited writers randomly—"over the transom," as they used to say—but their standard procedure, at least in the back of the book, was to hire guys who had worked on the *Yale Daily News* or the *Harvard Crimson*. Several young men from Harvard had been hired right after they graduated, including Jake Brackman (who later became a songwriter with Carly Simon), Rick Hertzberg (now a writer at the *New Yorker*), and as a graduate student, Ray Sokolov (a former writer and editor at the *Wall Street Journal*).

We also suspected that we had been discriminated against in pay as well as position. At one meeting, we decided to divulge our salaries. Phyllis Malamud, one of two New York bureau reporters, had been told she was the highest-paid woman in New York at $15,000. But it turned out that Lucy Howard and Pat Lynden were each making $18,000. "The suit was a sea change," Pat recalled. "Until then, coming from privileged backgrounds, we all felt we were special and therefore we were better than the other women. But while we were organizing, we started to like and trust each other. We figured we're all in this together and the risk is worth taking." Organizing became an unexpected bonding experience and, like D-Day, you never forgot who fought with you in the trenches.

Now that we had a deadline with the women's lib cover, we had to quickly convince everyone to take legal action. As budding feminists, we knew that the decision had to be made by consensus, so we invited about twenty women to meet Eleanor and hear her recommendations. We met on February 25, at Mary Pleshette's apartment, where women were sprawled over her colorful Moroccan carpet. "It was really exciting," remembered Mariana Gosnell, a reporter in the Medicine and Science sections who was a decade older than most of us. "Eleanor laid out our options, but we were a little timid by her standards. Some women thought it would affect their jobs. I felt good that we had some more radical, recent college graduates who were more confident than I was. I thought, this is the way it is and it wouldn't change. Still, I don't think it occurred to many of us that we could actually change the system."

There was a discussion about whether we should work through the Newspaper Guild, which represented *Newsweek* employees in contract negotiations with management. But the Guild, dominated by blue-collar men, had not been in the forefront of civil rights, let alone women's rights, so we nixed that. Then someone raised the possibility of sending a delegation to visit Kay Graham, thinking that as a woman she might be sympathetic. Others thought we should first go to the editors and give them one more chance. "Even I found it hard to stick it to them," remembered Judy Gingold. "I respected a lot of those people. Oz had three daughters and he was so proud that one of them had gotten eight hundred on her college boards. But all I could think of was, a lot of good that will do her! It was very difficult sustaining the belief that I was right, because how could I be right and Oz Elliott wrong?" Fay was reluctant to file any legal action. She kept asking, "Why can't we just talk to them?" and we kept saying, "It won't work, they won't listen."

There was one obvious reason it wouldn't work. Six months before we started to organize, ten of the senior writers on the magazine organized what became known as "the Colonels' Revolt." They were bitching about the usual issues of news-magazine writers: their ideas weren't listened to and they wanted a more personal voice in their stories. The writers held a meeting and drew up a list of "nonnegotiable demands," which is what all movements presented to the power structure in those days. They drew a map of the Wallendatorium on a chalkboard with arrows pointing to each office—wanting them to think they were plotting a sit-in—and purposely left it there, hoping it would be found. It was, and the Wallendas immediately met with the Colonels, not as a group but individually. "Every Wallenda was assigned to someone and I got Oz," recalled Peter Goldman. "They picked us off one by one. Some people got raises, some promotions, and we all got to recite our demands. But essentially nothing happened."

If the editors co-opted their most valued employees, we thought, why would they listen to their lowliest staffers? That's why many of us were willing to go to court. But Eleanor still had to convince us. We began meeting with Eleanor in the evenings, in what became a six-week boot camp in power politics. "It wasn't a case of me convincing you," she later said. "We met so many times precisely because the women had to convince themselves. You knew you were on the frontier and you all had to discuss what was happening. But I had to keep telling you the truth. You're the crème de la crème—what the hell are you afraid of? You're smarter than these guys, they're taking advantage of you, and when the court sees your credentials, their eyes will pop out."

Sitting in her apartment at 245 West 104th Street, Eleanor would cut and devour slices of raw onion—one of her pregnancy cravings—as she harangued us to screw up our courage. When we explained the researcher job and how all the decisions were made by men, she was shocked. "This is one of the great dictatorships in the history of magazines!" she exclaimed. She was also surprised by our naïveté. "You gotta take off your white gloves, ladies, you gotta take off your white gloves," she would say. At one point, fed up with us all, she yelled, "You God damn middle-class women—you think you can just go to Daddy and ask for what you want?"

We all were terrified of Eleanor but there was a method to her madness. She had to shape us into a tough, solid group. "Only one or two plaintiffs would have been very vulnerable at that early stage in a sex discrimination investigation," she later explained. "They could lose their jobs, even though there is a separate cause of action against retaliation. Or if they didn't lose their jobs, they're the ones who would be fingered, and everyone else would get the benefit of what a couple of people did." Even though she thought we had a strong case, Eleanor was worried about the fight. "If enough women would come forward, then there would be protection against you all becoming fodder," she recalled. "I didn't know if you would be fodder. I realized *Newsweek* was a liberal publication, so to speak. But when you go up against management—you go up against management."

CHAPTER 6

Round One

As HARD AS WE TRIED to keep our plans secret, they began to leak out. The Friday before we were to announce our lawsuit, Rod Gander invited Lala Coleman to lunch. They were friends—she was dating one of his reporters at the time—and the two would often go out for a few mint-flavored grasshoppers. At lunch, Rod asked her what was going on with the women. Suppressing her surprise, Lala coolly replied, "I don't know what you're talking about." "You can't even look me in the eye when you say that," he immediately shot back.

The next evening, after closing the Foreign section, Fay Willey was returning home with her groceries when the phone started ringing. She picked it up and was stunned to hear Oz Elliott on the other end. It turned out that one of the researchers in the Business section, who had been checking changes with writer Rich Thomas Friday night, had let it slip that the women were going to put out some sort of press release Sunday evening. Rich called Oz on Saturday and tipped him off. That evening, Oz told me years later, "I called Fay and said that I heard something big was going to happen with the women at *Newsweek* and that it would surface the following week." Oz pressed Fay to tell him what it was, saying the women should first come to management with their grievances. Fay was shaking. She greatly admired and respected Oz but she was scared of giving anything away. "In a very cold voice," Oz recalled, "Fay said she couldn't say anything, that the train was too far down the track." He made several attempts to convince her to tell him, appealing to her as a longtime, senior employee and a levelheaded one. Bravely holding her ground, she said simply that she would pass his message on to the women. "When I was told that Fay was involved, I felt it gave the whole thing gravitas," Oz told me. "She was no miniskirted recent grad from Radcliffe. She was part of the old guard."

Clearly worried about what was going to happen, Oz called Fay again Sunday morning, this time with a more serious concern. He reminded her that the press was under attack from the government and warned her that whatever the women were planning might have political repercussions for the magazine. In late 1969, the Nixon administration had begun its war on the "Eastern establishment elitist press." At one point Vice President Spiro Agnew declared that the *Washington Post* was part of "a trend toward monopolization of the great public information vehicles," saying that the *Post* and *Newsweek*, along with the Post Company's radio and television stations, "hearken to the same master." Oz appealed to Fay not to get the government involved and offered to meet with the women anytime. Fay again held her ground and promised to relay his concerns to the women.

There was one person we felt we should call: Helen Dudar. Pat Lynden offered to call her at home after we announced our suit. "That was incredibly helpful," recalled Peter Goldman, Helen's husband, "because Pat assured Helen that the suit wasn't personal—it was about going outside for someone to write the cover." Helen was part of the generation of women who had to make it on their own against great odds and she succeeded in every respect. "I idolized her," wrote Nora Ephron in a foreword to Helen's collected works, *The Attentive Eye: Selected Journalism*, edited by Peter. Nora, who worked with Helen at the *New York Post*, said, "Helen could do anything. She could write a lyrical feature piece, she could write hard news, and she was—in a city room full of world-class rewrite men—the greatest rewrite man of all."

Like many professional women of her generation, Helen hadn't embraced the women's liberation movement; she took the *Newsweek* assignment because she thought it was interesting. "She was in pre-feminist mode then," said Peter of his wife, who died in 2002. "I don't think she thought about the political context of the cover story. If I had been smarter I would have said this assignment has hair on it. But I wasn't smart then. You all woke me up and the assignment woke Helen up." For Helen, reporting on the new feminism was a voyage of self-discovery. "It was her consciousness-heightening period but I don't think she connected it with the *Newsweek* system," said Peter. "We used to talk about how one of the fringe benefits of *Newsweek* was that I had women pals for the first time in my adult life. But I wasn't bringing home that it was a caste system and that it wasn't fair."

When the couple discussed the assignment at home, "Helen was just communicating bits to me because she was assimilating it in bits," Peter recalled, "not in the sense of becoming an activist. She was like me on the civil rights movement—we were chroniclers. When Pat Lynden called, it was the first bell, an 'Oh my God' moment for both of us. Why didn't we get it? How could we—particularly me—not have figured this out? When the story of the legal action unfolded, it was like a revelatory experience."

The final irony of hiring Helen to write the *Newsweek* cover is that she ended up being a convert to the women's cause. Although *Newsweek*'s contents page, written by the editors, introduced the "Women in Revolt" cover in ominous tones, "A new specter is haunting America—the specter of militant feminism," Helen's report on the new feminism ended with the following thoughts:

> I have spent years rejecting feminists without bothering to look too closely at their charges. . . . It has always been easy to dismiss substance out of dislike for style. About the time I came to this project, I had heard just enough to peel away the hostility, leaving me in a state of ambivalence. . . . Superiority

is precisely what I had felt and enjoyed, and it was going to be hard to give it up. That was an important discovery. . . . Women's lib questions everything; and while intellectually I approve of that, emotionally I am unstrung by a lot of it. Never mind. The ambivalence is gone; the distance is gone. What is left is a sense of pride and kinship with all those women who have been asking all the hard questions. I thank them and so, I think, will a lot of other women.

The Sunday evening before we filed the suit, when we gathered at Holly Camp's apartment to work out the final details, Fay told us about Oz's calling her at home. She relayed how he reminded her of the Nixon administration's hostility toward the press and asked for another chance. Fay felt that Oz had made a good case, and once again she pleaded with us to go to the editors first with our grievances. We were shocked that Oz had found out about our plans but we were also impressed— and grateful—that Fay had fended off the boss and kept our secret. Still, we were convinced that filing a legal action was our best chance for change and protection. Our final act that evening was to sign the EEOC complaint, which had to be in the mail before midnight. As we solemnly lined up, I felt the thrill and the terror of what we were about to do. There was no turning back. One by one, we recorded our names on the historic document.

The next morning, thirty of us arrived at the ACLU an hour before the 10 A.M. press conference. We nervously started setting up the wooden chairs in the makeshift boardroom and then we waited—and waited. By 9:30, no one from the press corps had arrived. We started to panic. Our entire strategy hung on getting publicity. What if no one came? Finally some cameramen and reporters started filing in, including Susan Brownmiller, who had been invited by her former *Newsweek* colleagues to bear witness. When Gabe Pressman, the popular NBC reporter arrived, recalled Margaret Montagno, "I thought, 'Aha—this really is an event!'"

After the press conference, most of us in the back of the book and Business went back to the office. Judy, Margaret, and Lucy went to lunch at a small restaurant near the ACLU to celebrate. As they toasted the women's movement and each other, Judy kept yelling, "We did it, we did it!" The next morning, the women met again at the Palm Court in the Plaza Hotel with Pat and, over croissants and champagne, they read the newspaper accounts of the press conference out loud. "I was annoyed that I was called a respectable young woman," remembered Pat, "and amused that the *Daily News* called us 'Newshens'!"

When Lucy and Pat went into the office later that Tuesday morning, they ran into Oz on the eleventh floor. "How do you feel about what happened?" Pat asked him. Oz immediately invited them into his office, where they talked for forty-five minutes. "First Oz said how hurt he was," recalled Pat. "Then he asked, 'Why didn't you come to me?' Lucy said we had—we came many times in many ways. He listened to us but didn't concede anything." Lucy was insulted because Oz said, "I can understand you, Pat, but Lucy—you are such a nice girl."

Kermit Lansner, the magazine's editor, seemed to dismiss the whole thing. Whenever there was ever a ripple in the pond of tranquility at *Newsweek,* Kermit would typically say, "Madness . . . It's all mad." We thought managing editor Lester Bernstein felt betrayed, furious that these lowly employees had soiled his magazine's reputation. One editor, we were told, simply said, "Let's just fire them all." Only Oz took the lawsuit seriously. As the father of three girls, he was particularly chastened by the charges of discrimination against women. "My consciousness at the time was zero," he admitted to me before he died in 2008. "Here we were busily carving out a new spot as a liberal magazine and right under our own noses was this oppressive regime—and no one had a second thought! It was pretty clear to me on that Monday that the women were right."

That was one of the chilling contradictions of the culture: advocating civil rights for all while tolerating—or overlooking—the subjugation of women. "My theory is that we were all blind to the fact that we were sitting on top of a caste system," said Peter Goldman. "It was this '50s mentality and the fact that *Newsweek* was copying *Time.* It seemed natural that women were in servile roles and as you keep hiring, the overcaste and the undercaste become self-sustaining. By the time I got there in 1962, the men just accepted this as the way things were and I think the women accepted it the same way."

But after that Monday in March, it was a whole new story. Some of the correspondents in the field sent congratulatory cables. "The all male San Francisco bureau (and chief stringer Karen McDonald) say right on sisters," read a telex from bureau chief Jerry Lubenow and reporters Bill Cook and Min Yee. The female correspondents immediately signaled their support, especially Liz Peer in the Washington bureau. "Liz was a cheerleader," recalled Mimi McLoughlin, the Religion researcher. "She thought of herself as a woman who had succeeded on her own and somewhat distanced herself from it. But she'd always say, 'You guys are great.'"

Most of the writers supported their female colleagues. "My attitude was 'Go for it,'" recalled Peter Goldman. "We were in a 'movement' frame of mind and as soon as the women lit the match, it was obvious. I also thought doing it through a lawsuit was the right way. I had been covering the civil rights movement and Vietnam and I thought, 'Okay, here's one more revolution—this is inevitable and it had to happen.'" Harry Waters remembered viewing the women's plight less as a gender issue than as one of injustice. "I was a young guy who started as a fact checker," he said, "but I always knew—and was told—that I would get a shot at reporting, writing, and editing. For a young, ambitious, talented woman, that elevator was out of order."

Not everyone was espousing a new order, however. As in many organizations, it was middle management that was most resistant to change—in our case, some of the senior editors who ran the six editorial sections of the magazine. With the exception of my boss, Shew Hagerty, and Ed Diamond, none of the other senior editors had promoted a researcher to writer, nor had they hired a woman as a writer. In her memoir, Susan Brownmiller described being called into *Newsweek* several weeks after the press conference to meet with the Wallendas. They inquired whether she would be interested in coming back to the magazine as a writer, but she declined. "My idea of a cold-sweat nightmare was eighty-five lines for Nation on a Friday night—it still is," she wrote. Afterward, she was pulled aside by Lester Bernstein, her former boss when he was the senior editor of Nation. "When you worked here, Susan, did you have ambition?" he asked. As she noted in her book, "For two years not a week had gone by without my asking if I could 'do more.' He hadn't noticed."

After we announced our lawsuit, Oz sent a memo to the women Monday afternoon. Saying that he was "naturally dismayed at your evident unhappiness," he called for a meeting the next day at Top of the Week, the elegant penthouse of the *Newsweek* building where visiting dignitaries were entertained. Designed by I. M. Pei, Top of the Week had a sumptuous beige salon with luxurious couches and chairs, large and small dining rooms, and a kitchen. Before our Tuesday meeting with Oz, Eleanor had instructed us not to say a word until she got there, because she didn't want us to incriminate ourselves.

Oz had arranged rows of folding chairs for the women facing one of the soft suede couches where he had placed himself and Kermit. "Big mistake," Oz later told me. "The sofa was about a foot and a half lower than the chairs and now Kermit and I are looking up at forty-seven women—our knees under our chins. I said, 'I'd like to say a few words before we start,' and this cold voice from the back of the room says, 'Sorry, Oz, we're not going to do anything until our lawyer gets here.'

Oops, I thought, this is going to be a heavy session." We sat there awkwardly for a few minutes until Eleanor finally arrived. "In comes this very angry, very articulate, very smart, very pregnant, very black Eleanor Holmes Norton," Oz said. "I welcomed her and said, 'Please take a seat. I just want to say a few words to the women before we get started,' and she said, 'I'm sorry, Mr. Elliott, but this is *our* meeting—*we* will do the talking.' She had me splattered on the wall. Boy, she was tough. How much of that explosive nature was affected and how much was just sheer anger I don't know. I think a lot of it was playacting, but she was sharp."

The editors, who had supported the struggle for civil rights, were completely baffled by this pregnant black woman who questioned their commitment to equality. But they were also horrified that the women had, as they said, "hung out their dirty laundry in public." Eleanor had warned us that Oz would immediately ask why we hadn't come to him first with our dissatisfactions. Right on cue, that was his first question and we could barely stifle our giggles. "I was surprised by the anger of the women," Oz later told me. "But when I look back I'm only surprised that the women didn't wake up earlier."

Shamed and chagrined, Oz immediately agreed to enter into negotiations. He and Kermit, along with Grant Tompkins, *Newsweek*'s head of personnel, and Rod Gander, the chief of correspondents, represented management; Eleanor and ten representatives selected by the women composed the negotiating team (I was one of them). For several weeks we met in Oz's eleventh-floor office, a den-like room with bookshelves, a large wooden desk, a green patterned sofa, and matching green drapes. We had asked that as the proprietor of the magazine and one of the few female media owners Kay Graham attend the negotiations. But she declined, saying that the editors who ran the magazine would deal with the matter. "Kay was concerned, obviously," Oz told me, "but she never said, 'You've got to settle this Goddamn thing' or 'Screw them.' She never got involved."

As she wrote in her remarkably candid, 1997 Pulitzer Prize–winning autobiography, *Personal History,* Katharine Graham said that when she first took over the Washington Post Company, she felt inadequate as a company boss and a "pretender to the throne." A smart, talented young woman who had been a reporter for the *San Francisco News,* Kay had stopped working after she married Phil Graham. But after he committed suicide in 1963, she courageously stepped in to keep the paper in the family. Kay was immediately elected president of the Washington Post Company. Assuming she would be a silent partner, she was terrified. "I didn't understand the immensity of what lay before me," she later wrote, "how frightened I would be by much of it, how tough it was going to be and how many anxious hours and days I would spend for a long, long time." Six years later, she became publisher of the *Post,* a title both her father and her husband had held, but she was still riddled with feelings of inadequacy. "In the world today, men are more able than women at executive work and in certain situations," she told *Women's Wear Daily* in 1969. "I think a man would be better at this job I'm in than a woman."

Although Kay never commented publicly on our lawsuit, it was clear that she wasn't happy about it. A week after we filed charges in March 1970, in another interview with *Women's Wear Daily,* she was asked about the feminists at *Newsweek.* Kay replied that she encouraged her employees to speak their minds because people perform best when they have their say. Then she added, "Sometimes when I go home at the end of the day, I think they all have too damn much freedom to speak up."

One day in April, as we were meeting with management, Kay was spotted in her *Newsweek* office at the other end of the eleventh floor. When Eleanor heard this, she stopped the proceedings. "I understand Mrs. Graham is in the building," she said, "and I want her to come to this meeting. We will not continue these discussions until she comes." Kermit dutifully wandered off to find her and came back dragging a clearly uncomfortable Kay Graham, who sat down, tightly wrapping her legs around each other like a pretzel.

The topic that day was how women were excluded from meeting visiting dignitaries who came to the magazine. We were talking about Val Gerry, a researcher in the Foreign section who also reported on the United Nations. When a UN official came to *Newsweek* for lunch, Val had not been invited. Kay offered a response and to this day, nearly every woman remembers her words. "Well," she said, "I don't know why anyone would want to go to those lunches anyway. You know they're really very boring, and by the time you invite the four Wallendas, the Foreign editor, and the head of the UN and his entourage, there's really no place left at the table." We were flabbergasted. Clearly Kay was not a "sister." "When Kay said those lunches were so boring," said one researcher later, "it might have been boring to her because she had been involved in these kind of events her whole life!" After the meeting, Eleanor remarked that it was a good thing that Kay hadn't been in the negotiations after all.

Before the next meeting, Eleanor asked us whether there was anything in particular we wanted to ask for in the negotiations. We said that since the chief of correspondents was a senior editor, we felt that the longtime head of researchers, Olga Barbi, should also be promoted to that title. Positive that the men would go for it since they liked Olga and she had the power to hire and fire, Eleanor confidently made her pitch. The men rejected it outright, saying we were trying to elevate research and that Olga didn't do senior-editor kind of work. Afterward, Eleanor was furious that we had been so tactically stupid and excoriated us to never again ask for something when we weren't sure of the outcome.

But Eleanor held the editors' feet to the fire. At one meeting, Oz was explaining that hiring women writers was difficult because there were only so many slots open when he said, "You know, we've made a commitment on this magazine to get black writers, too." Eleanor immediately fired back, "All you're telling me, Mr. Elliott, is that now you've got *two* problems!"

Our negotiations moved rapidly, partly because Eleanor was pregnant and partly, although we didn't know it, because she had been approached by Mayor John Lindsay to be chair of New York City's Commission on Human Rights. The job was to begin April 15, a month after we filed our suit. (Many of us attended her swearing-in at the Blue Room of City Hall.) Luckily, most of the terms had been hammered out by mid-April. We had negotiated a memorandum of understanding, which stated that *Newsweek* was committed to "substantial rather than token changes." In the memorandum, the women agreed to accept management's "good faith" to "affirmatively seek out women"—including employees—for reporting and writing tryouts and positions; to integrate the research category with men; and to "identify women employees who are qualified" as possible senior editors. The agreement also stipulated that *Newsweek* would invite women to join editorial lunches, panels, campus speaker programs, and other public functions. To monitor the magazine's progress, management agreed to meet with our representatives every two months.

The language we settled for in the memorandum was vague. Quotas were illegal and although "goals and timetables" had been established as a method of relief in some legal cases, we didn't use them. Before he died in 2007, Rod Gander told me that Eleanor hadn't pushed for numbers because, "being pregnant, I think she was happy to get the thing done." Eleanor later admitted that she had to "turn this case around—I didn't get into depositions because I was trying to settle the case without going further." But she insisted that as far as setting goals and timetables, "it was not at all clear that the precedents had developed. All of the cases at that time had come out of the Deep South, where working-class black men were deliberately put into situations where they couldn't use the facilities but they could do the work. So the use of numbers had come out of harshly negative discrimination. I don't think we would have opened up numbers in this case."

We picked a historic date for signing the memorandum: August 26, 1970, the fiftieth anniversary of the passage of the Nineteenth Amendment. To celebrate women's right to vote—and to launch a new crusade for women's rights—Betty Friedan had called for a nationwide "Women's Strike for Equality" that day. Designed to appeal to both the older, liberal branch of the movement and the younger, more radical factions, the demonstrations were organized around three demands: equal opportunity in education and employment, free abortion on demand, and a network of twenty-four-hour, free child-care services. Women in more than forty cities and around the world participated.

The event was scheduled for 5 P.M. in New York, so that working women could attend, and many of us did. Reports said that between 25,000 and 50,000 women marched down Fifth Avenue, spilling over from the police-approved single lane to fill the street curb to curb. Carrying hand-lettered signs that read FIGHT SEXISM, WHISTLE AT TRUCK DRIVERS, and EVE WAS FRAMED, the women gathered for a rally in Bryant Park, behind the New York Public Library. Betty Friedan was joined on the platform by congressional candidate Bella Abzug, writers Gloria Steinem and Kate Millett, and our own Eleanor Holmes Norton. "Sex, like color, is a meaningless criterion and an oppression criterion when it is made a condition for a job," Eleanor told the crowd. Friedan ended the rally with a plea for unity. "We have learned that the enemy is us—our own lack of self-confidence," she said. "We know that the enemy is not men. Man as a class is not the enemy. Man is the fellow victim of the kind of inequality between the sexes that is part of this country's current torment and that is perpetrating violence all over the world."

But some men still didn't get it. Describing the event on the ABC evening news that night, anchor Howard K. Smith introduced his report by saying, "Three things have been difficult to tame: the ocean, fools, and women. We may soon be able to tame the ocean, but fools and women will take a little longer." In fact, it was the largest protest for women's rights since the Suffragettes, and it solidified Friedan's nascent National Organization for Women (NOW) and a scattering of women's lib groups into a national political movement.

When sixteen of us gathered in Kay Graham's eleventh-floor office on that Wednesday morning to sign the agreement, our spirits were high. We now numbered sixty plaintiffs, as more women from research, Letters, and Photo had joined the suit. Sitting at her conference table, the *Newsweek* managers—Osborn Elliott, Kermit Lansner, Rod Gander, and personnel chief Roger Borgeson—signed the 1,500-word document. Then they circulated it around the table to the women from the negotiating committee: Judy Gingold, Merrill Sheils (McLoughlin), Fay Willey, Madeleine Edmonson, Lucy Howard, Pat Lynden, Phyllis Malamud, Mariana Gosnell, Mary Pleshette, and me. Eleanor returned for the signing to join Mel Wulf, from the ACLU, and Kay Graham at the table. Kay said she was pleased that the signing had taken place on such a historic day and Oz congratulated everyone, adding, "I am sure that this agreement will contribute significantly to our editorial excellence."

As we toasted one another with wine afterward, we tried not to lord it over the editors but we couldn't conceal our triumph. We'd done it! We had forced management to at least acknowledge their prejudices and to promise to change their ways. We were still worried about what would happen to us and whether the editors would actually carry out Oz's orders, but we were hoping for the best. In a *New York Times* story about the agreement, titled "*Newsweek* Agrees to Speed Promotion of Women," I am quoted as saying, "We are very pleased with the progress so far," adding, "We feel a lot better now about things at *Newsweek*."

CHAPTER 7

Mad Men:
The Boys Fight Back

T HE FIRST SIGN OF TROUBLE came only weeks after the agreement was signed. Oz Elliott moved over to the business side as president of Newsweek Inc., leaving Kermit Lansner in charge of the magazine's day-to-day operations. Kermit was an intellectual and a creative man but he often was oblivious to what was going on around him. A paunchy man with the waddle of a duck, he would wander around the eleventh floor staring vaguely at the ceiling. Once, when he was walking through the copy area, a visitor saw him and said, a little too loudly, "What does that float represent?"

Kermit couldn't be bothered with enforcing our agreement, so the editors made the easiest changes first. They invited more women to Top of the Week lunches, panels, and public events and sent out several researchers to the bureaus on reporting internships. But when it came to giving women the chance to write, they were recalcitrant. Since we felt that most of the senior editors were biased, we had devoted five paragraphs in the memorandum to how reporting and writing tryouts were to be conducted. Each step—from requesting and evaluating the tryout to deciding whether she had made it as a writer—was to be done with the approval of top management.

The first researcher to ask for a writing tryout was Mary Pleshette, who had been freelancing for small publications. Jack Kroll, her senior editor, was immediately defensive, saying that he disagreed with her quote at the news conference—that discrimination was a "gentleman's agreement" at *Newsweek*. He agreed to give Mary a tryout but then gave her only a few pieces to write. There was no formal assignment schedule or evaluation of her writing. In fact, none of the pieces she wrote for him ever made it through the complete editing process; they just stalled on his desk. First Mary was annoyed and then she was angry. "I felt he gave me the tryout because he had to," she recalled. "At a certain point it was clear he was just going through the motions." At one point, Jack told Mary that he really liked a piece she wrote on Patsy Kelly, who played a sidekick in the old movies, but he never ran it. Instead, she sold it to *Newsweek's* syndication unit for publication in newspapers around the country. "Nobody wanted you to succeed," she later said. "I didn't feel the editors were doing hatchet jobs, but I felt it was an exercise in futility. There weren't many teeth to our agreement."

Lester Bernstein offered Pat Lynden a tryout in "Where Are They Now?," a section in the front of the book recapping what had become of once-famous people. Pat accepted but was wary. At the time, she confided to friends that "no matter how well I did, I thought I might fail so that the editors could point to me as evidence that women didn't have the right stuff to write for *Newsweek*." She later said, however, that "it was also clear that declining the offer was not an option. I had been one of the most outspoken women in our suit, I had the so-called track record, and "Where Are They Now?" was probably the easiest section in the magazine to write." Pat decided if she didn't make it, she could live with it. "I intended to leave *Newsweek* in a year or so," she recalled. "I was newly married, working on starting a family, and planning to move out west. I could afford to fail and if I did, it would show the editors' bad faith."

Pat's pieces ran for several weeks but she didn't get any feedback. "I didn't have a 'rabbi' among the top male writers or editors like the men who tried out always had," she said. Then *Newsweek* decided to do a feature on child care. Pat was given the assignment because she had written a cover story on the subject for the *New York Times Magazine* in February 1970. The senior editor on the story, Joel Blocker, told Pat to come to him with any problems or questions about the assignment and that he would be glad to help. She took him at his word and gave him her first draft. "The next thing I knew, he called me in to his office to say he'd turned over the assignment to Jerry Footlick," she recalled. "I asked what the problem was and said I wanted to fix it. But Joel shook his head and said

Jerry was doing the story. That was the end of my tryout and I returned to the New York bureau."

This was the problem we had anticipated in arguing for more women writers: the judgment of what is good reporting and good writing is purely subjective. "The senior editors are idiosyncratic," admitted Rod Gander in the negotiations, defending the editors. "Their views of what constitutes good *Newsweek* writing differ." Maybe so, but the editors were united in believing that no woman could do it. One was either "born" with the *Newsweek* style or not, they said, and it seemed that only men were born with it—whatever "it" was. According to Rod, it was "nearly impossible to make any kind of empirical set of credentials as to what makes a good *Newsweek* writer. We have had many writers who cannot do it although they produce beautiful stuff in other media. We have found people of no experience who can do it."

There were *Newsweek* writers who seemed to be born with the gift: Dick Boeth, Jack Kroll, Harry Waters, Pete Axthelm, and Liz Peer. The best was Peter Goldman. "Some of the top writers could go 180 degrees wrong, but Peter never went wrong," said Steve Shepard, the former head of the Nation section who edited him for four years. "I never saw any writer do as much work before actually writing the story. Peter spent hours reading the files from the reporters and background material, underlining everything in different color pens and pinning the files on his wall. When he sat down to write, he had so absorbed the reporting he was able to integrate it and compress it into a poetic style that was brilliant." But that was rare.

Most writers had to learn the newsmagazine formula, which differs significantly from the newspaper style. Newspapers use the "inverted pyramid" construction: the lead sentence or paragraph consists of the most important facts—who, what, where, when, why—and subsequent paragraphs contain information of decreasing importance, which allows editors to cut from the bottom for space. The newsmagazine story, at that time, was written in an authoritative voice that told the reader, "Here's what you have to know." Unlike newspapers, magazines put a premium on stylish writing with a beginning, middle, and end, and compressed as many details and as much color as possible onto the page. Mike Ruby, a writer in the magazine's Business section, used to call *Newsweek* writing f—k-style journalism: Flash (the lead), Understanding (the billboard—why is this story important), Clarification (tell the details of the story), and Kicker (bringing it all together with a clever ending). Dwight Martin, a senior editor at *Newsweek* and a former editor at *Time,* described it simply as "literary bricklaying—you're not born with it, it's a skill to be learned."

"It's such a constipated writing style and yet they elevated it to some mystical form," remembered Margaret Montagno. "Some guy who graduated from Harvard and came to *Newsweek* over the transom had it—he was a writer—while some woman who graduated from Radcliffe was only a researcher." Even women who had journalism experience, such as Mary Pleshette, Pat Lynden, and Susan Brownmiller—or who had worked on their college publications, as Nora Ephron, Jane Bryant Quinn, and Betsy Carter had—were still hired as researchers. When

Kermit Lansner was asked once why women such as Nora Ephron had to leave the magazine to write, he snapped, "*Newsweek* isn't a training ground, you know." But it clearly was for men.

Some men questioned whether forcing management to promote women from within was a good idea. One was Ray Sokolov, a *Harvard Crimson* alum who was writing in the Arts sections. "The researchers were problematic as a category," he recalled. "Almost none of them had a background in journalism." It is curious that none of the *Newsweek* editors had hired—or considered hiring—experienced women journalists from other publications. "There really was sexism at work in some way that made no sense," said Ray. "They could have found six women reporters in any of the daily journalism publications and not have had to wait for their potentially capable researchers to make it as writers."

In the mid-1960s, there were a few women writing at *Time,* where *Newsweek* editors often looked for talent. Some magazines, such as *BusinessWeek,* hired women as writers right out of college and all the major newspapers carried female bylines. When Katharine Graham suggested in the early 1960s that former *New York Times* art critic Aline Saarinen be hired as an editor at *Newsweek,* the editors dismissed her out of hand, she wrote, "condescendingly explaining that it would be out of the question to have a woman. Their arguments were that the closing nights were too late, the end-of-the-week pressure too great, the physical demands of the job too tough. I am embarrassed to admit that I simply accepted their line of reasoning passively."

After the agreement, however, the editors began pursuing female writers from outside the magazine as fast as they were scuttling the tryouts of women inside. The first woman they hired was Barbara Bright, who had been a stringer for *Newsweek* in Germany. She had returned to the United States and became a writer in Foreign. Then they approached Susan Braudy, an experienced freelancer for the *New York Times Magazine,* who went on to become a writer and editor at *Ms.* magazine and the author of several best-selling books. I had met Susan when we were reporting on the first Congress to Unite Women in August 1969, and we had become good friends. In December 1969, Susan wrote a freelance piece for *Playboy* on women's lib, but it never ran—Hugh Hefner spiked it. Hef's memo as to why he didn't like the piece was later leaked to the press by a *Playboy* secretary (who was promptly fired) and it became a cause célèbre. "What I want," Hef said, "is a devastating piece that takes militants apart. . . . What I'm interested in is the highly irrational, kooky trend that feminism has taken. These chicks are our natural enemy. . . . It is time to do battle with them. . . . All of the most basic premises of the extreme form of the new feminism [are] unalterably opposed to the romantic boy-girl society that *Playboy* promotes."

Joel Blocker, by now a senior editor in the back of the book, first contacted Susan because, he told her, *Newsweek* wanted to do a "sympathetic" story on the contretemps, which ran in

May 1970 (her own piece eventually ran in *Glamour* in May 1971). The following year, he offered her a tryout. Susan wrote in the back-of-the-book sections but struggled with writing *Newsweek* style. She and I talked often about this, but I was having my own problems with Blocker and wasn't much help. After a year, she left in the summer of 1972. "They wouldn't let me do my own reporting," she recalled, "and I didn't understand the condensation, the formulaic writing, and the kickers at *Newsweek*. But I learned a lot. I learned to write when I didn't like what I was writing."

Diane Zimmerman, a star reporter in the back of the book, had been writing occasional stories for the Medicine section and others. After we filed the complaint, she asked her editor, Ed Diamond, for a tryout. "With all his peculiarities, Ed was very fair and pushed for me," she remembered. "The Wallendas said they would do it but that they weren't ready yet. I tried to get a tryout for at least eight or nine months and I couldn't get one. The Wallendas didn't approve it." Diane left in 1971, when Shew Hagerty moved to the *New York Daily News* and hired her there.

There were also pockets of resistance by some writers and reporters. In February 1971, I received the following story suggestion via telex from Jim Jones, the crusty Detroit bureau chief: "A group of women's lib sows here, who are members of the Detroit Press Club, are demanding that they be admitted to the club's annual 'Stag Steakout,' a gridiron-type affair where the insults and language are a deep blue. . . . Now it appears the club's board of governors may bend and admit the broads at the do in March (partly this is because a governor or two has a mistress or two among the libbies and are afraid that they'll get cancelled out if they don't vote favorably). This is a teapot tempest, but I'm advised the *NY Times* is working up a story involving the hassle, and maybe you'd want to take the edge off that."

Infuriated, I telexed Jones back ordering a fifty-liner, with a zinger at the end. "Allowing for your clearly sexist item, appreciate as objective an account as possible." For that, I was called into Rod Gander's office and, with Jones on the phone, told we had to settle our differences amicably. We grudgingly did but the story never ran.

By March 1971, the women's panel realized that management wasn't living up to even the spirit—much less the letter—of the agreement in recruiting women writers, inside or out. Once again, we contacted Mel Wulf at the ACLU, who wrote to the editors requesting a meeting "since there are failures involving the pace of implementation" of the agreement. He also noted that "it is unethical and a breach of the agreement to set up your obligation to seek out blacks as in some way mitigating your obligation to rectify the imbalances effecting [*sic*]women." Eleanor Holmes Norton, now chair of the New York City Human Rights Commission, also sent a letter recommending that the women's representatives no longer meet with management unless accompanied by an attorney. The editors immediately promised that the meetings would be more productive without a lawyer present. We reluctantly agreed, continuing to meet over the summer and into the fall.

One of the major problems in recruiting women writers was that vacancies were not posted. The editors simply continued to recruit through the old-boy network. At one meeting, Oz admitted that the editors didn't have any "resources" for finding writers; they just asked friends and colleagues in the business, obviously all male. Nor did editors honor their commitment to report what efforts had been made to find a woman when a man had been hired. Asked whether the Nation editor would show the panel some proof that he had searched for a woman in filling a recent opening, Oz simply said no, adding that if a good writer "came down the pike," he would not want to go searching for a female just to show us they had looked for one.

In July, Lester Bernstein promised to come up with some suggestions for better recruitment but when we met again in September, he said that after talking it over with some of his colleagues, he had thought better of it. At the same meeting, executive editor Bob Christopher said that if *Newsweek* were forced by law to set up a recruitment program, the editors would simply make up a list of resources and then ignore it. Kermit Lansner, clearly exasperated with the whole process, insisted that *Newsweek* didn't need to change its recruitment policies. "Writers come to the magazine over the transom," he said, "and women aren't coming. We can't do anything if they're not interested." We told him to go out and look for them. Then, for a good ten minutes, he lamented that actually nobody wanted to come to write for *Newsweek* anymore. In the end, management never gave us an explanation of what efforts, if any, they had made to find a woman for the last five writing slots filled by men.

We did have some success getting women into the reporting ranks. After a summer internship in Chicago, Lala Coleman became a correspondent in San Francisco in the fall of 1970. Sunde Smith was promoted from Business researcher to reporter in the Atlanta bureau and Mary Alice Kellogg went to the Chicago bureau. Ruth Ross, an experienced black reporter who had left *Newsweek* to start *Essence* magazine, returned to the New York bureau in 1971. We also got our first female foreign bureau chief when Jane Whitmore, a reporter in Washington, was given that position in Rome in 1971. Management also started hiring men as researchers and finally, after ten years as head researcher in the Foreign department, assistant editor Fay Willey was promoted to associate editor.

But there were casualties. When Trish Reilly, one of the most talented young women on staff, was sent to the Atlanta bureau for a summer internship in 1970, the move terrified her. "I was such a depressive, anxiety case," she recalled. "I was horrified at the thought of being shipped off someplace but I couldn't say anything because the women were being set free." The most helpful person was the bureau's Girl Friday, Eleanor Roeloffs Clift. Eleanor, whose parents ran a deli in Queens, New York, had dropped out of college and gotten a job at *Newsweek* in 1963 as a secretary to the Nation editor. She was later promoted to researcher and transferred to Atlanta in 1965, when her husband found work there. "Eleanor was the office manager but she ran the bureau," said Trish. "She gave out the assignments, she did everything, including some reporting." Indeed, when some of the New York women called Eleanor to say she should stop doing reporting until the editors gave her a raise and a promotion, Eleanor refused and continued her dual roles.

One night Trish was in Birmingham, Alabama, covering a school desegregation story. "I was staying in a crummy Holiday Inn all alone with the Coke machine running outside my door," she recalled. "I thought, 'If I have to do this the rest of my life, I will slit my wrist.' To another woman this would have been a shining moment—covering desegregation in Birmingham! But it totally threatened who I was, being given this adult responsibility, and I was miserable and I couldn't tell anyone."

Trish returned to New York after the summer and was offered a permanent spot as a reporter in the Los Angeles bureau. This sent her into a tailspin. "It was announced that I was going to LA and I couldn't face it," she remembered. "I told Rod [Gander] I couldn't go. I knew if you turned down a promotion it was the end of your career, but that was fine. I just wanted to be a researcher." The only person she confided in was Ray Sokolov, a close friend. Ray told her the editors were bewildered by the fact that Trish had turned down the offer, and they didn't like it. "Apparently the editors were surprised that a lot of women hadn't come forward to be reporters and writers," she later said. "But I understood that because I was one of those women. The women's movement helped me accept the fact that women were equal to men as intellectuals, but it didn't change who I was inside. A lot of women were prepared socially and emotionally for it, but for those of us who were traditional women, you couldn't switch off overnight just because we won a lawsuit." In fact, Trish thought many of us were too abrasive and too ambitious. "I just didn't think girls should behave like that—take a man's job," she later said. "I found it a little improper."

Little did she know that some of us "ambitious" types were as conflicted about pushing ourselves forward as she was. I constantly struggled with confidence issues. In 1970, Shew Hagerty, who had promoted me, moved to another department and the new editor was my old boss, Joel Blocker. Since working for Blocker as a secretary in the Paris bureau, I had been writing for nearly a year in New York. But Blocker still saw me as a secretary and told me quite clearly that I would have to prove to him that I could write. Week after week over the next eighteen months, nearly every story I handed in was heavily edited or rewritten. I was so miserable I started looking for another job and thought about leaving journalism. Though I didn't think the lawsuit was the reason he was punishing me, it didn't help. I was barely holding on to my job.

By the fall of 1971, a year after the editors committed to "actively seek" women writers, *Newsweek* had hired three women—Barbara Bright, Susan Braudy, and Ann Scott (Crittenden), a researcher at *Fortune*—and nine men. Three *Newsweek* staffers, Pat Lynden, Mary Pleshette, and Barbara Davidson, a Business researcher, had failed their writing tests. The women's panel was fed up. In October, we reported our frustrations to our colleagues. Furious at management's intransigence, we once again decided to hire a lawyer. Since Eleanor Holmes Norton could no longer represent us, we were directed to a new clinic on employment rights law at Columbia Law School. One of the teachers was twenty-seven-year-old Harriet Rabb, who agreed to represent us.

Good girls revolt: When *Newsweek* published a cover on the new women's movement on March 16, 1970 (above), forty-six staffers announced we were suing the magazine for sex discrimination (seated from left: Pat Lynden, Mary Pleshette, our lawyer, Eleanor Holmes Norton, and Lucy Howard. I am standing in the back, to the left of Eleanor Holmes Norton).

Newsweek—Tony Rollo

Newsweek—Bernard Gotfryd

The Ring Leaders: When Judy Gingold (top left, in1969) learned that the all-female research department was illegal, she enlisted her friends Margaret Montagno (top right) and Lucy Howard (bottom, with Peter Goldman in 1968) to file a legal complaint.

Newsweek

On the job: Reporter Pat Lynden had written cover stories for other major publications (with writer David Alpern in 1966).

Newsweek—Tony Rollo

Covering fashion: I was the only woman writer at the time of the suit (with designer Halston and Liza Minnelli in 1972).

Newsweek

The "Hot Book:" Editor-in-chief Osborn Elliott transformed *Newsweek* in the Sixties. He called the gender divide a "tradition," but became a convert to our cause (1974).

At the top: When *Newsweek* owner Katharine Graham (with husband, Philip Graham, in 1962) heard about our lawsuit, she asked, "Which side am I supposed to be on?"

The Editors: We called them "the Wallendas" a joking reference to the high-wire circus act (clockwise from top left, in 1969: Oz Elliott, Lester Bernstein, Robert Christopher, and Kermit Lansner).

A key recruit: Fay Willey wanted research—and researchers—to be more valued at *Newsweek* (1967).

Newsweek—Bernard Gotfryd

Self doubt: Trish Reilly was afraid to say she didn't want to be promoted (1970).

Newsweek—Robert R. McElroy

Success stories: Religion researcher Merrill McLoughlin (left) went on to co-edit *US News & World Report* and reporter Phyllis Malamud became *Newsweek*'s Boston bureau chief (right, with writer Ken Woodward in 1971).

Newsweek—Tony Rollo

On the move: Elisabeth Coleman was given the first bureau internship in Chicago in the summer of 1970 (below) and became a reporter in San Francisco later that year.

Jeff Lowenthal

No chance: Mary Pleshette was given one of the first writing tryouts but her pieces just sat on her editor's desk (1967).

Newsweek

Historic moment: We signed our agreement on August 26, 1970, the fiftieth anniversary of the suffrage amendment (seated clockwise from top left: Eleanor Holmes Norton, Oz Elliott, Kay Graham, Kermit Lansner, Roger Borgeson, Rod Gander, me, Mariana Gosnell, Lucy Howard, Madeleine Edmondson, Fay Willey, Judy Gingold, and Mel Wulf from the ACLU).

Smiles all around: After the signing everyone was hopeful, but the optimism didn't last long (seated clockwise from left: Mel Wulf, Eleanor Holmes Norton, Oz Elliott, Kay Graham, Kermit Lansner, Roger Borgeson, and me; standing from left: Jeanne Voltz, Lauren Katzowitz, Sylvia Robinson, Harriet Huber, Abby Kuflik, Judy Harvey, Mary Alice Kellogg, Joyce Fenmore, and Lorraine Kisley).

Our Brenda Starr: Reporter Liz Peer was a gifted journalist but the editors wouldn't send her to Vietnam (1971).

My mentor: Writer Harry Waters said that for women at *Newsweek* the elevator up "was out-of-order" (1978).

Newsweek—Wally McNamee

Newsweek—Bernard Gotfryd

Civil rights: "My attitude was, 'Go for it,'" said star writer Peter Goldman (1968).

Newsweek—Bernard Gotfryd

The Famous Writers School: Dick Boeth taught the first writer training program for women with Peter Goldman (1972).

"Female Writer Seligmann": Jeanie Seligmann was the first researcher to become a writer after the lawsuit (1973).

Newsweek—David Alpern

Newsweek—Robert R. McElroy

Victory at last: Our second lawyer, Harriet Rabb, prevailed and later represented the women who sued the *Reader's Digest* and the *New York Times* (1972).

Courtesy of Columbia Law School

Liberated: Reporter Mariana Gosnell (here in 1967) wrote her first book at age 62.

The Critic: Writer and editor Jack Kroll was brilliant, but recalcitrant (1976).

The boss and me: Looking back, Oz was the first to say, "God, weren't we awful?" (1975)

Learning the ropes: Media reporter Betsy Carter went on to start *New York Woman* magazine and write novels (here with striking printers in 1974).

Tough call: Diane Camper was one of the black researchers who decided not to join our suit (1977).

A star is born: Eleanor Clift rose from Girl Friday to *Newsweek*'s White House correspondent (in 1976, with Vern Smith, left, and Joe Cumming, Jr., in the Atlanta bureau).

The boys' club: Integrating the story conference (clockwise from left, editor Ed Kosner, Larry Martz, Peter Kilborn, Russ Watson, Dwight Martin, and me, 1977).

Breaking the barrier: My official photo as *Newsweek*'s first female senior editor, September 1, 1975.

Newsweek—Bernard Gotfryd

Forty years later: In March 2010, three young women (from left) Sarah Ball, Jesse Ellison, and Jessica Bennett wrote their story in *Newsweek*—and kept ours alive.

Elizabeth Weinberg

CHAPTER 8

The Steel Magnolia

HARRIET SCHAFFER RABB was the opposite of Eleanor—a petite Texan with a soft Southern accent and a steel-trap intellect. She was also four months pregnant. Harriet had grown up in Houston, the daughter of two physicians. Her parents practiced in the same building: her father, a general practitioner, at one end; her mother, a pediatrician, at the other. Her father's practice and examining room were integrated, but he kept his waiting room segregated because he thought people would feel more comfortable that way. Her mother's practice was mostly white. When her father was serving in World War II, Harriet's mother took her on her nightly rounds or to the Jefferson Davis charity hospital where she trained nurses. "I admired her beyond description," said Harriet. "When the phone rang at home and a patient would ask,

'May I speak to Dr. Schaffer,' I would always have to say, 'Which one?' She was Doc Helen and he was Doctor Jimmy. I thought they were amazing and wanted to be a doctor until I took biology in college and couldn't stand the labs."

Harriet's family was active in the Jewish community, and she was president of her Jewish sorority, but she felt the sting of anti-Semitism in high school. "The Jewish kids did very well in honor society, drama, and debate," she explained. "We went to the nationals on the debate team and won a lot of prizes. But when the head of the school would announce the prizes for debate, he would never pronounce our names correctly. He would say 'Schaffner' or something like that. They were unhappy with us. We could not be cheerleaders because nobody would have ever voted for us."

Knowing what it felt like to be an outsider, Harriet got involved in the voting-rights movement and other civil rights issues when she went to Barnard College in New York City. She was elected president of her freshman class and became chair of the Honor Board senior year. "I liked the process of listening to the evidence and thinking about it," she recalled, "and at some point realized I wanted to be a lawyer." She went on to Columbia Law School and got a summer internship with Kunstler, Kunstler and Kinoy, founded by the well-known civil rights lawyers Bill Kunstler and Arthur Kinoy (Michael Kunstler, Bill's brother and partner, was not involved in their civil rights work). That summer, in 1964, two white civil rights workers, Michael Schwerner and Andrew Goodman, and their black colleague, James Chaney, disappeared in Mississippi. The

Schwerner family was a client of the law firm, so Kunstler and Kinoy tried to get the FBI involved, saying that the kids had been kidnapped. The FBI declined, saying there was no evidence of a crime, and certainly not of a federal crime, so they had no jurisdiction. "There were about five interns at the law firm," Harriet remembered, "and Arthur [Kinoy] said, 'Here's the library, there's the wall of US statutes. Divide it up any way you want to. I want every single one of those books read by the end of this week and I want you to use your imagination to find any potential statute that could be a basis of the FBI getting into this investigation.' And we did. We found a document to persuade the FBI that they needed to get into it. Of course by then, the kids were long dead."

After law school and a brief marriage, Harriet got a job at the Center for Constitutional Rights, which Bill Kunstler and Arthur Kinoy had set up in Newark, New Jersey. The center represented members of Students for a Democratic Society and the Student Nonviolent Coordinating Committee, several of the Weathermen who blew up the West Eleventh Street town house, and the black militant H. Rap Brown. "The first time I ever appeared in a court by myself it was with Rap," Harriet recalled. "He was there for taking a gun on an airplane." At the time, Harriet was dating a law school classmate, Bruce Rabb, who was working on civil rights in the Nixon White House and whose father, Maxwell Rabb, later became President Ronald Reagan's ambassador to Italy. Kinoy was worried about the relationship. He told Harriet that his clients wouldn't trust her because of her close relationship with a Republican working in the White House. He said she would have to get another job. She was disappointed but understood. She quit the law firm and worked for a year for Bess Myerson, then New York City's commissioner for consumer affairs.

In 1970, Harriet and Bruce married and moved to Washington. She tried to get a job in civil rights but she was rejected, she said, either because she was white or because her husband worked in the Nixon administration. Then she found out about an opening as clerk to the US Court of Appeals for the District of Columbia, where David Bazelon was the chief judge. But two of the judges on the panel had checked Harriet's extensive FBI record and objected to her appointment. They also threatened to call the White House to get Bruce fired because his wife had worked with Kinoy and Kunstler.

Judge Bazelon called her in and told her that her FBI file troubled the people on this court; then he asked her to withdraw her application. "Bruce and I talked about it," she recalled. "I said, 'I don't want to run away. I'm not ashamed of what I've done.'" She told Judge Bazelon that she wasn't going to withdraw her application. With tears in his eyes, she remembered, he said, "You're making me ashamed because these judges have told me they won't work with me on the court if I hire you, and I don't have the courage to resist because I feel responsible and the court has to work well. You have the courage not to do this. So I'm not going to give you a job but I'll find you a job." He found her a position at Stern Community Law Firm, which handled public interest cases.

Bruce and Harriet moved back to New York in 1971, and she began teaching a clinic on employment-rights law at Columbia Law School with George Cooper. George, an expert in Title VII, had won a grant from the EEOC to train lawyers on enforcing the new antidiscrimination laws. Harriet spent the summer learning the syllabus on employment rights law. When we approached her in October 1971, she had just started teaching, and she and George began to educate us on building a better, stronger case. "The *Newsweek* case was challenging because it wasn't an assembly-line job," recalled George. "It was a subjective test [of talent], so the challenge for the lawyers is to take the subjectivity and say that on a group basis it turns out to be biased."

Harriet mobilized her law school class to start taking histories of all the women involved, which could serve as statistical evidence of discrimination and as depositions if necessary. She and George also prepared a detailed chart of prior discriminatory practices, violations of the agreement, and continuing discrimination in every category, outlining the charges and then the methods of proof. "You say, here are the credentials of all the men—where they went to school, what their grades were, what their experience was—and you compare the members of the aggrieved class with the people who got what they wanted," George later explained. "You show there's no difference in any measurable things—everybody went to an Ivy League school— and you force them to come back and respond to them using class data." It was a far different approach from that of the fiery

Eleanor Holmes Norton. "Harriet was just right for us," recalled Mimi McLoughlin. "Different talents for different times."

Just before her first encounter with the editors, George took Harriet to lunch at the Columbia Faculty Club to discuss the case. When they got there he said, "I'm not going with you to the *Newsweek* meeting." Harriet was stunned. "The bottom dropped out for me," she recalled. "While I was objecting, he said, 'You don't need me, it'll be fine.' It was my lack of confidence. I had done a lot of things but I was new to Title VII." George continued his involvement with our case, but Harriet was out front. "I knew her background," he later said. "I thought she was great. I knew she could do it."

At Harriet's first meeting with management on December 7, 1971, she proceeded to point out how the magazine was violating the memorandum of understanding by not affirmatively seeking out women to try out as reporters and writers. Only 23 percent of the newly hired writers were female, but 39 percent of the newly hired researchers were male. Of the four *Newsweek* women who had tryouts, three had failed. In November 1971, Jeanie Seligmann, the Medicine researcher, became a writer in the back of the book, the first woman staffer to be promoted. (From that point on, her boss, Dwight Martin, teasingly called her "Female Writer Seligmann.") Kermit Lansner had asked Phyllis Malamud to try out as writer but she declined, citing management's hostile attitude toward the women trying out. In a follow-up meeting on January 5, Rod Gander said that "most of the women on the staff haven't enough experience in writing to show to their proper advantage under a systemized approach in a tryout." But management refused to define what a tryout actually involved. Rod noted that in the case of men on the staff who came in as researchers or junior writers and got promoted, "the ones who have succeeded best have succeeded under . . . a flexible lack of ground rules."

In one meeting Grant Tompkins, the head of personnel, asked if, since the magazine was in the midst of "very difficult" Newspaper Guild negotiations, we would postpone our meetings until those were finished—which we declined to do. The Guild, which was voluntary, had become a pet project for the women. It was dominated by men from Makeup and Photo, and very few editorial employees were members. Two Nation researchers, Noel Ragsdale and Nancy Stadtman (whom we feminists called Stadtperson), encouraged us to join the Guild to make it more responsive to women's needs, which we did. In 1970, we elected Nancy an officer of the Guild and two years later, she became chair, the first female in that position. "Some of the union men had daggers out for me until the first contract," Nancy recalled. "We got a good maternity policy but we also got a paternity leave clause, the first one for a news publication."

Management still seemed stumped about how to move forward, and at the December and January meetings, they asked *us* for constructive solutions. Harriet sent a detailed document suggesting a program for training women writers and specifying goals and timetables for the complete integration of women into the magazine. When we met again on March 8, 1972, the editors refused to make any commitments to changing their policies. Harriet replied that if they wanted us to continue talking, management should come up with suggestions for progress within two weeks. Two weeks and two days later—and only after the women's panel had called an urgent meeting of the women—Harriet received a hand-delivered note from Grant Tompkins ignoring our request and again "welcomed" Harriet's thoughts on how to increase the number of women writers and reporters while improving the representation of the other groups.

On March 28, the women's panel called an emergency meeting, at which we summarized the history of our negotiations and presented a list of grievances. There were now five new women writers on the magazine (Sandra Salmans, a graduate of Columbia Journalism School, had been hired in Business), but since the lawsuit, at least fourteen men had been hired as writers, almost three times as many men as women. In the research category, twelve people were hired from the outside, eight of whom were men. Rod Gander told us that four other women from outside were asked to try out at *Newsweek,* but they had declined. "After one and a half years, we feel that there is no further purpose to be served by meeting with management," we said in our report. "The continuing consultation has become, finally, a means for management to present apologia for every breach of the memorandum and thereby to get away with doing nothing at all for *Newsweek* women. . . . In our opinion, the women should either go ahead and take legal action or else resign themselves to the present situation and discontinue all attempts to right it through mass movement."

Then Harriet spoke. She said that if we wanted to take action, she recommended we do two things: file a new complaint of discrimination with the EEOC and simultaneously sue for breach of contract with the New York State Division of Human Rights. Should we lose the breach-of-contract suit, our federal case would not be prejudiced. Should we win it, we would gain immediate court-ordered relief. After a few questions we decided to take a straw vote. Of the thirty-one women present, twenty-nine voted to file complaints in both jurisdictions, one voted to file only in state court, and one voted to use the legal machinery of the Guild. We sent a memo to the absent women asking for their opinions as well.

I was amazed by the vote. I couldn't believe that two years after our lawsuit—after several women had been trained, promoted, and co-opted with titles—the group was still willing to go through another legal action, with all the recriminations and unpleasantness that would inevitably ensue. We "good girls" had become radicalized. "The first time, I was very nervous," recalled Mimi McLoughlin. "Were we right? Could I defend what we were doing? The second time around I was angrier because I thought they were just stringing us along." Even Harriet was impressed. "I thought the *Newsweek* women were incredible—all of you," she said. "You were committed to *Newsweek* but you wanted opportunities."

For Harriet, we were probably her first clients who wanted to change the system from within. "I learned a great lesson from you," she told me. "After we started meeting with management, I was concerned that management would try to speak to you all individually. So I remember saying to you, 'Lynn, if Oz calls you and asks you to come to his office, you tell him everybody needs to go through your lawyer.' And you said, 'I work for this man and if he asks me to go to his office, I need to go there.' It was really evidence of how young I was to take this on. I wasn't thinking how life was for my clients, partly because I was a teacher. For me, it was breaching the barriers while you all were working there with men who were superiors or jealous. Eleanor and I were litigators. We came in wanting to win. It was so much more complicated for you."

We continued negotiating with management in the spring of 1972 while we planned our next action. During the increasingly difficult discussions about how to increase the number of female writers, we realized that the women needed a writer training program to combat the subjective—and, we thought, biased—tryout system. To teach the course, we recruited two of the best writers on the magazine, who immediately agreed. After proposing the course to the editors, one of them snidely asked, "Well, who would you get to teach this course?" When we said, "Peter Goldman and Dick Boeth," they were silenced.

The Famous Writers School, as it was called, was an eight-week seminar that began in the summer of 1972 and lasted for three semesters, training more than twenty-five women. As Peter Goldman taught it, the opening conversation was about demystifying *Newsweek* writing. He would start his writers with a short seventy-line story from a single reporter's file. Then he moved on to longer stories incorporating files from multiple bureaus. One week, everyone had to write a "Newsmaker," the gossipy items in the most popular section of the magazine. "It was distilling down a story to its essence, a reduction in cooking," Peter recalled. "It had a beginning, middle, and end and it had structural demands. Lucy did a perfect Newsmaker." Each week, Peter did a one-page critique of the women's copy but we were so terrified that the results would be transmitted to management that the women decided to use pseudonyms. "In the beginning, there were several pieces by 'Jane Eyre' and 'Emily Bronte,'" Peter said, "but within two weeks everyone knew who it was."

Dick Boeth, one of the most creative writers on the magazine, had his own method of teaching and in his course he wrote a hilarious spoof of the *Newsweek* style. To explain the various ways one could start a *Newsweek* story, he enshrined "The Wonderful World of Ledes" (purposely misspelled to distinguish it from other pronunciations of "lead"). Some of the best were:

- Action—little picture: "Henry Kissinger had not even finished shaving the stubble from his girlfriend's chin early one morning last week when his tubside hotline to the White House began beeping insistently. At the other end was President Richard Nixon himself and his voice was grim. 'Hank,' the President said, 'hold onto your Barbasol. We're moving seven divisions into the Dominican Republic before lunchtime.'"

- Historical: "Not since the Roman proconsul Fabian Cunctator marched steadily backwards for two years before invading elephants of Hannibal has a commander-in-chief sought victory in retreat with the stubborn insistence of President Richard Nixon. But last week the harassed President tired of the waiting game. Without informing anyone but the White House telephone operator, who had to make the necessary calls, Mr. Nixon dispatched seven crack divisions of Marines in a dramatic amphibious invasion—aimed not at enemy strongholds in Vietnam but at the undefended beaches of the Dominican Republic."

- Anecdotal: "One February afternoon early in his Administration, Richard Nixon was bobbing around on a rubber duck in the lagoon fronting on his house in Key Biscayne, Fla. 'You know,' the President said reflectively to C.R. (Bebe) Rebozo, who was paddling nearby, 'they all think I came down here to make points for the Southern strategy. What all those pundits don't realize is that a guy will do almost anything to get away from those Washington winters.' Last week the President's search for sun took on new and potentially explosive international dimensions, as Mr. Nixon ordered seven divisions of U.S. Marines ashore in the Dominican Republic in a wholly unexpected dawn invasion."

- General lede: "With only three weeks to go until Election Day, Richard Nixon seemed to be a President with all his options foreclosed. Saigon, Manila and Honolulu had fallen in successive weeks to 'Un-American elements,' the most recent Gallup poll had reflected a new if razor thin edge for George McGovern, and Pat Nixon had filed for a legal separation. In a bold (some say reckless) attempt to recoup his political fortunes, the President last week dispatched seven Marine divisions to seize control of the Dominican Republic."

Yes, it was definitely newsmagazine formula, but when done well it could be brilliant.

CHAPTER 9

"Joe—Surrender"

WHILE WE WERE GEARING UP for a second lawsuit, the women at the *Washington Post* were getting restless. Several years earlier they had complained about discrimination, including the lack of women in decision-making positions. That prompted Ben Bradlee, the paper's executive editor, to issue a directive in June 1970 underscoring the "equality and dignity of women." Promising to "use all our resources to combat discrimination against women," Bradlee decreed that words such as "divorcee, grandmother, blonde (or brunette) or housewife should be avoided in all stories where, if a man were involved, the words divorcee, grandfather, blonde or householder would be inapplicable. In other words, they should be avoided. Words like vivacious, pert, dimpled or cute have long since become clichés and are droppable on that account alone."

THE GOOD GIRLS REVOLT

Two years later, on April 12, 1972, fifty-nine women at the *Post* sent a letter to Bradlee and Katharine Graham, among others, noting that women were losing ground at the paper. According to their statistics, women made up 15 percent of the *Post's* staff in June 1970; in March 1972, they made up only 13 percent of the staff. There were no women assistant managing editors, news desk editors, or editors in the Financial, Sports, and Outlook sections, nor were there any female foreign correspondents or sports reporters. This time the *Post's* management responded with specific goals and actions. Among other things, Bradlee promised "to increase substantially, and as fast as possible, the number of women on the newspaper, especially in top and middle management." He also insisted that "there is and shall be no discrimination in the assignment of women to breaking stories involving action and/or violence." The *Post* immediately established an internal equal employment opportunity committee and instituted a monthly status report on the employment of women and blacks. (The *Post* women ended up filing charges of discrimination two years later with the EEOC, which ruled in their favor.)

Also in April 1972, a group of black reporters at the *Post* called the Metro Seven filed a complaint with the EEOC charging the paper with racial discrimination in promotion and hiring, especially with regard to the lack of black editors. Bradlee and managing editor Howard Simons quickly negotiated a deal, hiring, among others, Dorothy Gilliam, a former *Post* writer whom they promoted to assistant editor. Gilliam was the first black editor of the reconfigured Style section. "It

140

was shortly after [the Metro Seven settlement] that I was sought out," said Gilliam. "I can't help but think there was some connection."

Meanwhile, Kay Graham had undergone her own form of consciousness-raising. As one of only two women publishers of a major newspaper (the other was Dorothy Schiff of the *New York Post*), Kay was feeling isolated in the professional world, worried, as she wrote, that she would "appear stupid or ignorant when she was the only woman in a room full of men." Her close friend at the *Post* was Meg Greenfield, the deputy editor of the editorial page, who had achieved her success before the women's movement. (In her early days at the *Post,* Meg had a sign on her office door that read, IF LIBERATED, I WILL NOT SERVE.) But Meg, like Kay, was often the only woman in the room and together they decided to "think through" how they felt about women's lib. They started by reading books, among them *The Second Sex* by Simone de Beauvoir.

Then Kay met Gloria Steinem. Gloria had been writing a political column for Clay Felker at *New York* magazine when she began thinking about starting a feminist magazine (the first issue of *Ms.* magazine appeared as an insert in *New York* in December 1971). When Gloria was seeking an investor for her start-up, Felker introduced her to Kay. "She told me that if they put up money, they—the *Post*—would have to own it," Gloria told me later. But Kay gave her $20,000 in seed money and asked Gloria to talk to her about the new feminism. At the time, Kay wrote, "I couldn't understand militancy and disliked the kind of bra-burning symbolism that appeared to me like man-hating." But Gloria "more than any other individual, changed my mind-set and helped me grasp what the leaders of the movement—and even the extremists—were talking about." Around that time, Kay even asked her longtime executive assistant, Liz Hylton, who came from West Virginia, to please stop saying "yes, ma'am."

One day, Kay asked Gloria to come to lunch at the *Post*. "She wasn't being taken seriously by the men she employed," Gloria recalled. "She had invited Joe Alsop to lunch and asked me to explain this to him while she was sitting right there! I was trying to do Feminism 101 and be reasonable and persuasive about women's issues in general. It was as if she was calling me in to argue with someone she didn't want to argue with." Among the things they discussed was the fact that the *Post* wouldn't hire newsgirls to throw the paper on people's porches in Chevy Chase, Maryland. "After the lunch," said Gloria, "Kay told me that she had gotten so mad at some employee who told her they couldn't have newsgirls, she threw an ashtray at him. I was impressed because she was usually so reserved."

Kay also had Gloria talk to Oz Elliott about the *Newsweek* women. "I remember meeting Gloria in Kay's office and she was very helpful to me," he told me. "I was impressed with how constructive she was in suggesting how management should deal with the situation." When Kay discussed *Newsweek* with Gloria, however, "all I remember was trying to talk her out of being angry at Eleanor Holmes Norton," Gloria said. "Kay never really forgave Eleanor. She felt wrongly accused—her world had been wrongly accused—and Kay felt Eleanor crossed the line. She felt *Newsweek* was unfairly targeted, but separate from that was Eleanor and her style." Later on, when Gloria found herself on the opposite side of Eleanor on an issue, "I could see what Kay meant," she said. "Eleanor is scary, very scary. She's tough—and she should be."

I, too, felt Kay's disapproval—or perhaps it was disappointment. Because of my father, she probably felt that I was part of the *Post* family, which I felt as well. After all, she was responsible for my entrée to *Newsweek* and now I was the apostate suing her magazine. Many years later, when she was making a speech at *Newsweek* and recounting the history of the women's lawsuit, she stopped and said, "and some of the suers are in this room!"—and pointed to me. Whatever the reason, I thought she never forgave me for being disloyal and I felt a coolness in our interactions after the suit. It wasn't overt. She was always gracious to me, and from time to time she would ask me to come to her office to tell her how things were going with the women's movement at *Newsweek*. Over the years, I grew to admire Kay's courage, especially during Watergate, and as she became more confident, her sense of humor became more evident. At a *Newsweek* sales conference in Puerto Rico one year, Kay came out to walk with some of us on the beach. It had been a cloudy day, but when she appeared the sun suddenly came out. Kay looked up at the sky, opened her arms, and said mischievously, "Now you know why they call me the most powerful woman in Washington."

Primarily, however, I was concerned about my father's feelings since I now found myself in the unusual position of suing

his boss. Dad loved and respected the Grahams and had a special fondness for Kay. When I called him after we filed the first
complaint, he listened and never questioned or criticized my
actions. At the same time, I knew he was worried about how
Kay would feel. "He was nervous," recalled my brother Maury.
"He didn't want anything that was untoward to happen to the
Post and to Kay in particular." If he ever spoke to Kay—or she
to him—about my role in the suit, he never told me. But I
know he felt torn by his loyalty to her and his love for me. In
1974, Kay gave my father a gala dinner dance to celebrate his
fifty years at the *Washington Post*. Before I flew down to Washington for the event, my father phoned me and gently asked
whether I was planning to shake Kay's hand on the reception
line, clearly wanting to avoid an embarrassing incident. "Of
course," I said. "I'm not angry at her personally, just at the men
who run her magazine." I think he was relieved, and it turned
out to be a warm, wonderful evening.

Meanwhile, our negotiations with management were leading nowhere. After the March 1972 straw vote, the women met
again and formally voted to once again take legal action, this
time in two jurisdictions. On May 16, 1972, we announced
that fifty women had filed a second complaint against
Newsweek with the EEOC "because sex discrimination at the
magazine remains essentially unchanged." Two weeks later,
Margaret Montagno was the lead plaintiff on a complaint filed
with the New York State Division of Human Rights "on her
own behalf and behalf of the 50 or more female employees
similarly situated." In a half-page, single-spaced paragraph,

enumerating all the ways the magazine discriminated against women, Margaret charged *Newsweek* with unlawful discriminatory practice, ending the complaint saying, "Because I am a woman I believe I have no chance to become a senior editor or part of top management at *Newsweek*. Because I am a woman I believe I have very little chance to become a writer, bureau chief or reporter at *Newsweek*. I believe that to be a woman at *Newsweek* is to accept a permanent position in those lower paying and/or less prestigious jobs restricted to or predominantly held by women."

At the end of June 1972, Oz Elliott returned as editor-in-chief of *Newsweek* after serving on the business side. "I was astonished no progress had been made," he told me years later, "and I was surprised by the anger of the women. They were angrier than they had been two years before. One of the first things I did was to put the women's issues at the top of my list."

Oz immediately hired Shana Alexander as the first female columnist in the history of *Newsweek*. Shana had been the "first" in several publications: the first female staff writer and columnist for *Life* magazine and the first female editor of *McCall's*. But she quit *McCall's* in 1971, saying that it was a token job in a sexist environment. (Shana left *Newsweek* in 1974 and was replaced as a columnist by Meg Greenfield of the *Washington Post*.) As a concession to the women inside *Newsweek*, Oz also promoted Olga Barbi, the chief of research, to senior editor. The women were pleased for Olga but it didn't satisfy our demands to have a woman editing one of the major sections in the magazine. (On the business side, my friend Valerie Salembier was appointed *Newsweek's* first female ad sales representative in May 1972.)

Then there was silence. Between May and September 1972, we had no meetings with *Newsweek's* management. That summer, while the *Newsweek* women were being "trained" at the Famous Writers School, women from outside the magazine were being hired as writers without any trouble, and some without much experience. In July 1972, at the Democratic convention in Miami, Oz met Maureen Orth, a member of a guerrilla TV collective from San Francisco called TVTV. Maureen had graduated from Berkeley with a political science degree, had served in the Peace Corps in Colombia, and earned a master's degree in journalism at UCLA with an emphasis on documentary film. In 1971, she was pitching a story to *New York* magazine on the Cockettes, a group of celebrated hippie drag queens from San Francisco who came to New York where they were a big flop. "Clay Felker [the editor of *New York*] told me he'd pay me $500 and then have Rex Reed put his own lead on it and cut me out completely," she recalled. "I refused and gave it to the *Village Voice*." The story, one of a dozen she had written, ran on the front page.

Maureen came to New York in September and looked up her Berkeley schoolmate Trish Reilly at *Newsweek*. Trish asked whether she was interested in writing since the editors were desperately trying to hire women because of the lawsuit. Maureen had an interview with Rod Gander, and then spoke to Oz. "Oz said, 'Well, I think if we're going to hire women writers we're just going to have to make a decision to hire them,'" she recalled. She was sent to Jack Kroll, the Arts editor, "because I came from the West Coast and they thought he would 'get' me." Kroll said he would talk to Rod but added, "There's no way you can be hired as a writer because there are a lot of women waiting in the wings to be hired." Maureen told him about Oz's remark to just start hiring women.

A few weeks later, Kroll invited Maureen to lunch at the Gloucester House on East Fiftieth Street, the editors' favorite dining establishment for Saturday lunch. The expensive fish restaurant, staffed exclusively with black waiters, offered such *spécialités* as shrimp wrapped in bacon and French-fried zucchini strips stacked like Lincoln Logs. Over martinis, Kroll offered Maureen a job as a writer in the back of the book for $14,000 a year. She began in October 1972.

A month earlier, Linda Bird Francke, a contributing editor to *New York* magazine, was looking for a staff job when she got a call from Clay Felker, her boss. "He said, 'You've got a job at *Newsweek*,'" she recalled. "I was startled. I subscribed to *Time* and had never even read *Newsweek*, let alone considered it a job prospect. But Clay was insistent. 'Just call this number,' he said. 'They're waiting to hear from you.'" Linda went to 444 Madison Avenue, bought a copy of *Newsweek* in the lobby, quickly looked it over, and proceeded upstairs to meet with Russ Watson. "Without any preamble, he offered me any one of four sections: Life & Leisure, Nation, Foreign, and one other," she recalled. When she said that Life & Leisure sounded fun, he retorted, "No, no, that's considered a women's ghetto. You want to be on the front lines in Nation or Foreign, don't you?"

She reiterated that she preferred Life & Leisure, so he went on to discuss salary. "Well," he said, "I'm authorized to offer you anything up to $19,000, so let's make it simple and say $19,000. When can you start?" "And so," said Linda, "I commenced on my totally unexpected and unsought job without anyone looking at a single clip. Maureen Orth came in the same way. We were all hired in an instant to offset the women's suit."

Kay Graham, meanwhile, was feeling under pressure. With blacks suing the *Washington Post,* the *Post* women pushing for change, and now a second lawsuit by the *Newsweek* women, she called in Joseph A. Califano, Jr., the corporate attorney for the Washington Post Company. Califano was an old Washington hand, having served as special assistant to President Lyndon B. Johnson before joining the law firm of Edward Bennett Williams in 1971. "Kay said, 'I want you to straighten this out,'" Joe recalled. "She wanted it settled, no question about that, but we didn't want quotas. Nobody wanted quotas, certainly not Oz. I called Alan Finberg [*Newsweek's* general counsel] and said, 'Let me start by dealing directly with the women's lawyer.' That was Harriet Rabb."

Joe wrote to Harriet requesting a meeting with her and the women's committee on September 13, 1972. When we met, he had brought along a young associate, Rich Cooper, who seemed to object to every suggestion we had to move forward. In all our meetings that fall, Rich played bad cop and Joe, the avuncular good cop. Harriet was probably used to such legal maneuverings, and she had a few of her own. "I thought Harriet was a good lawyer," Joe said. "However, I have a recollection of her saying, 'I want you to listen to all these women to get you sensitized'—not something I appreciated her lecturing me about."

On October 6, Joe wrote Harriet a letter saying the September meeting "encouraged our hope that we are reasonably close on a number of the issues." But then he went on to shoot down almost every recommendation we made: a grievance procedure the women proposed was already provided in the Guild contract; he had investigated charges that back-of-the-book reporters were discriminated against as compared to bureau reporters, who did similar kinds of work, and concluded that "there is no substance to the suggestion"; and punitive enforcement provisions were not acceptable—instead management would provide detailed periodic reports for ensuring performance under the agreement. Joe ended the letter by stressing that it was in the interest of both *Newsweek* and the women to settle their differences amicably because "litigation is likely to be long, expensive and divisive."

By this time, "goals and timetables" had become common legal tools in job discrimination cases, and Harriet recommended them in her letter back to Joe that same day. She proposed that by December 1973, one-third of the writers and one-third of the foreign and domestic reporters should be women. She stated that priority should be given to in-house women for writing positions and that a woman writer should be placed in each of the seven editorial departments, including in the hard-news Nation, Foreign, and Business sections and not just in the feature-laden back of the book. The letter also stipulated that the percentage of male researchers should approximately equal the percentage of female writers on staff. There was a long section outlining procedures for recruiting and in-house tryouts. Finally, she insisted that one of the next three openings for senior editor should be filled by a woman.

That was the real sticking point. Mariana Gosnell, the Medicine reporter on our committee, pushed hard for a woman senior editor. "I remember saying that until they put a woman in the holy top bunch, they would have it in their heads that a woman couldn't be a Wallenda," she said. The editors refused, saying that the women couldn't dictate who would be in management. We said we wouldn't sign an agreement that didn't include a woman in the meetings where the decisions were being made.

"I went into the negotiations knowing we were going to end up with goals and timetables," Joe remembered. "In the beginning, Oz was not for that. He viewed goals and timetables as locking him into things he didn't want to do. But then we got into this argument about having one or two women senior editors. I'm not sure whether Katharine was or wasn't for them, but at some point I sat down with her and said, 'If you want to settle this you're going to have to do something like this. We're going to make sure that everybody knows they have a real opportunity and it's palpable, it's there. The only issue is who's going to get it and when.'" According to Joe, Kay's view was, "if we're going to do this, we want as much talent up in New York as possible so we can make the right pick."

Joe called *Newsweek*'s Washington bureau chief, Mel Elfin, to find out whether any women on the magazine were qualified to be a senior editor. Mel recommended Liz Peer, who was working for him in the bureau. When she was in Paris in the mid-1960s, Liz had wanted to go to Vietnam, but *Newsweek* wouldn't send a woman to cover a war. Instead she returned to the Washington bureau in 1969, where she covered the State Department, the White House, and the CIA. "I think Katharine may have known Liz," Joe later said, "and I think she was more comfortable knowing that there was someone she knew who was capable of doing this, if she turned out to be the person. I was just surprised that Liz Peer was the only person outside New York that they thought worthy." (For her part, Liz confided to a friend that she felt Kay Graham didn't want her to be the first woman to succeed.)

Joe asked Oz to interview Liz Peer as a candidate for senior editor. "Mel had told Liz that it would cost, like, 25 percent more to live in New York than in Washington, and he told her, 'You gotta get more money and you gotta get this and you gotta get that,'" Joe recalled. "In the course of the meeting with Oz, Liz asked about salary and Oz, who was in the middle of a difficult divorce and sick and tired of talking to women about money, made some snide remark. When I asked Elfin about getting Liz to New York, he said it wasn't a good meeting. I think Oz was just very unhappy."

Once Joe was assigned the *Newsweek* case, I found myself in an awkward position as a member of the women's committee.

THE GOOD GIRLS REVOLT

My older brother, David, was a law partner of Joe's at Williams, Connolly & Califano, so I didn't discuss our case with him. But at one point I was so annoyed with Rich Cooper's sarcastic remarks that I called David to ask about him. David said Rich really was a good guy, very smart, and then explained that he was just doing his job. Then David called me one day to tell me a story, laughing on the phone. Joe had come into his office complaining about the *Newsweek* negotiations. "These women are really tough," David recalled him saying. "They don't give an inch and your sister is one of the ringleaders. I don't know what to do." At this point David looked up from his desk and said simply, "Joe—surrender."

The negotiations carried on through the spring of 1973. On May 21, Mariana Gosnell noted in her diary that we "just spent the day negotiating with the lawyers about our women's agreement. It's still being haggled over and they keep backtracking and driving us mad. Men are REALLY pigs"—short for "male chauvinist pigs," the worst thing you could say about a man in those days. By June, Joe had finally convinced *Newsweek*'s management to accept goals and timetables for a female senior editor. "Katharine was fine so long as there was talent," Joe recalled. "I think Oz took it reluctantly, but he took it because Katharine was aboard. His divorce had an enormous impact on him. It was a bitter, bitter fight, and whatever was going on with his wife was consuming him."

On June 28, 1973, we announced that fifty *Newsweek* women had signed a second, twenty-two-page memorandum of understanding with management. We also withdrew our complaints with the EEOC and the New York State Division of Human Rights. The new memorandum stated that by December 31, 1974, approximately one-third of the magazine's writers and domestic reporters would be female and by the end of 1975, one of every three people hired or transferred to the staff of foreign correspondents would be a woman. We gave management more than two years—until December 31, 1975—to appoint a female senior editor in charge of one of the seven editorial sections of the magazine.

Newsweek also committed to providing writing and reporting training programs for women, an arbitration procedure, and reports three times a year on the magazine's affirmative actions. Editors now had to fill out forms on all the applicants for researcher, reporter, and writer vacancies, noting their age and gender, whether they had applied to or been approached by *Newsweek,* their experience and education, samples of their work, whether an interview was held and by whom, and the result: if rejected—why, if kept on file—why. The document, witnessed by Rich Cooper, was signed by Oz and Harriet and the six women on our committee: Connie Carroll, Merrill Sheils (McLoughlin), Margaret Montagno, Mariana Gosnell, Phyllis Malamud, and me. *Newsweek* paid Harriet $11,240 in costs and fees, payable to the Employment Rights Project at Columbia University.

According to Joe, Kay was pleased that it was settled. "She was sympathetic, but I had no sense of her being a feminist in any way at all during the *Newsweek* negotiations," he said. "She really was a business woman and a publisher, but she had a sense of fairness. I don't think she ever would have done any-thing she didn't think was right." We finally felt the system would change. One unnamed member of the women's com-mittee was quoted in the press release saying, "All of the women at *Newsweek* worked very hard to bring this about, and we feel it's a great accomplishment, not only for us, but for other women in the media. The strength of this agreement—its specific goals, timetables and training programs—shows the strength of *Newsweek*'s commitment to equal employment for women. We think congratulations are due all around."

Again, we didn't ask for back pay. "It was a failure of will and imagination," said Harriet, looking back. "It was either your judgment or ours that if we asked for money, they wouldn't settle without litigation." At the time, recalled Harriet, the *Newsweek* case was fairly straightforward. "You all didn't have different job categories or salaries," she said. "You were a ho-mogeneous class. Guys had better opportunities but they looked like you in background and qualifications."

Indeed, our case was relatively simple compared to Har-riet's discrimination suits against the *Reader's Digest* in 1973 and the *New York Times* in 1974, both of which included women in different job categories and on the business side. The women at the *Reader's Digest* "were treated worse," said Harriet. "At the *Digest,* corporate was resistant because they felt they were good to women. There were women who worked in 'Ful-fillment,' filling subscriptions—one of the least fulfilling jobs ever. In the morning, you could order dinner for two, three, or four people because Mother *Reader's Digest* wouldn't want you to go home without food, and women should feed their families well." But when it came to giving the women higher pay or promotions, the *Digest* was not so concerned. "There were end-of-the-year reviews with two lists of names—the editors and the ladies, who were also editors—and the factors for promotion. 'He's a family man, we need to help. She's a single woman, doesn't need more.'"

At one point, the *Digest* even went after Harriet. The plaintiffs had asked her to talk to an open meeting of other female employees who might want to learn about their case and either join or support them. Some *Digest* loyalists taped her remarks and turned the tape over to the company's lawyers. "The *Reader's Digest* filed a sanction against me saying I had breached legal ethics by encouraging people to litigate, that I was 'ambulance chasing' to get clients," Harriet explained. "It was scary because they were after my license. I wrapped myself in the flag and told the judge that management didn't want people to tell them their rights and that's what I did and I'm proud of it." The judge dismissed the *Digest's* motion from the bench. In the end, the *Digest* settled and 5,635 women plaintiffs got $1,375,000 in back pay—about $244 each.

In the case of the *New York Times,* said Harriet, "management really took off on the women and trashed them, unlike *Newsweek's* management, which didn't fight ugly. The *Times* women were angrier than the *Newsweek* women, in part because they were older and because many of them came out of the labor union movement. They also had seen their salaries because the union saw salaries, and there's nothing like money to make you angry."

The *Times* women began organizing in 1972, right after we filed our second suit in May. "Grace [Lichtenstein, a young *Times* reporter] kept saying, 'What are we doing sitting around like this when the *Newsweek* women are stirring things up?'" recalled Betsy Wade Boylan, the named plaintiff on *Elizabeth Boylan v. The New York Times Company.* In the spring of 1973, six *Times* women hired Harriet to represent them and in November 1974, filed a class action lawsuit. Management was furious. At one point, according to Harriet, Arthur Ochs "Punch" Sulzberger, Sr., publisher of the *New York Times* and a former trustee of Columbia University, called Michael Sovern, then dean of Columbia Law School, and asked whether he thought that what Harriet was doing with these cases in her law clinic was legitimate. "He led Michael to believe that he really wanted to stop the lawsuit, that he thought it was unfair," recalled Harriet. "Michael refused, and didn't tell me about it until the case was over."

Four years later, as the *Times* women were preparing for a September 1978 court date, a machinists union strike hit all three New York daily newspapers in August. The *Times* settled the suit in October, though the strike didn't end until November. The case had gotten so poisonous that going to court probably would have damaged not only the paper but also the women. Still, said Harriet, "I think they settled because if their defense was that the women weren't promoted because they weren't any good, then these were the same women—Nan Robertson, Marilyn Bender, Eileen Shanahan, Grace Glueck—whose bylines were in the paper." The *Times* ended up paying $350,000 to settle the suit, $233,500 of which went to back pay for the 550 women and $15,000 was divided among the plaintiffs and women who had testified in depositions. Employees with twenty or more years of service were given $1,000 with the others paid on a sliding scale down.

Afterward, several of the original editorial plaintiffs saw their careers stall—or worse. "We did a brave and a noisy thing and we knew it wasn't going to be for us," said Betsy Wade. Eileen Shanahan, a top financial reporter in the Washington bureau, left the *Times* in 1977, before the settlement. "I had repeatedly asked for editing jobs and couldn't get them," she later said. "That's one of the reasons I left. The other was knowing what retaliation was going to come from the suit." (Ironically, Shanahan went to work as the assistant secretary for public affairs officer for Joe Califano, who had become the secretary of Health, Education, and Welfare in the Carter administration). Grace Glueck, a gifted writer whose stories often ended up leading the culture page, was never made a top arts critic, while Joan Cook, a talented reporter, editor, and ideas person, was relegated to day rewrite, a backwater of the news department.

When she began organizing the women in 1972, Betsy Wade had been in a high-ranking position as head of the foreign copy desk. Getting nowhere, she took a position during the litigation as assistant travel editor so that she would be in a protected Guild job. She ended her career at the *Times* writing the "Practical Traveler" column, a secure but going-nowhere job. "I was sidelined because I was a woman," she recalled, "and I wasn't going to be promoted to the jobs that the people I trained were going to be promoted to."

"We were born ten years too early," said Grace Lichtenstein. "If I were born ten years later, I would have been a sportswriter. If Betsy were born twenty years later, she would have been managing editor or executive editor and certainly foreign editor." Although she felt disheartened by how little credit they got from young journalists "who don't understand all the opportunities that have opened up for them," said Grace, "we changed the way the *New York Times* looks at news." For Betsy Wade, the lawsuit "was the most important thing I did in my life." But she insisted it also had a broader impact. "It was important at the *Times* but it was even more important for the great newspapers out there," she said. "That's why the women at *Newsweek* were so important, because they were so early and people said, 'Holy Hosanna.' The *Newsweek* suit created a mold that showed that it could be done."

Anna Quindlen, who was hired at the *New York Times* at the age of twenty-four, considers herself one of the beneficiaries of the lawsuit. "I was convinced that I was hired because I was a whiz journalist," she said. "But I was hired there because of six courageous women who brought the women's suit. They weren't going to get a lot out of it, but I did. I call it the gift that keeps on giving. I was editor of the metropolitan section at twenty-nine and an op-ed columnist at thirty-three." Quindlen left the *Times* in 1995 to write novels, very successfully, and then went to *Newsweek* as a columnist in 1999, a position she held until 2009. "So you could say I was also the beneficiary of the *Newsweek* suit in taking over Meg Greenfield's spot on the back page."

At the *New York Times*, said Anna, "The women's suit changed the paper a lot! The content changed. Look at my 'Life in the 30s' column [which she wrote in the mid-eighties]. That was a direct result of the women's suit. One letter to my column said, 'I never thought the *New York Times* would write about what I was thinking about.' We understood the readers—a population that male editors had never known about." She also said the lawsuit changed who ran the paper. "Now we have women on the masthead," she added. "I never thought in my lifetime I'd see a woman on the *New York Times* masthead."

Gail Collins, the former editorial page editor of the *New York Times* and now an op-ed columnist and best-selling author, also credits the pioneering women. I first met Gail in 1973 when she invited me to speak to women journalists in Connecticut about our lawsuit. Gail was running the Connecticut News Service, which she had started in 1972 after covering the state legislature for the weekly *Fair Press*. "The idea of inviting you was not in the context of a suit," remembered Gail. "It was rather getting you to inspire everyone." But according to Trish Hall, the current op-ed editor at the *New York Times* who was then at the *New Haven Journal-Courier,* after my talk the women decided to sue. On October 4, 1974, fifteen women filed sex discrimination charges with the EEOC against the New Haven Register Publishing Company.

Gail was not part of that suit, but she extols all the women who put their jobs on the line. "I arrived in New York approximately one second after the women at places like the *New York Times* and *Newsweek* had filed lawsuits," she recalled. "The women who fought those fights were not the ones who got the rewards. People like me, who came right behind them, got the good jobs and promotions. I know many of the heroines of those battles and they aren't bitter. They're still very ticked off at their former employers, but they're very happy and proud of the women who came after and got the opportunities that rightfully should have been theirs. To me that's the definition of a great heart."

CHAPTER 10

The Barricades Fell

WOMEN'S PROGRESS TOOK a dramatic leap in the 1970s when Congress, the courts, and the media began responding to feminist demands. Between 1971 and 1974, Congress extended employment benefits to married women working in the federal government, prohibited sex discrimination in Social Security and other pension programs, and proscribed creditors from discriminating against women (until then, women couldn't get credit—or credit cards—in their own name). In 1972, Title IX of the Education Amendments Act banned sex discrimination in education programs and activities, giving women equal access to advanced math and science courses, medical and vocational schools, residential facilities, and in 1975, college sports. When twenty-nine-year-old Billie Jean King, who had been campaigning for equal prize money for women athletes, defeated fifty-nine-year-old tennis champion Bobby Riggs in three straight sets in the 1973 "Battle of the Sexes," she legitimized women's professional sports and inspired female athletes everywhere.

Politically, feminists were beginning to enter the national arena and their agenda was shaped around issues affecting women's lives. In 1964, Patsy Mink (D-HI) was the first Asian American elected to Congress, and in 1968 Shirley Chisholm (D-NY) became the first African American woman representative. They were followed by social activist Bella Abzug (D-NY) in 1970, civil rights leader Barbara Jordan (D-TX) in 1972, and a thirty-one-year-old lawyer named Pat Schroeder (D-CO) in 1973. Chisholm, Abzug, Betty Friedan, Gloria Steinem, and Eleanor Holmes Norton, among others, founded the National Women's Political Caucus in 1971 to increase the participation of women in political and public life. Two years later, the National Black Feminist Organization was formed. Its "statement of purpose" declared that

> the distorted male-dominated media image of the Women's Liberation Movement has clouded the vital and revolutionary importance of this movement to Third World women, especially black women. The Movement has been characterized as the exclusive property of so-called white middle-class women and any black women seen involved in this movement have been seen as selling out, dividing the race, and an assortment of nonsensical epithets. Black feminists resent these charges and have therefore established The National

Black Feminist Organization, in order to address ourselves to the particular and specific needs of the larger, but almost cast-aside half of the black race in Amerikkka, the black woman.

Meanwhile, sex discrimination suits were proliferating, including one against the giant telephone company AT&T. The largest employer of women, the Bell System (of which AT&T was a part) classified jobs by gender, prevented women from serving as line workers, and denied women the promotions it offered to men. The suit was settled out of court in 1972, when AT&T agreed to a multimillion-dollar payment to workers and promised to end the company's discriminatory practices.

In 1971, a young feminist attorney named Ruth Bader Ginsburg successfully argued before the US Supreme Court that an Idaho law giving preference to men as executors of estates was unconstitutional. That decision was the first time the court ruled that the Fourteenth Amendment's equal protection clause protected women's rights, which over the next thirty years was used to strike down many laws discriminating against women and men. In 1973, as a result of *Roe v. Wade,* the Supreme Court established that a woman's right to a safe and legal abortion, with certain qualifications, was a fundamental liberty under the US Constitution.

But there were several significant defeats. The Equal Rights Amendment, which passed Congress in 1972, failed to get ratification from enough states to become law. In 1971, Congress had approved the Comprehensive Child Development Act, which would have provided child care on a sliding fee scale to working parents as a matter of right. However, President Richard Nixon vetoed it, saying it would commit "the vast moral authority of the national government to the side of communal approaches to childrearing over against [*sic*] the family-centered approach."

At the same time, the mainstream media were spreading the feminist message in the public arena. By the end of 1971, stories on the new women's movement had appeared on the covers of *Time, Newsweek,* the *New York Times Magazine, Look, Life,* the *Atlantic,* and the *Saturday Review.* There was also a spate of "first" stories in the media—the "first woman" firefighter, police officer, stock broker, auto mechanic, telephone installer, you name it. The exploding coverage of the feminist movement not only was changing old institutions, it also was creating new ones. Feminist bookstores, magazines, coffee shops, and health care clinics were springing up, bringing women's previously private issues into the public domain.

Distrusting the coverage of the women's movement in the mass media, feminists focused their press on their own experiences and testimonies. Beginning in 1968, publications calling for social change—liberation or revolution rather than just equality—began to proliferate, including the *Voice of the Women's Liberation Movement* out of Chicago, *No More Fun and Games* in Cambridge, Massachusetts, *Lilith* in Seattle, and *Notes from the First Year* in New York (which published Anne Koedt's famous 1970 essay on "The Myth of the Vaginal Orgasm"). In all, more than five hundred feminist periodicals were published between 1968 and 1973.

Ms. magazine, which began publication in 1972, had a major impact on the media as the first mainstream publication written, edited, owned, and operated by women. It featured cover stories on domestic violence and sexual harassment, commissioned a national study on date rape, and publicized such issues as sex trafficking and the sexist portrayal of women in advertising. In 1973, a group of women in Boston who had been studying their own anatomy and sexuality published *Our Bodies, Ourselves,* which revolutionized how the world looked at women's health and popularized the radical notion that women's bodies were as worthy of research as men's.

Inside the traditional media, women at newspapers, television networks, and local TV stations were busy forming committees and filing lawsuits. In early 1972, the Federal Communications Commission granted a petition from the National Organization for Women requiring that women be included in affirmative action programs for radio and television stations as a condition for the renewal of their broadcast licenses. That same year, NOW filed a petition to deny the license renewal of WABC-TV in New York and of WRC-TV in Washington, D.C. In February 1973, fifty women at NBC filed a sex discrimination complaint with the EEOC, the US Department of Labor, and the New York City Commission on Human Rights, which "found cause to believe" the complaint had merit. NBC conceded that "the commission's report for the years 1967 to 1972 reflects the historical trends in American society—that women have been under-utilized in managerial positions and over-utilized in clerical positions." (The case would be settled in 1975 for $2 million, awarding $540,000 in back pay to 2,600 women—between $500 and $1,000 each, with more going to the original sixteen plaintiffs.)

Things were more complicated for the women at Time Inc., partly because they were older and better paid than we were and partly because the leaders of their movement didn't involve all the women employees from the very beginning as we had. (*Time* magazine, however, counted six women among its fifty-six writers.) In March 1970, a reporter for the British news-magazine the *New Statesman* called a female *Fortune* employee and asked whether, after the *Newsweek* women sued, the women at Time Inc. were planning any action. That spurred a small group of women at several Time Inc. magazines to start meeting secretly. They decided to file sex discrimination charges with the New York State Division of Human Rights. When the complaint was ready to be signed, they called a meeting of the rest of the women to enlist their support. But, as one woman put it, it turned into "the Bay of Pigs," a similarly ill-fated mission. Some women who had made it out of the research ranks didn't feel discriminated against, others wanted to go to management first, and a number of women did not like having the decision imposed upon them.

A group of sixty Time Inc. women actually split off into a dissident group and drew up a petition simply to "bear witness" to the truth of the allegations of discrimination, which they presented to top management. Two months after our legal complaint, on May 1, 1970, ninety-six women at Time Inc. filed a sex discrimination complaint against *Time, Life, Fortune,* and *Sports Illustrated.* Seven months later, in February 1971, a conciliatory agreement was signed between 147 women and management stipulating, among other things, that the Human Rights Commission would monitor the company's progress in interviewing, hiring, and promoting women on a quarterly basis. We were envious of this legal accountability, but in the end, it fizzled out.

At *Newsweek,* we were moving ahead. After we signed the second memorandum of understanding with management in June 1973, more women were given tryouts as reporters and writers, and some were promoted. Lucy Howard, who had refused a bureau internship in 1972—"I was always the last person to try something," she explained—was sent to the Washington bureau in 1973 to fill in during Watergate. The following year, she returned to New York to work in the newly created Justice section. "Technically I was a researcher but I never checked a story—I was reporting," she recalled. "One of the women told me that according to Guild rules, if you don't check anything for six months they have to promote you." After six months, Lucy went to Ed Kosner, the managing editor, and showed him that she had not fact-checked a single story. She was promoted to reporter in 1974. "I was pushed into it," she said. "I was asked to do the reporting and I was a good girl, so I did it. I was competitive and I didn't want to get left behind, but I didn't think of this as a career until long after the suit."

Pat Lynden left the magazine in May 1971, when she got pregnant. Margaret Montagno ended up writing in Nation and

Religion before moving to *Newsweek*'s international edition, which, she said, "I preferred because it was much less pressure." Judy Gingold was given a writing tryout in "Where Are They Now?" but it didn't work out. As Judy's close friend, I was upset, knowing how smart and talented she was. I went to Ed Kosner and suggested that he give her a tryout editing the guest essays in the "My Turn" section. Until then, Ed had been selecting the pieces himself, but he was taking on more responsibility for editing the magazine, so he agreed. Not surprisingly, Judy was brilliant at it, especially handling famous contributors, such as Henry Kissinger and Lionel Tiger. She was promoted to "My Turn" editor in 1974.

When Mimi McLoughlin, the Religion researcher, had a writing tryout, she showed so much talent that Dwight Martin hired her. "If I have to have one of these women, I want to have a good one," he said. Mimi became the Education writer, where she proved to be a star. Mariana Gosnell, the Medicine and Science reporter, also tried out with Dwight, but after writing in Education and on *Newsweek International,* she languished and returned to her old position in the back-of-the-book. "I preferred reporting," she recalled. "I was always very verbose and didn't like to do the seventy-liners."

Even after she had turned down a promotion to be a reporter in the Los Angeles bureau, Trish Reilly found herself being groomed as a writer in the Arts sections. Her editor, Jack Kroll, kept giving her story assignments. "I don't know why I was targeted for success," Trish recalled. "I just assumed that Jack was under pressure to promote women." After a year or so, Jack told Trish he was going to promote her to writer and she panicked. "I felt so humiliated and ashamed that I was being given these opportunities and couldn't say, 'I don't want to be a writer,'" she explained. "I remember walking out of Jack's office saying, 'I've got to get out of here.'" In 1973, she bolted to CBS News.

I was doing better as a writer since my boss and nemesis, Joel Blocker, was fired in 1972. I felt vindicated. The senior editors who filled in liked my copy and in August that year, I was assigned my first cover story. It was on Halston, a young fashion designer who outfitted fashionable ladies, including Kay Graham, in chic Ultrasuede shirtdresses and sweater sets with wraparound skirts. I spent days hanging out with Halston, going to Studio 54, and interviewing his clients, including a heady lunch on his terrace with actress Liza Minnelli and photographer Berry Berenson, designer Elsa Schiaparelli's granddaughter. Given that we had sued *Newsweek* three months earlier—and kept asking to give the women a chance to succeed—I felt under enormous pressure. In a letter to my parents, my husband described my agony: "Lynn just wrote her first cover story. She had trouble sleeping at night and it was a sure sign of maturity. In the past, if she was nervous she would fall asleep in a second. Oz decided to cut short the chain of command and the article only went through one set of hands before he had a look at it. He was delighted with the story and gave it a very light edit." Afterward, Oz sent me a note that revealed questionable taste but unquestionable enthusiasm. It said, "Congratulations on losing your virginity in such style."

Over the next year, more women from outside were being hired as writers. Susan Fraker, who had graduated near the top of her class at Columbia Journalism School, got a job on *Newsweek*'s international edition in August 1973, the only woman writer on that staff. "I learned about the women's suit months afterwards," she recalled, "but clearly that must have been why I was hired." That fall, Margo Jefferson became the first black woman writer at *Newsweek* and the first woman to write in the Arts department, an area populated in the general press by many female bylines. "I was a direct beneficiary of the women's suit," said Margo, who went on to become a Pulitzer Prize–winning critic for the *New York Times,* "and I was stunned by the systemic, genteel, upper-middle-class sexism of the place." When she was being interviewed by Jack Kroll, movie critic Paul Zimmerman wandered in to ask Kroll a question. Recognizing Margo from Columbia Journalism School, where he taught an arts writing course, he said, "You were one of Judy Crist's students. I wanted one of my best students to get an interview here but he didn't because he wasn't black or a woman." Margo was stunned. Kroll made a little joke that got Paul out of the office, "but that's how angry, how beleaguered and besieged and maltreated certain kinds of men were already feeling," she said.

By then, there were several black reporters at *Newsweek* and at least one bureau chief, but there was never any attempt to organize among them. "There wasn't a critical mass of blacks on the magazine," recalled Margo. "Although if there were more than two of us standing together talking, you could guarantee that someone would walk by and say jokingly, 'Planning an uprising?'"

When it came to finding a female senior editor, the editors first looked outside the magazine. I was told that they approached Gloria Steinem, who wasn't interested because she was editing her own magazine, *Ms.* Gloria later told me that she couldn't remember whether she was asked but, she added, "it would make perfect sense because at a certain point, I became like José Greco—I was the only Spanish dancer they knew." In the end, they decided to see whether a *Newsweek* woman could do the job. "I think after the Helen Dudar thing, they thought the women would be really mad if the first woman senior editor came from outside," recalled Ed Kosner. "And as for inside, there weren't too many candidates."

Oz offered Liz Peer a tryout as a senior editor in the summer of 1974. Liz had returned to New York in May 1973 as a swing writer in various back-of-the-book sections. In 1974, she won a Page One Award for her cover story on Barbara Walters (in her stylish prose, Liz described Barbara's probing interrogations as "some of the toughest questions in TV journalism—dumdum bullets swaddled in angora"). Liz was by far the most senior and most talented woman on the staff, and it was right that she would be the first to shatter *Newsweek*'s glass ceiling. But Liz was complicated. "Liz was very ambitious and not easy," said her close friend, sculptor Helaine Blumenfeld. "When the armor was on, she was clever, brilliant, and sassy. But nobody really knew her. She was so sweet, so vulnerable— just a gorgeous human being." With her spiked heels and conical bras, she always talked about her "beaux" and was famous for hanging a full-length ball gown—and feather boa—on her office door to show that she had better things to do after work. On seeing a dress hanging on her door one night, Dwight Martin popped into her office and said, "I know where you're going, Liz—to a women's lib meeting."

Oz had wanted Liz to be the first female senior editor. But although she was the consummate *Newsweek* writer and reporter, she wasn't cut out to be an editor. "She was very talented," recalled Ed Kosner, *Newsweek*'s managing editor at the time, "but she wasn't a good manager." She could be volatile. Her tryout ended when she threw an ashtray across the room because she was furious at someone or something. "They immediately said it was because she was a woman," recalled Nancy Stadtman, "but Russ Watson [another senior editor] used to throw things, too." (Betsy Carter said Russ once threw a typewriter at her.)

When Liz was trying out in the fall of 1974, I was on leave, trying to save my failing marriage. Unfortunately, the feature film that Jeff made had not done well and in 1973, he moved to Los Angeles to find work. For more than a year, we had been commuting back and forth every six weeks. Jeff desperately wanted me to move to LA, but I didn't want to give up my job until I was sure he could earn a steady living. In October 1974, I took a three-month leave of absence to see if we could make a go of it. Things were better there, and I felt that before any decision was made, we needed to live together again. In December, I came back to *Newsweek* and asked Ed Kosner for another, longer leave beginning February 1. I also offered to do some work out of *Newsweek's* LA bureau. Ed said fine.

As I was cleaning out my office in January, Ed called me down to his office. "I'm going to complicate your life," he said. "How?" I asked. "I want you to try out as a senior editor," he replied. I was surprised and, frankly, unnerved. How could I do this now? What would happen to my marriage? Would Jeff understand? Not to mention the job—was I up to it? Could I really do the work? Could I edit guys who had been my bosses and were far more experienced than I was? And, every editor's nightmare, would I be able to rewrite a cover story or a disastrous feature that needed to be turned around overnight? Not wanting to show my doubts or fears, I told Ed I was flattered and would talk it over with my husband.

I went home that night worried about telling Jeff the news. But as I mulled over Ed's offer, I found myself getting more and more excited just thinking about it. I had been working at *Newsweek* for ten years and writing for almost six. How could I turn down this opportunity to move up the ladder? To be the first woman senior editor? I knew Jeff would be disappointed, that he was counting on our being together in LA, as was I. But a tryout lasted only a few months and I wasn't sure I would get the job anyway—I just knew I wanted to try.

I called Jeff and told him about the offer. I said I had to stay in New York, that I felt I needed to prove to myself that I could—or couldn't—be an editor, and that if I never tried out, I would never know. There was silence and then Jeff said, "Either you come to Los Angeles or our marriage is over." I was shocked. I couldn't believe he really said that. He couldn't mean it. My stomach began to churn and it took me a minute to find my voice. Shaking, I told him that if he didn't understand how important this was to me after all these years at *Newsweek,* then he must not love me. He said that of course he loved me, which is why he wanted me in Los Angeles. We talked a few more minutes but there was nothing more to say.

The next day I had an appointment with my therapist at lunchtime. I remember walking into his office, sitting down, and saying, "Well, I guess my marriage is over." I was so confused between feeling elated by Ed's offer and feeling depressed that my husband couldn't understand the opportunity I was handed. It clarified some things in my mind that I had been talking about with my shrink: why our life always seemed to revolve around him and what I had to do for myself after spending so many years encouraging him. I walked out of the office still not believing that after seven years our marriage was actually ending. That night, Jeff called me from LA. He apologized and told me he loved me. He said he would come back to New York to be with me. The next month, he returned and found a job directing a soap opera.

My tryout lasted several months that spring of 1975. I was nervous and exhausted, staying late several nights a week to get the job done. But I quickly realized that I enjoyed editing more than writing. I felt more suited to it and it fit my nurturing personality. I had lots of ideas and a strong sense of structure, and I enjoyed working with talented writers, relishing the give-and-take in making their work better. What proved more daunting was being the only woman in the story meetings. Despite Ed's support, it was clear that most of the editors didn't take me seriously. In a room filled with testosterone and egotism, I had to learn to speak up and defend my stories and my writers. As I struggled to push myself forward, I was surprised by the passivity of some of the men. One of my former editors, who was always insisting that he had fought hard for our stories, just rolled over whenever he encountered an objection from the top guys. And he wasn't the only one.

My relationships with my writers were more rewarding. The most surprising was with Harry Waters, my old boss whom I now was editing. Mensch that he was, Harry couldn't have been more supportive or less threatened. We continued to work well together and I always valued his counsel. Ken Woodward was more skeptical of the decision to let me audition for the job. Ken was the longtime Religion writer at *Newsweek* and a man with old-fashioned values. But he was a good writer and an expert on religious topics. One day, Ken came into my office to tell me that initially he had been against my becoming a senior editor. He was against affirmative action and felt I was being considered only because I was a woman. But he had changed his mind after he realized I really was interested in the material and not just using the position as a stepping stone to get ahead, as had the men before me. He also told me that he had never asked to leave early to attend his son's baseball game because he was afraid to say that to a male boss; instead, he would say he had a doctor's appointment. But he felt that he could tell me the truth and I would understand. We had come to a truce.

That summer, Jeff and I went on vacation to Los Angeles to visit Mary Pleshette and Jack Willis, who had married and moved there. We decided to drive to the Grand Canyon and we were there when, on August 1, Oz announced that he would move up to become editor-in-chief and that Ed Kosner would be the next editor of *Newsweek*. When we got back to LA, Mary told me that Ed had phoned and to call him in New York. When I reached him, Ed told me his news. I was very happy for him and gave him my congratulations. Then he congratulated me. He told me that he had decided to promote me to senior editor and had already announced it effective September 1.

I'm sure I thanked him but I remember only that I was dumbfounded. I hadn't expected Oz to leave so soon, although it was clear that Ed was the next in line. Nor was I given any indication that I was even succeeding in my tryout. Although many of my ideas were picked up and my stories were getting through, I had no idea whether I was doing well. When I asked Ed years later, "Why me?" he said, "You had an editor's mind. You could see structure and you didn't have the kind of ego that had to be out there. The best editors were analytical and if our edited stories didn't sing, it was because we were on deadline and fixing a structural problem. And, no disrespect, but you had an iron ass. You would sit in the chair and work until it was done—late nights, late hours, and all."

I was pleased with Ed's confidence in me. He had been my mentor and was good to me, but it turned out that he wasn't exactly an equal-opportunity employer. When I returned to New York, Ed proudly told me that he was raising my salary from $27,000 to $32,000. Then I found out that Charlie Michener, another writer who had been promoted to senior editor in the Arts sections, would be making $40,000 a year. I couldn't believe it! Consciousness finally raised, I confronted Ed. He explained that my percentage raise was much higher than Charlie's, which meant only that I was making much less to begin with. Since Ed had already announced my promotion, I had him cornered. I told him that I wouldn't take the senior editor job unless I got the same amount as a man doing the same work. He reluctantly agreed and I felt great. When I called my parents to tell them the good news, my father was thrilled and cheered me on. My mother's response was true to form. "Now you'll never have children," she said.

Three weeks later, I encountered the editing nightmare I feared. On Monday, September 22, Jacqueline Kennedy Onassis announced she was taking a job as a consulting editor at Viking Press. *Newsweek* decided to crash a six-column story describing "Jackie on Her Own," to be reported and written by Liz Peer and edited by me. I was nervous about how Liz would respond to my editing her, but she was a pro. We discussed the story and she spent the week gathering information. On Friday evening, around six, I got the first half of her story. Unlike most of her pieces, this one just didn't work, and I was dismayed that Liz hadn't nailed it. I showed it to my top editor, Ed Klein, who agreed and told me the story had to be rewritten. Normally I would talk through the problems with the writer and let her fix it. But Liz was still writing the second half of the piece and I needed her to finish. So I shut my door and began to rewrite the copy. When Liz handed in the last part, she came into my office and I explained what I was doing and why. She took it well, but she was exhausted and said she didn't want to work on it anymore. I stayed until 4 A.M., returned early Saturday morning to finish the story, and handed it in by noon. It sailed through. I was relieved that I had passed the test, but I will always appreciate Liz's professional behavior. She never held it against me.

Becoming the first female senior editor in *Newsweek's* forty-two-year history was a personal as well as a professional victory for me. I had never thought of myself as ambitious. I had been lucky in that most opportunities had come to me—I didn't have to ask for them. I pushed myself forward by looking around and saying, "Well, if that guy can do it, then I surely can." Now I had to recognize that I did have drive (my preferred word to "ambition") and some talent. I was anxious about succeeding in my new job, but for the first time I felt confident in my career, armed with the kind of outside affirmation that I—and many of the women I knew—needed. It was one thing for your parents or teachers to tell you how good you were; it was another for the world to chime in.

Professionally, my elevation broke the editorial barrier. Now women had a voice in the meetings, a representative in management, and an advocate for them and for their story ideas. There was still resistance. I was told that Bob Christopher, the executive editor, said that my becoming a senior editor was the worst mistake management ever made. But it didn't matter. This time, something truly had changed. We *Newsweek* women, who had never wavered in demanding our rights, had finally prevailed in our five-year fight for equality. I was amazed that as one of the women who had been a leader in the lawsuit, I was rewarded with being named the magazine's first female senior editor. That wasn't true for most women on the front lines in the media lawsuits. But the barricades were falling, and women were rushing in.

CHAPTER 11

Passing the Torch

B ETWEEN 1975 AND 1985, women pushed their way into
every position on the magazine except top management.
Liz Peer, who was promoted to Paris bureau chief at the end
of 1975, was sent to cover the war in Somalia in 1977 as
Newsweek's first female war correspondent. Elaine Sciolino,
hired as a researcher in the international edition in 1970, flew
to Iran in February 1979, on the same plane as the Ayatollah
Khomeini, where she covered the Iranian Revolution and
then the hostage crisis. (She later became Paris bureau chief for
the *New York Times*.) In December 1976, Eleanor Clift from the
Atlanta bureau rode into Washington with Jimmy Carter as
Newsweek's White House correspondent, the first female newsmagazine reporter to cover the president in the West Wing
(not the first lady in the East Wing).

Phyllis Malamud was promoted to Boston bureau chief in 1977 and Mimi McLoughlin became one of the magazine's star writers and editors. In the early 1980s, Mimi became the first female to edit the Business section and then National Affairs, the most important section on the magazine. Mimi had that natural newsmagazine talent: as a writer, she could synthesize pages of files on nuclear power and polish off a complicated and comprehensive cover story the next day; as an editor she had a nose for news and a keen ear for the language. She was also popular with her troops—tough when she needed to be but never leaving bruises—and we loved that she could drink any of the boys (including the "big boys") under the table.

During the years of our lawsuits, *Newsweek*'s coverage of women was beginning to change, although an August 1971 cover story on Gloria Steinem ("The New Woman"), reported by three women and written by Dick Boeth, "a writing minority of one," still carried the sexist subline, "A Liberated Woman Despite Beauty, Chic and Success." A content analysis of the magazine between 1969 and 1975 by a student at the University of Missouri showed that the number of lines devoted to women or women's issues nearly doubled in those six years, the greatest increases coming in the Sports and Business sections. Most sexist adjectives had been deleted, and when bylines were added in 1975, women writers and reporters were highly visible, especially in the Religion, Medicine, and Justice sections.

With more women reporting, writing, and editing, there were more diverse story ideas, more quotes from female experts, and fewer cheesecake photos in "Newsmakers." As fatigue from

Vietnam and Watergate took hold, the news focus began to shift inward and the back-of-the-book areas became more important. As we had predicted, women brought new ideas to the magazine. In my first few years as senior editor, I was averaging almost a cover a month in my five sections (News Media, Television, Life/Style, Religion, and Ideas), including "Who's Raising the Kids?" "Living with Dying," "How Men Are Changing," and "Saving the Family," the first newsmagazine special report on such family issues as stepfamilies, family therapy, and how the family is portrayed on TV.

Unfortunately, my family wasn't saved. In November 1976, after nearly nine years of marriage, Jeff and I separated. The confidence I had gained on the job allowed me finally to deal with the problems in my marriage. We had tried everything, including couples counseling, but nothing seemed to work. One day, when I was telling my therapist that Jeff wasn't giving me what I needed emotionally, my doctor simply asked, "Is he unwilling or unable?" That's when I realized I had to leave. I felt very sad but also relieved. I think Jeff knew it was over, too, and he moved back to California soon afterward.

I became consumed with work and as luck would have it, that paid off professionally and personally. Not only did I flourish as an editor, but I also found the right man. Steve Shepard was hired at *Newsweek* as a senior editor in the Business section in May 1976. Steve had been a top writer at *BusinessWeek* and was on leave at Columbia University's Graduate School of Journalism to direct the Walter Bagehot Fellowship, a mid-career business journalism program he had created with his friend Soma Golden from the *New York Times*. When he came to *Newsweek* in 1976, Steve was married, as was I, and we became friends, collaborating on several *Newsweek* covers and feature stories. Steve couldn't help but notice the close camaraderie on the magazine. "Gosh, there's so much sex at *Newsweek*," he said to me shortly after he arrived. Assuming this was standard practice at most weeklies, I asked whether this wasn't true at *BusinessWeek*. "Not like this," he replied.

From the beginning, everyone respected Steve and he was regarded as a "comer" at the magazine. In story meetings, he was smart, sensitive, and supportive of his writers and reporters. I admired how he was able to cut through all the posturing and get to the essence of the idea. But I also thought Steve was cute. A great dresser, with a tall, slim body to show off his English double-breasted suits, Steve sported aviator glasses and longish hair that curled around his neck. Although he had grown up in the Bronx, he was nothing like those "pushy Jewish guys" from New York my Jewish mother had warned me about. He was soft-spoken and had an impish sense of humor. We got along well. He gave me wise advice about my writers and stories, and when he had his doubts, I supported his move to edit the National Affairs section in early 1977.

And that's where things stood when Steve's marriage ended in June 1977. I had been single for almost a year, going out with various guys but not really involved with anyone. (I did have a few dates with Warren Beatty, which set the office chattering for months.) In September, Steve asked me out. Although I was very tempted, I thought that dating a colleague, even one on an equal level, wasn't wise. We were in the same meetings every week and if things didn't work out, it would be awkward. So I refused several times. Finally he stopped asking. Annoyed, he told me that if I ever wanted to go out with him, I would have to do the asking.

The following month, in October 1977, Steve had proposed a cover story on "Is America Turning Right?," a prescient topic three years before Ronald Reagan was elected president. For the cover, he borrowed one of my writers, David Gelman, who could be eloquent on conceptual topics. The Friday night before the cover closed, I went down to the eleventh floor to see how David was doing. Unfortunately, the story wasn't in great shape, but Steve assured me that they would fix it and it would be fine.

At home on Saturday, I felt bad for Steve and David. But sitting alone in my bachelorette sublet on East Sixty-Ninth Street, I realized that what I really felt was stupid. Here was this great guy at *Newsweek* whom I really liked, and I was crazy not to go out with him. On the pretense of finding out how the story came out, I called Steve at the office on Saturday around 5 P.M. He assured me that David had turned the cover around and it was about to go to the printers. "Well, to thank you for all your hard work, I'd like to take you out to dinner," I said. There was a silence at the other end. Clearly he had other plans. Finally he said, "Okay, I can change some things and meet you for dinner."

We met at La Goulue, a little French bistro on East Seventieth Street, right around the corner from my apartment. Steve had the usual Saturday night dinner that editors often ordered to celebrate the magazine's closing: a martini, a big fat steak, french fries, and a glass of red wine. We chatted about the cover story and Reagan and all the *Newsweek* gossip. At dessert, I asked if he would like to share some profiteroles. Steve confessed that he had never had profiteroles, so we ordered some. I dug my spoon into the creamy pastry puff dripping with chocolate and offered him the first taste. Our eyes met and, as we say in Yiddish, it was *bashert*—destiny. We went back to my apartment after dinner, where I realized that not only did I like this man, I was falling in love with him. From then on we were a couple and to this day, we celebrate our first-date anniversary on the last Saturday night in October.

In the beginning, we kept our relationship secret. It helped that we worked on separate floors and reported to different Wallendas. Although as single senior editors there was no ethical issue, reporters are professional gossipmongers and we didn't want to deal with the rumors. In February, we decided to go on vacation to Virgin Gorda and the only people we told were our two bosses. At dinner the first Friday night at Little Dix Bay, we toasted each other, thrilled that we were looking at the moonlit Caribbean rather than working at *Newsweek* until two in the morning. Just then, a waiter brought over a bottle of wine. We looked around the restaurant and didn't recognize anyone. Bewildered, we finally saw the card. It read, "Enjoy! From all your friends at *Newsweek*." The surprise had been staged by my Sports pal Pete Bonventre, whose brother worked at Little Dix. Those *Newsweek* reporters were good! Steve and

I married in September 1979, and when I left on maternity leave in November 1980, I was given a big send-off at Top of the Week. It was another breakthrough—*Newsweek*'s first pregnant senior editor.

In the 1980s, *Newsweek* did better in hiring and promoting women than most media organizations, but progress was slow and painful. There were backtracks and broken promises, injustices and discrimination—and still no women were at the top. When I went on maternity leave, I told the editors to fill my senior editor slot, because I wanted to work part-time when I returned. But there were other candidates who could have risen up the masthead. Mimi McLoughlin, who had the talent and experience to become the first female assistant managing editor, left the magazine in 1986 when she and her husband, Mike Ruby, another *Newsweek* editor, departed for *US News & World Report*. In 1989, they became coeditors of *US News*, making Mimi the first woman to edit a national newsmagazine. Annalyn Swann, a music critic at *Time*, was hired at *Newsweek* as a writer in the Arts sections and took over as senior editor in 1983. At one point Kay Graham, a friend of Annalyn's family, had encouraged her to think about becoming a Wallenda. But, Annalyn later recalled, in talking to Rick Smith, then the editor of *Newsweek*, "He told me that any Wallenda should be seasoned by front-of-the-book experience as well as back-of-the-book."

In 1986, Rick changed his mind. He hired Dominique Browning from *Texas Monthly* as the senior editor for my old sections. Two years later—and eighteen years after our first lawsuit—Rick promoted Dominique to assistant managing editor (AME), the magazine's first female Wallenda.

After Dominique left in 1992, several women became AMEs, but none of them made it to the very top. Alexis Gelber, a former National Affairs editor and AME, was a strong contender, but she was married to Mark Whitaker, who became the editor of *Newsweek* in 1998, the first African American to lead a national news magazine. That put Alexis out of the running. Ann McDaniel, who ran *Newsweek's* award-winning Monica Lewinsky coverage as Washington bureau chief—and held the title of managing editor—was a favored candidate, but she didn't want to leave D.C. In 2001, Don Graham hired her as vice president of the Washington Post Company. Dorothy Kalins was hired in 2001 as *Newsweek's* executive editor, the number-three position, but as an accomplished lifestyle editor and founder of *Metropolitan Home, Saveur,* and *Garden Design* magazines, she clearly would never become the top editor of a newsmagazine.

Every masthead is a snapshot of a moment in time: women do better at some times than at others. That's natural, as long as progress flows as well as ebbs—and that usually depends on the person at the top. Some editors, such as Rick Smith and Maynard Parker, worked well with women and hired or promoted many of them. Others seemed to feel more comfortable with a circle of men. In 2008, Don Graham appointed Ann McDaniel to the newly created position of managing director of Newsweek Inc., overseeing both the business and editorial sides of the magazine. It was the second time, since Kay Graham, that *Newsweek*'s editor reported to a woman.

***

AND THAT'S WHERE things stood in October 2009, when Jessica Bennett, Jesse Ellison, and Sarah Ball persuaded their editor to let them write a story about young women in the workplace today. Since the piece was bound to be controversial, the editor, Marc Peyser, kept it under wraps until it was ready. "The three of us had so much fun working on the story," said Jesse. "We felt like there were echoes of what you all had done forty years earlier—the secrecy of it and the sisterhoodness of it!" They decided not to put their names on an early version that went to the top editors. Instead, they bylined the story "the Dollies," the patronizing name given the Nation researchers of old. "Marc was worried about repercussions and he thought it would be safer if we didn't sign it, just for the first draft," explained Jessica. "He thought it would make the editors think more about who—and how many people—were saying this. But his biggest concern was that they could hold it against us and if it never ran, it would hurt us."

The women submitted the story to the editors right after Thanksgiving. Then they heard nothing. In January 2010, various editors responded with particular points and fixes they wanted made. The story went from 2,500 words to 6,000 words, then to 3,000 words and finally back to 2,000 words. When Peyser felt it was ready, he resubmitted it. That's when

Newsweek's editor, Jon Meacham, decided to recuse himself from overseeing the story. "That was a perfect, silent way of killing it," explained Jessica, "because nobody would make any decisions without Meacham's approval."

For two months there was no word from the top, and the fortieth anniversary of our lawsuit was approaching in March. "At that point, I was physically ill, going from lethargic to depressed to angry," said Jessica. "Jesse lost her voice, Sarah was crying, and we were a mess. We felt if this didn't run we would have no faith in humanity." As a reminder of the history of discrimination at *Newsweek* and the fortieth anniversary news peg, the three women pinned up copies of the 1970 "Women in Revolt" cover over their desks.

At one point, *Newsweek*'s general manager, Ann McDaniel, asked to see them. "She was coming from a management perspective," recalled Jesse. "She wanted to see if we had legitimate complaints about the way we were treated, but we didn't say anything. She talked about convening monthly lunches where we would talk about the women, but none of that happened. It was good to talk to her but it was unclear what her motives were."

Then they met with Mark Miller, *Newsweek*'s editorial director, and begged him to run the cover. Miller asked whether the women had been personally discriminated against. "Our strategy was to be positive," said Jesse. "We felt that the more we said we were discriminated against, the less [likely it was] they would run the piece. So we talked about how it's not really about *Newsweek,* it's bigger than *Newsweek,* it's a cultural thing."

Marc Peyser was upset that the women hadn't relayed their personal grievances. He called Miller and told him about the women's experiences—and the piece got going.

The four-page story, "Are We There Yet?," finally ran in the March 22, 2010 issue, almost forty years to the day that we had charged *Newsweek* with sex discrimination. Leading with our landmark suit, the women questioned how much had actually changed for women since 1970, not only at the magazine but in the workplace in general. They cited statistics showing that full-time working women who *haven't* had children still make seventy-seven cents on the male dollar and that in their first job out of business school, female MBAs make $4,600 less per year than male MBAs. In the media, they wrote, "female bylines at major magazines are still outnumbered by seven to one; women are just 3 percent of Fortune 500 CEOs and less than a quarter of law partners and politicians."

They also wrote about *Newsweek*. In 1970, women made up 25 percent of the editorial masthead; forty years later that number was 39 percent. (Overall, they pointed out, 49 percent of the entire company was female.) But perhaps the most damning statistic they cited was that "men wrote all but six of *Newsweek*'s 49 cover stories last year—and two of those used the headline 'The Thinking Man'" ("The Thinking Man's Guide to Populist Rage," for example). Then, to cover their tracks, they wrote,: "We should add that we are proud to work at *Newsweek*. (Really, boss, we are!) We write about our magazine not because we feel it's worse here, but because *Newsweek* was once ground zero for a movement that was supposed to break at least one glass ceiling." The women explained how "somewhere along the road to equality, young women like us lost their voices. So when we marched into the workforce and the fog of subtle gender discrimination, it was baffling and alien. Without a movement behind us, we had neither the language to describe it nor the confidence to call it what it was." Recognizing that sexism still exists, they said, "is one of the challenges of the new generation."

The response inside *Newsweek* was overwhelmingly positive from the young female and male staffers. "One woman said, 'I can't believe you guys did this—I truly thought there was no chance in hell it would see the light of day,'" recalled Jessica. "The only negative response we got was hearing that the middle-aged editors thought we were very entitled, that we were just complaining and didn't appreciate what we had. But it sparked a lot of conversation among the young women in the building." After the story came out, several women got promotions and there were more covers about women, written by women. Jon Meacham never spoke to the women about the story.

Five months later, in August 2010, the Washington Post Company sold *Newsweek* for $1 plus its liabilities to ninety-two-year-old audio pioneer Sidney Harman. The magazine had been hemorrhaging revenue and readership for years, but Harman thought it had value and he had the money to invest in it. After a very public search for a new editor, Harman made news again. In November 2010, he announced that Tina Brown, the first female editor of *Vanity Fair* and the *New Yorker*, would become editor-in-chief of *Newsweek* in a joint venture with her website, the *Daily Beast*. It happened almost by accident, but forty years after forty-six terrified young women sued *Newsweek* for sex discrimination, there was finally a female name at the very top of the magazine's masthead. Tina tipped her hat to us in her press interviews. "A merger has created what the lawsuit couldn't," she told National Public Radio. In her first editor's letter, she said she was "honored to be the first female editor of *Newsweek*," but unaware of the behind-the-scenes details of our lawsuit, she also wrote, "I'm both humbled and grateful to know that the trail was blazed long ago, and that Kay Graham blazed it. This issue is dedicated to her memory and inspired by her example."

But Tina couldn't make a go of it. *Newsweek* folded its print edition on December 31, 2012, and went digital. Five months later, owner Barry Diller said he was exploring a sale of what was left of *Newsweek*. It was an inglorious end to a once great magazine.

Today many women hold senior positions at other news organizations, but few have made it to the top. The *New York Times* has the best record. Janet Robinson was president and CEO of the New York Times Company from 2004 until 2012 and in June 2011, Jill Abramson was appointed to the paper's highest editorial position. The *Washington Post* has a female publisher, Katharine Weymouth, Kay Graham's granddaughter; Gracia Martore is president and CEO of Gannett; Mary Junck is chairman, president, and CEO of Lee Enterprises; Kathleen Carroll is the top editor of the Associated Press; and Debra Adams Simmons, an African-American, is editor of the

Cleveland Plain Dealer. At one time, the *Chicago Tribune,* the *Oregonian,* the *Philadelphia Inquirer,* the *Des Moines Register,* and the *St. Paul Pioneer Press* all had women editors, but none do today. *Time* magazine has never had a female managing editor nor has a woman run the news operations of ABC, CBS, CNN, MSNBC, or Fox News. In July 2012, Patricia Fili-Krushel became chair of NBCUniversal News Group, and in May 2013, she appointed British ITV editor Deborah Turness as president of NBC News—the first woman to head a network news division.

It's hard to believe that two generations later there are still so few females in the executive suite. Who would have thought it would take so long? We believed the lack of advancement was merely a pipeline problem: once there were enough women in the workforce, they would naturally advance—all the way to the top. We didn't realize how hard it would be to change attitudes and stereotypes. There still are not enough stories on women's issues, not enough women quoted as sources, and not enough women editorial writers and commentators. Perhaps most important for women's advancement, there still is no private or public support for working families, who rely primarily on mothers to care for the children. According to the 2011 Global Report on the Status of Women in the News Media, conducted by the International Women's Media Foundation, the regions with the most women at the top of their news organizations are those with the best support system for parents: the Scandinavian countries, Europe, and Eastern Europe.

Oz Elliott once said that the two most important things that happened in the twentieth century were civil rights and women's rights. As in the civil rights movement, the women's movement didn't solve all the problems, but our actions at *Newsweek* continue to have an impact. "Finding out about the lawsuit and writing the story was a real turning point for me," said Jesse Ellison, who took the *Newsweek* buyout in December 2012 and is now a freelance writer. "It was hugely empowering and put a finger on what we were feeling—tremendous self-doubt. Once I understood that things aren't just my problem, they're *a* problem, it made me bolder, more willing to push for my stories and realize that I am as smart as the dude sitting next to me." Jesse found that in working on the *Newsweek* story, "there was an element of personal growth in our own journey and how that compared to—and was reflected in—learning about your journey. As we kept rewriting the *Newsweek* piece, it made the story more effective and strengthened my voice."

For Jessica Bennett, now a freelance journalist and editor-at-large for Sheryl Sandberg's Lean In Foundation, "It was our modern 'click!' moment," she explained. "Now I see almost everything through a gender lens. I'm writing a lot about women's issues. Part of me doesn't want to be pigeonholed as the women's writer, but I am naturally drawn to these stories in ways I never was before." Learning the history of our lawsuit, she said, was a "sub-education—it's become so useful to me, thinking about stories, knowing the background and how things evolved. It's enabled me to understand what's changed and what hasn't."

Sarah Ball didn't consider herself a feminist before she started working on the *Newsweek* story. "I'm just young enough not to have ever been in a situation before *Newsweek* where there were more men than women," she said. "I only knew 'feminism' as a denigrating term. Doing the story, it was fascinating to dive back to its beginnings and understand how feminism was—and is—such a necessary term to use and to espouse. I'm now aware that we didn't just get this one day. There were a lot of women who got this for us and I'm glad I will never be ignorant of what came before."

Sarah was particularly moved by a fortieth reunion of the original *Newsweek* plaintiffs at my home in June 2010. "I'm so grateful that I can put a face to the people I owe this incredible debt," she told me. "I had so many meaningful conversations that night with very smart, educated women who have a lot of history and a lot of experience. There was something about the way that experience resonated with you all—it was so important a cause, so much bigger than yourselves, and so selfless risking the job you already had rather than just protesting from outside. I don't know if anything would make women coalesce like that today. It made me feel very jealous, as if our generation missed out on something."

Jesse and Jessica acknowledge they also feel a bond with us, although we are old enough to be their mothers. "There was a sense of a *Newsweek* culture that hadn't really changed—even to calling the editors the Wallendas—so we could share these stories from forty years apart," said Jessica. "We have a great feeling for the women who came before us, who were proud of what we were doing and were supporting us in our fight. I used to keep the 'Women in Revolt' cover over my desk and it still gives me chills when I see it. It was an honor to be associated with it."

The women's movement is an incomplete revolution. Many issues remain unsolved for this generation, including the continuing stereotyping of women, the increasing sexualization of society, and the infighting that still exists in the women's movement. After the *Newsweek* piece was published in March 2010, the feminist blog *Jezebel* attacked the young women for a narcissistic "focus on your magazine and its past covers, and your childhood, and your issues with the F-word." It also excoriated them for not including women of color in their story. "If the actual staff of *Newsweek* doesn't include much in the way of diversity," *Jezebel* opined, "isn't it time to utilize those reporting skills of which the traditional media is supposed to be the last guardians?"

Stunned by the criticism from their fellow feminists, Jessica and Jesse answered *Jezebel* in a blog they had started called *The Myth of Equality*. They pointed out that the women they interviewed for the piece were either directly involved in the suit, wrote about it, or had recent books, articles, or studies related to women in the media and in the workplace. "We should also note—and this was one of many things that didn't make it into the final piece—that the women of color at *Newsweek* didn't sign onto the suit in 1970, for various reasons," they wrote. The *Jezebel* experience cut deep. "You can argue about sexism," said Jesse, "but in the feminist blogosphere, there's a strange infighting that happens that's destructive. When *Jezebel* attacked us,

I felt like I lost a best friend. Nobody can be feminist enough. I see so much of that on these sites. Feminism takes on an exclusionary sensibility and competitiveness."

This year, the political attacks on reproductive rights have begun to galvanize this generation. "Just as we grew up being told we could 'do anything we put our mind to,' we took having freedom over our bodies for granted," said Jessica. "Plan B [the morning-after pill] has been around since I was a teenager, available over the counter. I'm sure the Right would like to argue this made me a bigger slut—it didn't—but it did make me assume that these kinds of rights would always be available to me. So here we are, suddenly having to fight for something we never had to think much about."

As they see their friends having babies, these young women also worry about how to balance work and family. "The idea of being able to 'have it all' is still prevalent," said Sarah Ball, who left *Newsweek* in 2010 and is deputy editor of Vanityfair.com. "It's become easier because you can work remotely, but it still eats at your core. It's what a lot of my friends talk about." Free and accessible child care has always been a fundamental demand of the women's movement, but the legislative efforts to pass such measures have failed. "Everything that our generation asked for as feminists was getting the identical things of what boys had—access to the Ivy League or professional schools or corporate America," said psychiatrist Anna Fels. "Women now are up against a much deeper structural problem. The workplace is designed around the male life cycle and there is no allowance for children and family. There's a fragile new cultural ideal—that both the husband and wife work. But when these families are under the real pressure of having a baby or two, there's a collapse back to old cultural norms and these young parents go back to the default tradition."

While women are increasingly taking on leadership positions in what are considered "caretaking" professions—medicine, social work, teaching, and even politics—in other professions, such as business and law, said Fels, "there's still a huge backlash against women who are openly ambitious and there are fewer women at the top. The data show that once you're a mother you're written off in terms of a career. Some of it is prejudice and some of it is reality. If husbands don't change their roles, if family structure doesn't change, and if corporate attitude toward families doesn't change, then women are in a lose-lose situation."

Facebook's Sheryl Sandberg agreed. "We reward men every step of the way—for being leaders, for being assertive, for taking risks, for being competitive," she said in 2012 at the World Economic Forum in Davos, Switzerland. "And we teach women as young as four—lay back, be communal. Until we change that at a personal level, we need to say there's an ambition gap. We need our boys to be as ambitious to contribute in the home and we need our girls to be as ambitious to achieve in the workforce."

Jessica, Jesse, Sarah, and many of their friends are already working on these problems. "Five years ago we didn't really talk about women's issues," said Jessica. "Only when we got to the workforce did we start to care about gender issues. Now a lot of young women are realizing sexism still exists. They're writing about it and starting blogs about it. I think something's happening."

This recognition of sexism in the workplace perhaps explains why this young generation loves *Mad Men*. My generation identifies with the sexualized office culture, the subjugation of women, the 1960s clothes, and the scotch-soaked parties. That was our life. I always thought that younger women viewed the TV series simply as a historic costume drama. But they understand that the most compelling part of the show takes place in the office and they relate to that. They see how Peggy, the talented, ambitious secretary who becomes the first female copywriter, and Joan, the smart, voluptuous office manager, battle sexism at work. "Peggy's having this feminist awakening," said Jessica, "and many of the things she talks about are things women still debate."

In 1970, we challenged the system and changed the conversation in the news media. For the women who participated in the lawsuits, the struggle rerouted our lives, emboldened us, and gave many of us opportunities we never would have had. It made *Newsweek* a better place to work and a better magazine. Like us, today's young women are challenging assumptions and fighting their own, more complicated battles in the workplace. They, too, are having a feminist awakening. We are standing in their corner and rooting for their success. For we now see that as with *Mad Men,* our history isn't just history. It has become a legacy for the young women who followed us.

EPILOGUE:

WHERE THEY ARE NOW

I T HAS BEEN FORTY-THREE YEARS since we became the first women in the media to sue for sex discrimination. All of us are proud of the historic role we played but the effect of the lawsuit on our lives has been mixed. For some women, it opened doors and offered career choices they never would have imagined. For others, it remains the high point of their professional lives. For a few, it's a bitter reminder of regrets and never-realized ambitions. But for all of us, now in our sixties and seventies, it was an experience that changed our perspectives about ourselves, about men and women—and womanhood—and about justice and ambition.

Judy Gingold. As with many of the women on the front lines of a legal complaint, the mainspring of our movement never fully benefited from her courageous act or her enormous talent.

Judy's last job at *Newsweek* was editor of the "My Turn" section, which she enjoyed, shepherding essays from prominent experts and everyday readers. In 1982, she left the magazine and went to Los Angeles with her husband, David Freeman, a screenwriter. In LA, Judy did some book reviews for the *Los Angeles Times* and freelance pieces for the *Wall Street Journal*. She continued her interest in feminism as a fellow at the Institute for the Study of Women and Men in Society at the University of Southern California, where Betty Friedan led a feminist think tank, and at the Center for the Study of Women at the University of California at Los Angeles.

In 1996, Judy wrote a groundbreaking piece on liposuction, which was published in the *Atlantic*. Recently, she has worked on several health topics and written some lighter, more humorous pieces. "The *Newsweek* suit was the most worthwhile thing I've ever done," she told me. "I can't think of anything I've done subsequently that comes close." Looking back at her role in starting it all, she said, "I am very proud of my part in the suit. Pride is what enables people to make that psychic switch, whether it's black pride, gay pride, or women." Though Judy feels that the suit didn't help her professionally, she believes it helped her grow personally. "I was a good girl," she said. "I learned something about the world and found the courage not to be a good girl."

Lucy Howard. Lucy spent her entire career at *Newsweek*. After reporting for the Justice section in New York, she returned to the Washington bureau in 1976 and worked as a correspondent there for ten years. When Lucy came back to New York, she wrote for the Periscope section and eventually was promoted to senior writer. Lucy took a buyout in 2002, leaving *Newsweek* after thirty-nine years. "I should have pushed myself more," she said, "but I'm not going to look back and say, 'Boo-hoo.' I have no regrets about staying, but the most enduring pleasure is the amazing range of people I worked with, and the lasting friendships I made." Lucy went back to her roots: she bought several small shares in racehorses and became active in environmental issues in Maryland. She never married.

Margaret Montagno Clay. Although Margaret enjoyed her stint writing on *Newsweek*'s international edition, "I never really thought of myself as a journalist nor thought I had a future as a journalist," she said. In the summer of 1978, she married Pete Clay, a scientist and inventor, and left *Newsweek* later that year. Since 1981, Margaret has lived in Los Alamos, New Mexico, where she has raised two children and done volunteer work.

"To me the situation at *Newsweek* was glaringly unfair and totally at odds with the editors' liberal views," she said. "When Oz said this wasn't discrimination but a long-held tradition, it was staggering." At the time of the lawsuit, Margaret recalled, "I knew this was not a just way to run the world but I didn't have a vehicle for it. I went to some early consciousness-raising groups where everyone sat around until they arrived at some consensus. The lawsuit seemed like a better route to change. You could actually do something about it with people whose abilities were known to you. It was the most concrete thing I've ever done."

Pat Lynden. Pat was going to be a journalist no matter what, just not at *Newsweek*. She was still a reporter in the New York bureau when she married Allen Gore, a police detective, in August 1970, the month we signed our first memorandum of understanding. She left *Newsweek* in May 1971, when she was pregnant with her son, Richie. Pat has worked as an editor on several magazines, including *Viva, Connoisseur,* and *Longevity,* and freelanced for others, including *New York Woman,* founded and edited by Betsy Carter, a former *Newsweek* researcher. Now divorced and a grandmother, she is a freelance writer and editor and is currently writing a novel.

Pat looks back on *Newsweek* with mostly positive feelings. "I loved the smart, interesting people, the lifelong friends I made," she said. "But I don't feel good about the fact that journalistic advancement for us didn't come from hard work and talent, as it did for the men. I adored reporting and would have given anything for a foreign bureau assignment, but that was out of the question. To this day I'm sad that I never got a crack at that professional experience."

For Pat, the lawsuit was a vindication of our belief in ourselves. "During those many nervous-making months when we were planning our action—right up to the day of the press conference—we proved to ourselves, and finally to the guys, just how smart and capable we were," she said. "It was amazing how clueless and dumbstruck they were by what we pulled off!

Of course, our action took place in the cauldron of the women's movement that was roiling every household in America. But we contributed a nice piece to that history and I'm glad I was part of it."

Fay Willey. Fay was an example of why the women's movement at *Newsweek* didn't necessarily work for everyone. Fay never wanted to be a writer, but feeling pressured by several women to move up the ladder—and seeing others try out who knew far less than she did—she relented, tried out, and was promoted to a writer in the Foreign section in May 1973. Her pieces were smart, especially on Communism, but rarely led the section. When *Newsweek* started a Japanese-language edition in 1984, the editors asked Fay to teach the Japanese how to make a newsmagazine. Two years later, she returned to the Foreign section as a writer. Although Fay was always proud of her part in the lawsuit, she has said that she regretted being talked into becoming a writer. She felt she didn't have the overall influence at the magazine that she once had as chief researcher. In 1988, Fay took a buyout with sixty-four other staffers. After a brief marriage in college, she never remarried and continues to be actively involved in the world of foreign affairs and the arts in New York and in London, where she lives for several months a year.

Merrill (Mimi) McLoughlin. Mimi is an example of what women can accomplish if given the chance. From Religion researcher to writer to the senior editor for National Affairs,

Mimi had a meteoric rise at *Newsweek*—and then rose higher. In 1986, she left to go to *US News & World Report* with her husband, Mike Ruby, also a *Newsweek* editor, where they became coeditors in 1989. Mimi was the first woman to edit a national newsweekly. In 1999, they left *US News* and are now living in the Southwest, writing and coauthoring books.

"The women's movement at *Newsweek* was definitely a turning point for me," said Mimi. "Had it not opened the doors, I probably wouldn't have hung on—I would have looked for another thing to do with my life. I wanted to be a doctor or I might have become a full-time mother. I didn't want to be an editor, ever—even at *US News*—but I liked writing." For Mimi, the lawsuit was a great confidence builder. "Coming together in a group was a very liberating experience," she said. "I can't imagine doing it on my own, but we had that sense that we were acting together and that it was a just cause." "When you look back," she added, "*Newsweek* ended up in a very good place."

Trish Reilly. Trish was so smart and talented, yet she was unable to benefit from the women's movement. In 1973, she left *Newsweek* in a panic but found herself just as anxious at CBS News. "I wound up doing very well there," she recalled, "but it still didn't change who I was. With every success, I became more depressive." After her three-year contract ended, Trish married and moved to Los Angeles. Six years later, she got divorced and moved back to Northern California, where she got a license doing real estate appraisals for probate court until she retired in 2000. "I never pursued anything that would make me a star or put me out there like that," she said. "Working for probate court didn't threaten my image of myself as a 'good girl' who didn't seek attention, who didn't seek higher achievement. I had that fire of youth that propelled me out of Alameda, but I never could overcome that other part of myself that said, 'Who do you think you are?' I understand the other part of this—the women who didn't push themselves."

Looking back at her *Newsweek* experience, Trish said, "Ultimately the women's movement helped me relate to men like an equal, but I was so entrenched in traditional values that it wasn't until my forties that I finally realized it. On the one hand I'm very sad about what could have been for me, but I don't feel regret. There are women who never tried. I can take pride in what I did do."

Liz Peer. Liz was at the top of her game in the 1970s. She had been a star reporter and writer at *Newsweek* and was promoted to Paris bureau chief, covering Western Europe and North Africa. In 1977, she finally got her wish to be a war correspondent—in Somalia. Liz won an award for her reporting there but riding in a Land Rover with no springs, she suffered a broken coccyx, causing a cycle of chronic pain. That same year, her father committed suicide—seventeen years after her older brother was found dead in a New York City rooming house, also an apparent suicide.

In 1978, Liz married at the age of thirty-nine. She continued to write in the back of the book, but her pain began to affect her personality and slow her journalistic skills. She became more erratic, more difficult, and more depressed, and by 1982 her marriage had disintegrated. In April 1983, according to a *Manhattan Inc.* article by Gwenda Blair, Bill Broyles, the new editor of *Newsweek,* terminated Liz but offered her a deal: *Newsweek* would help her find a new job and if she couldn't find one, she could freelance and do consulting work for the magazine. Liz was distraught. "What always concerned me about Liz was that her identity was completely with *Newsweek,*" recalled her friend Linda Bird Francke, a former *Newsweek* writer. "She would start every sentence with 'We feel, we know, we think'—meaning her and the magazine. You can't lose yourself so much. When she got fired, I knew terrible things would happen. That completely destroyed her."

Liz was negotiating with the magazine for health insurance and was even considering suing *Newsweek* when the editors, seeing her deterioration, offered to hire her back. According to Gwenda Blair, when they didn't promise her a level of work comparable to what she had done in the past, she turned them down. She was to go on permanent medical disability in July 1984, but on the evening of May 26, Liz put on a pale blue negligee, laid out her favorite ball gowns, and propped her feather boa around a mirror. Listening to French songs on the stereo, she wrote letters to her mother and her estranged husband. "I don't like the person I've become," she wrote to her husband. "I'm dog-tired living with an ice pack belted to my rear and I can't bear the sense of failure that stretches from my first waking moment until I fall asleep. . . . When friends ask why, tell them it's simply seven years of pain."

She drank some wine and swallowed pills. She was forty-eight years old.

"They could have kept Liz," said Linda Francke, still bitter today about what happened to Peer, as many *Newsweek*ers are. "She could have written something. She would have taken less pay. She would have done anything. They didn't need to fire her but they did. After speaking at her funeral, I walked out of the church and burst into tears. Several editors were there, looking stricken, and they came up to me and said. 'We didn't know, we didn't know.' And I said, 'You're assholes for not knowing.'"

Mary Pleshette Willis. During Mary's writing tryout for Jack Kroll, which was going nowhere, her fiancé, Jack Willis, was hit by a wave while body surfing off Long Island and broke his neck. It was July 1970, two months before they were to marry. Mary immediately took a leave from the magazine until November and, she recalled bitterly, "Kroll never called once to find out how Jack was."

Luckily, Jack Willis recovered, and he and Mary married the following year. In 1972, the couple wrote a book about their experience, *But There Are Always Miracles.* "When the advance was more than I was making at *Newsweek,* I quit," said Mary. In 1975, Mary and Jack moved to Los Angeles when their book was optioned for a television movie, which they cowrote as well as several other made-for-TV films. They moved back to New York in 1978 with their two daughters, and Mary freelanced and wrote afternoon TV specials. She published her first novel, *Papa's Cord*, in 1999, still freelances, and is writing another novel.

"I felt I was one of the early guinea pigs," said Mary, looking back on her *Newsweek* experience. "Had I stayed, I might have gotten some of the benefits of the suit, but I left before there was really any change. The highlight of my time at *Newsweek* was filing the lawsuit."

Diane Camper. Diane was one of the black researchers who decided not to join the lawsuit. In 1971, she was sent on a summer training program to the San Francisco bureau and the following year was promoted to a reporter in *Newsweek's* Washington bureau, covering the Watergate break-in and trials. Diane took a leave in 1976 to go to Yale, where she earned a master's degree in law. She returned to the Washington bureau the following year to cover the Supreme Court. In 1983, the *New York Times* editorial board hired Diane to write on education, welfare, and other social issues. She left journalism briefly to go to the Annie E. Casey Foundation as public affairs manager in 1997. In 2004, Diane went to the *Baltimore Sun* as assistant editorial page editor until June 2008. She is currently communications officer at the Public Welfare Foundation in Washington, D.C. She never married.

Thinking about the situation of women then and now, Diane said, "Whatever oppression I felt then, I identified [it] more as a racial thing. But I do know that women, particularly black women, have suffered. To that extent, I think we could have identified on both a racial and gender basis without compromising the racial piece of it. I have probably benefited by being both black and female, so I identify now in a more positive way with both race and gender."

Elisabeth (Lala) Coleman. Lala had been a reporter in *Newsweek*'s San Francisco bureau for three years when she was hired away by KQED-TV in 1973. The following year she went to work for ABC News before becoming press secretary to California Governor Jerry Brown in 1976. She resigned in 1978, when she married Rock Brynner, Yul Brynner's son. Lala came back to New York, got divorced, and started working for a media communications firm. She joined American Express in 1990, rising to vice president of international public affairs and communications before retiring in 2004. She is currently writing a memoir.

"The *Newsweek* lawsuit played a huge role in my life," said Lala. "I was immediately dispatched to a bureau and then given the first bureau reporter opening. If we had not filed, others probably would have, but I suspect they would not have been as successful as we were."

Phyllis Malamud, Jeanie Seligmann, and **Mariana Gosnell** were *Newsweek* lifers. Phyllis was promoted from New York reporter to Boston bureau chief in 1977 and returned to New York in 1983, where she became editor of the "My Turn" section. In 1986, at the age of forty-eight, Phyllis married *Newsweek*'s longtime Medicine editor, Matt Clark. She and

Matt took a buyout in 1988 and have since retired. "The suit was helpful in getting me the Boston bureau chief position," said Phyllis, "and that was helpful in terms of establishing myself as a manager."

Jeanie Seligmann worked at *Newsweek* for twenty-eight years. After being promoted to writer in 1971, she became editor of the Letters section in 1999 and took a buyout in 2002, retiring at fifty-seven. She never married. "Without the women's suit, I don't think I would have had the gumption to push for a tryout," said Jeanie. "I was much more of a follower than a leader. I guess my consciousness got raised."

Mariana Gosnell left *Newsweek* in 1988, after twenty-six years. "I often thought about leaving but I couldn't figure out a better job," she said. On her off-hours, Mariana got a pilot's license and in 1961, she bought a single-engine airplane. At one point, she took a three-month leave of absence and flew solo across the country. In 1994, when she was sixty-two, Mariana published a book about her bird's-eye journey in her plane, *Zero Three Bravo*. In 2007, she wrote another called *Ice: The Nature, the History, and the Uses of This Astonishing Substance*, which the *New York Times* reviewed and pronounced "remarkable." "I wasted too many years at *Newsweek*," said Mariana, who had a long-term relationship but never married. "It was a lack of knowing one's possibilities and a lack of belief in your capabilities. Doing the flying book gave me more of a sense of accomplishment, but the reporting at *Newsweek* determined a lot about how I write." Sadly, Mariana died unexpectedly in March 2012.

Eleanor Clift. One of Washington's most respected reporters and commentators, Eleanor credits the *Newsweek* women's suit with giving her the first boost. "It was this great unseen hand in New York that gave me the entrée to ask for a reporting internship," she recalled. In 1970, Eleanor was the Girl Friday in the Atlanta bureau. After her reporting internship in the summer of 1971, she was promoted to correspondent in Atlanta and started covering Georgia Governor Jimmy Carter. Her big scoop was getting Hamilton Jordan's game plan for how Carter could win the presidency. In 1976, Eleanor followed Carter to Washington as *Newsweek*'s White House correspondent. She left *Newsweek* briefly in 1985 to go to the *Los Angeles Times* but returned to the Washington bureau thirteen months later. She covered Capitol Hill and then the White House again from 1992 to 1994. Eleanor is currently a contributing editor at *Newsweek* and a regular on the syndicated TV show *The McLaughlin Group*.

Married to Brooks Clift (Montgomery Clift's brother) from 1964 until their divorce in 1981, Eleanor has three sons. In 1989, she married fellow journalist Tom Brazaitis, who died of kidney cancer in 2005 at the age of sixty-four. Three years later, she wrote *Two Weeks of Life: A Memoir of Love, Death, and Politics,* which weaves the experience of Tom's death with the events surrounding the Terri Schiavo case during a two-week period in March 2005.

When she first heard about the women's suit, Eleanor recalled, "I thought there was a lot of anger at *Newsweek* on the part of the men and the women. But in the end, I think it changed the chemistry of the magazine and how we looked at gender. It wasn't about ego—this was before bylines. It was about women wanting to be in the game and it was a group effort."

Jane Bryant Quinn. Jane was the only woman to hold positions at opposite ends of the *Newsweek* masthead. After leaving the *Newsweek* clip desk "with great pleasure" in 1962, she went to *Look* magazine and then was hired by McGraw-Hill to cofound a personal finance newsletter for *BusinessWeek* magazine. She was listed on the masthead as J. B. Quinn, "because women weren't thought to know anything about personal finance." A young mother in need of a job, she reluctantly agreed to the byline, but "I compensated by listing my entire staff— male and female—by their initials, too." Six years later, when she became the newsletter's publisher, she switched the masthead to full names.

In 1974, Jane started writing a personal-finance column for the *Washington Post* syndicate and in 1979, she was hired back at *Newsweek* as the magazine's first female business columnist, alongside economists Paul Samuelson and Milton Friedman. "To come back to *Newsweek* as a respected columnist was a wonderful feeling," said Jane. "I always loved *Newsweek,* but I was angry and sorry there had not been a place for me there."

In addition to *Newsweek*, Jane wrote for many publications and authored several books. She married again, had another child, and after her husband died, remarried in 2008. In 2009, Jane and her husband, Carll Tucker, started what is now The

Daily Voice, an online community news company. "Although I wasn't active in the women's movement," she said, "I was—and am—proud to declare myself a feminist. I love and respect all those rude and noisy women whose protests—even the silly protests—achieved so much for women's freedom and choice. It wouldn't have happened if the movement had been left to polite girls like me, who said 'please' and 'thank you' and imagined we could advance, in a man's world, on merit alone. We and our daughters and our granddaughters are all standing on the shoulders of those tough and insistent personalities who wouldn't be appeased. Equality is never given, it is taken—and they took it for all of us."

Eleanor Holmes Norton. Still a firebrand, Eleanor Holmes Norton continues to fight for civil rights, women's rights, and the rights of the residents of Washington, D.C. After representing the *Newsweek* women in their first lawsuit, Eleanor became head of the New York City Human Rights Commission in 1970, where she held the first hearings in the country on discrimination against women. In 1977, President Jimmy Carter appointed her to chair the Equal Employment Opportunity Commission, the first woman to hold that position. Eleanor returned to her hometown and in 1990 was elected a delegate to Congress for the District of Columbia. In her position she serves and votes on committees but is not permitted to vote on the final passage of legislation. In 1993, Eleanor divorced her husband after an income-tax scandal. She continues to serve in Congress and as a tenured professor of law at Georgetown University.

Looking back on her first meeting with the *Newsweek* editors, Eleanor said, "they were so awkward and didn't know how to deal with you, the women, or with me. Oz became a good friend and so did Katharine Graham, but here they were, the pillars of progressive America being confronted with a discrimination suit—how embarrassing." One thing Eleanor regrets is not speaking to the black researchers about joining our suit. "I would have convinced them, I know I would have," she said. "At that time, it was very hard to go behind you all, but I'm sure they would have all been with you today."

Eleanor still regards our lawsuit as a seminal case for women. "This was a case that some would say that you could not win because there was no precedent," she explained. "But discrimination is discrimination and your case paralleled any case in which there were qualified blacks at the bottom and whites at top. I didn't understand why this should be any different."

Harriet Rabb. After the *Newsweek* case, Harriet became the go-to lawyer for sex discrimination lawsuits. She represented the women at the *Reader's Digest* in 1973 and those at the *New York Times* in 1974. Harriet continued as director of the Employment Rights Project at Columbia Law School until 1978, where she also served as a professor, director of clinical education, assistant dean for urban affairs—the first woman dean—and vice dean. In 1977, when Joe Califano was appointed secretary of Health, Education, and Welfare in the Carter administration, he called up his old *Newsweek* adversary and asked whether Harriet would be interested in working for him. She declined, but the offer came around again. In 1993, Donna Shalala, the new secretary of Health and Human Services in the Clinton administration, hired Harriet as her general counsel. Harriet returned to New York in 2000 and is the vice president and general counsel of Rockefeller University.

"Look at what we took on," said Harriet. "The *Washington Post* and the *New York Times*—it doesn't get any tougher than that. What you all did gave other people the courage to do it as well. The *Newsweek* women were not waiting for God to descend and fix it for all of us. A pool of New York journalists rising up made a picture for every woman in other papers around the country."

Harriet believes not only that our case was important, but that it continues to be relevant. "It's not over," she said, "and it's never going to be over—the realization that people always have to have somebody who's the other, that justice is so hard to come by, that fairness is so hard to come by. You hope that it will get better, and it does get better. But backsliding is so much easier than forward progress and there always has to be somebody who's willing to step forward. You provided the role models. You all had options. You could have personally had an easy row to hoe. But it just wasn't who you all were. For you, it was the integrity of the case, to do the right thing. It's not that there wasn't courage involved. It took courage, but it was just some well of integrity and decency that says this isn't right. And that's at least as great a virtue as courage."

Oz Elliott. Although his first impulse was to justify the discrimination of women at *Newsweek* as "a newsmagazine tradition going back almost fifty years," Oz turned out to be a quick and lasting convert to our cause. After we had negotiated our first memorandum of understanding in August 1970, Oz thought the mechanisms were in place for progress. When he returned to the editorial side in June 1972, just after we had sued the second time, he made women's advancement a priority. At that point, Oz was going through his own transition. He was getting divorced and had just started seeing Inger McCabe, who had been married to a *Newsweek* correspondent in the Far East. Inger was an independent woman—a talented photographer and entrepreneur who started a successful design business called China Seas. "Oz loved women," said Inger, who married Oz in 1974. "He adored women and yet he didn't pay enough attention to them. He wasn't thinking!"

When Oz left the magazine in 1976 to become New York City's first deputy mayor in charge of economic development, there was a big party at Top of the Week. As he recalled in his memoir, "The women of *Newsweek* who had fought so strenuously for their rights gave me a suitably sexist scrapbook chronicling their victory." In 1977, Oz became dean of the Columbia University Graduate School of Journalism, stepping down in 1986. He also chaired the Citizens Committee of New York, an organization he helped found in 1975 that encourages local volunteerism. He died of cancer in 2008.

To his credit, Oz was always honest about his role in *Newsweek's* discrimination against women. When he became friendly with Ellen Goodman in later years, she recalled, "He was the first to say, 'God, weren't we awful? Can you believe that it was like that then? All those [talented women] who left, as well they should have—why did they ever stay?' Oz would preempt the discussion but in my mind, there would still be this connection to the women whose careers were basically ended by that [discrimination]. People did something and it had terrible effects on other people. Then they changed and the world changed and Oz certainly changed. I was very fond of him."

We all were. Just before he died, I asked him if there was anything he regretted. "Looking back," he said, "I would have been more sensitive about what it was all about before the storm broke. And in retrospect, I'm sure I would have said something different than that it was a newsmagazine tradition!"

As for me, I always say I am an affirmative-action baby and proud of it. After being promoted to *Newsweek*'s first female senior editor in September 1975, I worked in that job until I left on maternity leave in November 1980, when our daughter, Sarah, was born. When I returned six months later, I negotiated a three-day week to work on special projects. During that time, I packaged seven *Newsweek* cover stories into books, helped turn one of them into a CBS Reports television documentary, and launched *Newsweek on Campus* and *Newsweek on Health,* specialty magazines that were distributed on college campuses and in doctors' offices. In 1982, Steve and I had our son, Ned, and two years later I returned full-time as a senior editor, often filling in as a Wallenda.

In 1991, after twenty-five years at *Newsweek,* I left to become editor-in-chief of *Working Woman,* a monthly magazine started in the mid-1970s when women were flooding into the workforce. I loved having my own magazine, especially one geared to professional and business women, but it was severely underfinanced (it closed in 2001). In 1996, I took a job as East Coast managing editor/senior executive producer of MSNBC.com, a new Internet–cable TV news venture created by Microsoft and NBC. Working in New York, my team was responsible for creating the Internet content for NBC News and MSNBC cable programs and personalities. It was exciting to be in this new world of digital journalism and I learned a lot. But since broadband—so critical for NBC's video—wouldn't happen as quickly as we had hoped, I started to get restless. After a brush with breast cancer (I'm fine), I decided to leave MSNBC.com in March 2001. Since then I have freelanced, tutored in a public school, and been active on the boards of the Women's Rights Division of Human Rights Watch and the International Women's Media Foundation, which supports women journalists around the world.

My husband, Steve Shepard, left *Newsweek* in 1981 to become editor of *Saturday Review,* a weekly literary magazine with a distinguished history. But it was on its last legs and folded a year later. Steve was wooed back to *BusinessWeek* as executive editor and became editor-in-chief in 1984, a position he held for twenty years. In 2004 Matthew Goldstein, chancellor of the City University of New York, asked him to create a new Graduate School of Journalism at CUNY. As a product of public schools in New York and a graduate of City College, Steve was thrilled to design the only publicly funded graduate school of journalism in the entire Northeast and he has been the founding dean ever since. We have been blissfully—and blessedly—married for more than thirty-three years.

My father, who died in 1998, continues to have an enormous influence in my life. He suffered from a damaged heart valve but was writing up to the very end, at nearly ninety-three. The day before he died, on June 4, 1998, he wrote his last column, which was published alongside his obituary. His seventy-five-year writing career provided a front-row seat to the most awe-inspiring sports moments of the twentieth century, yet his columns had never been collected. In early 2003, my brothers and I decided to edit a collection of his sports columns, along with George Solomon, former sports editor of the *Washington Post* who had worked with Dad for twenty-five years. *All Those Mornings . . . At the Post* was published by PublicAffairs in 2005, on what would have been my father's hundredth birthday.

I was fortunate to be working and without children when the women's movement came along. If it hadn't been for the lawsuit, I never would have become a senior editor at *Newsweek,* a thrilling job that taught me so much about the world, about managing people, and about myself. I am forever grateful to the women who pushed us, the lawyers who represented us and the men who supported us. The lawsuit not only changed my life, it changed my thinking about women: about how we are raised, how we realize our ambitions, how we balance the demands of a career while raising a family. It also set a path for me for the rest of my life: to help other women. In telling our history, I hope our daughters come to understand that sisterhood is powerful, that good girls can revolt, and that change can—and must—happen.

THE GOOD GIRLS
WHO SIGNED ON FOR THE GOOD FIGHT

**THE FORTY-SIX WOMEN WHO FILED THE FIRST
EEOC COMPLAINT (IN THE ORDER IN WHICH
THEY SIGNED), MARCH 16, 1970:**

Virginia Adams
Susan Agrest
Holly Camp
Elisabeth Coleman
Barbara Davidson
Nancy Dooley
Valerie Gerry
Marianna Gosnell
Judy Gingold
Lucy Howard
Janet Huck
Patricia Lynden
Phyllis Malamud
Margaret Montagno
Mary Pleshette
Noel Ragsdale
Trish Reilly
Sylvia Robinson
Susan Sands
Merrill (McLoughlin) Sheils
Joan Spack
Nancy Stadtman
Lynn (Povich) Young

Sheila Younge
Jeanne Voltz
Jean Seligmann
Abigail Kuflik
Harriet Huber
Lynn Allegaert
Eileen Pond
Judy Harvey
Madeleine Edmonson
Joanna Cole
Ellen Jurow
Karla Spurlock
Marjorie Lester
Helen Willingham
Fay Willey
Ann Ray Martin
Diane Zimmerman
Jean MacGregor
Alden Cohen
Marie Whiteside
Constance Bessie
Constance Carroll
Sunde Smith

THESE FOURTEEN WOMEN ADDED THEIR NAMES ON MARCH 24, 1970:

Priscilla Baker
Deborah Beers
Pat Conway
Dale Denmark
Joyce Fenmore
Susan Fleming
Constance Guthrie
Alison Kilgour
Janet MacDonell
Madlyn Millimet
Ann Schumacher
Ruth Werthman
Lisa Whitman
Gwendolyn Wright

THE WOMEN WHO SIGNED THE SECOND EEOC COMPLAINT, MAY 16, 1972:

Katrine W. Ames
Linda B. Backstein
Bonnie K. Bell
Andrea Besch
Connie Bessie
Susan Braudy
Barbara Bright
Barbara Burke
Holly Camp
Constance W. Carroll
Babette W. Carter
Alden D. Cohen
Barbara L. Davidson

Allison W. Dimond
Madeleine Edmonson
Susan (Moran) Fleming
Jane M. Friedman
Sandra Gary
Judith Gingold
Marianna Gosnell
Constance Guthrie
Hilary Horton
Clare Howard
Lucy Howard
Janet Huck
Sally Hunter
Alison Kilgour
Lorraine Kisly
Abigail Kuflik Kimball
Laurie Lisle
Jean L. MacGregor
Anne N. McGinn
Phyllis Malamud
Ann Ray Martin
Werner Michel
Margaret Montagno
Patricia C. Reilly
Sandra Salmans
Ann M. Schumacher
Jean A. Seligmann
Merrill (McLoughlin) Sheils
Nancy Stadtman
Elizabeth Wasik
Marie Whiteside
Lisa Whitman
Fay Willey
Lynn (Povich) Young

ACKNOWLEDGMENTS

W HEN I LEFT *NEWSWEEK* in 1991 after twenty-five years, I took
home the documents surrounding our 1970 lawsuit. By then, no
one seemed interested. I was going to send them to the women's archives
at Radcliffe's Schlesinger Library, which had requested the material, but
I got sidetracked. In 2006, when I finally had time, I realized that to make
sense of the papers I had to write a narrative. I started contacting the
women involved. When the history grew to 30,000 words, I knew this
was a story that should be told.

Interviewing people about what happened forty years ago, however,
was a challenge. My own memory proved inaccurate in several instances
and other people's recollections contradicted one another. I have tried my
best to reconstruct what happened using documents, interviews, and research. However people remember it, I am hoping that, as T.S. Eliot said,
"the end of all of our exploring will be to arrive where we started and know
the place for the first time."

I interviewed over forty people who were at *Newsweek* at the time, including, just before he died, Oz Elliott. All of them contributed facets of
the story and I deeply appreciate their help. But this tale could not have
been told without the testimony and insight of Judy Gingold, Lucy
Howard, Peter Goldman, Pat Lynden, Margaret Montagno, Trish Reilly,
Mary Pleshette Willis, Harry Waters, Mariana Gosnell, Franny Heller
Zorn, Betsy Carter, Phyllis Malamud, and Elisabeth Coleman. I am indebted to them for their time and their support. I also want to thank our
two inspiring lawyers, Eleanor Holmes Norton in the first lawsuit, and
Harriet Rabb, whose files on the second lawsuit were invaluable.

In capturing what *Newsweek* was like in the early sixties, I relied on
the vivid memories of Jane Bryant Quinn, Ellen Goodman, and Nora

Ephron. Gloria Steinem, Betsy Wade, Anna Quindlen, and Gail Collins provided essential information on the tenor of the times.

When I started reporting, I didn't know Jessica Bennett, Jesse Ellison, and Sarah Ball, three young women working at *Newsweek*. I am so grateful to them for keeping our story alive. I am also proud that they now call themselves feminists and are passionately carrying on the fight for women's rights. At *Newsweek/Daily Beast*, Sam Register, director of the library, and photo editor Beth Johnson were especially helpful.

I want to thank my friend Peter Osnos, founder of PublicAffairs, who was an early supporter of the project, and PublicAffairs' publisher, Susan Weinberg, and senior editor and marketing director, Lisa Kaufman, who were enthusiastic about the book from the very beginning. I am particularly indebted to Lisa, my editor, for her sage advice and suggestions in helping me shape the story. Managing editor Melissa Raymond kept me on track, and assistant director of publicity Tessa Shanks provided creative and expert guidance. My lawyer, Jan Constantine, general counsel at the Authors Guild, shepherded me through the contract and made smart recommendations.

Throughout this project, I was encouraged by many close friends. I am especially grateful to Jack Willis, Sarah Duffy Edwards, Rosemary Ellis, Polly McCall, and Letty Cottin Pogrebin who urged me to keep going whenever I got stuck.

I could not have written this book without the loving support of my husband, Steve Shepard, a brilliant editor who makes everything in my life better. As I was laboring with my book, Steve began to write a memoir of his life in journalism, from *Newsweek* and *BusinessWeek* to the CUNY Graduate School of Journalism. It's called *Deadlines and Disruption: My Turbulent Path from Print to Digital*. As luck would have it, our books were being published in the same week.

Our children, Sarah and Ned, bring joy and meaning to my life every day. May this story inspire them to speak up and make a difference.

NOTE ON SOURCES

Most of the information in this book comes from my interviews, original documents or copies of documents, and books, which are listed in the bibliography. All other sources are cited by chapter.

All quotations from Susan Brownmiller are from her book *In Our Time: Memoir of a Revolution* (New York: Dial Press, 1999).

Here, in alphabetical order, are the people I interviewed:

Leandra Hennemann Abbott, Katrine Ames, Sarah Ball, Jessica Bennett, Helaine Blumenfeld, Susan Braudy, Kevin Buckley, Joe Califano, Diane Camper, Betsy Carter, Susan Cheever, Phyllis Malamud Clark, Margaret Montagno Clay, Eleanor Clift, Elisabeth Coleman, Kate Coleman, Gail Collins, George Cooper, Madlyn Millimet Deming, Dorinda Elliott, Inger Elliott, Osborn Elliott, Jesse Ellison, Nora Ephron, Karla Spurlock Evans, Anna Fels, Joe Ferrer, Penny Ferrer, Susan Fraker, Linda Bird Francke, Rod Gander, Judy Gingold, Peter Goldman, Ellen Goodman, Mariana Gosnell, Trish Hall, Lucy Howard, Liz Hylton, Margo Jefferson, Vajra (Alison) Kilgour, Ed Kosner, Lynn Langway, Grace Lichtenstein, Diana Elliott Lidovsky, Pat Lynden, Ann Ray Martin, Merrill McLoughlin, Joe Morgenstern, Eleanor Holmes Norton, Barbara Bright Novovitch, Maureen Orth, Anna Quindlen, Jane Bryant Quinn, Harriet Rabb, Noel Ragsdale, Trish Reilly, Elaine Sciolino, Jeanie Seligmann, Steve Shepard, Sunde Smith, Ray Sokolov, Nancy Stadtman, Gloria Steinem, Annalyn Swan, Rich Thomas, Jeanne Voltz, Betsy Wade, Harry Waters, Fay Willey, Mary Pleshette Willis, Diane Zimmerman, Franny Heller Zorn.

PROLOGUE: WHAT WAS THE PROBLEM?

Page xiii **Hadn't Maria Shriver's report:** Maria Shriver and the Center for American Progress, *The SHRIVER Report: A Woman's Nation Changes Everything*, ed. Heather Boushey and Ann O'Leary, October 16, 2009; www.american progress.org/issues/2009/10/womans_nation.html.

Page xiv **A crumpled Post-it note marked the chapter:** Brownmiller, *In Our Time*, 140.

Page xv **Joe Halderman, a CBS News producer:** Richard Huff, George Rush, and Samuel Goldsmith, "David Letterman Reveals $2M Sex Affair Extortion Plot; CBS News Producer Robert [Joe] Halderman Busted," *New York Daily News*, October 2, 2009; www.nydailynews.com/entertainment /television/david-letterman-reveals-2m-sex-affair-extortion -plot-cbs-news-producer-robert-halderman-busted-article -1.379822#ixzz1oYaHuIBT.

Page xv **That same month, ESPN analyst Steve Phillips:** Jeane MacIntosh and Dan Mangan, "ESPN's Steve Phillips in Foul Affair with Production Assistant," *New York Post*, October 21, 2009; www.nypost.com/p/news/national/item _bLw9UoSAQJwJLU4ZDXvvDO#ixzz1oYWPQC9L.

Page xv **In November, editor Sandra Guzman:** Sam Stein, "*New York Post* Lawsuit: Shocking Allegations Made by Fired Employee Sandra Guzman," *Huffington Post*, November 10, 2009; www.huffingtonpost.com/2009/11/10/shocking -allegations-levi_n_352314.html.

Page xv **"At this moment, there are more females":** Nell Scovell, "Letterman and Me," Vanityfair.com, October 27, 2009; www.vanityfair.com/hollywood/features/2009/10/david -letterman-200910.

Page xvii **"the problem that had no name":** Betty Friedan, *The Feminine Mystique* (New York: W.W. Norton and Co., 1963), p. 57 in later editions.

Page xviii **In the 1950s, full-time working women:** Borgna Brunner, "Help Wanted—Separate and Unequal," *The Wage Gap: A History of Pay Inequity and the Equal Pay Act*, Infoplease

.com; www.infoplease.com/spot/equalpayact1.html#ixzz1o
YPDhqqg.

Page xviii   **Until 1970, women comprised fewer than 10 percent:**
Claudia Goldin and Lawrence F. Katz, "On the Pill:
Changing the Course of Women's Education," *Milken Institute Review* 3 (2nd quarter 2001): 14; www.economics
.harvard.edu/faculty/goldin/Papers.

CHAPTER 1 "EDITORS FILE STORY: GIRLS FILE COMPLAINT"

The description and quotes about the *Ladies' Home Journal* sit-in are from
Brownmiller, *In Our Time,* 83–92.

Page 9   **In the next few years, women sued:** Kathleen L. Endres
and Therese L. Lueck "Media Report to Women," in
*Women's Periodicals in the United States: Social and Political
Issues* (Westport, CT: Greenwood Press, 1996), 202.

Page 9   **In 1974, six women at the *New York Times*:** Nan Robertson, *The Girls in the Balcony: Women, Men, and the New
York Times* (New York: Random House, 1992), 168.

Page 9   **in 1975, sixteen women at NBC:** Arnold H. Lubash, "$2
Million NBC Pact Is Set as a Settlement with Women of
Staff," *New York Times,* February 17, 1977.

Page 10   **When Oz Elliott and *Newsweek* chairman Frederick
"Fritz" Beebe telephoned her:** Katharine Graham, *Personal History* (New York: Alfred A. Knopf, 1997), 425.

Page 11   **In her insightful book:** Anna Fels, *Necessary Dreams: Ambition in Women's Changing Lives* (New York: Pantheon
Books, 2004).

Page 12   **Sheryl Sandberg, chief operating officer of Facebook:**
"Sheryl Sandberg Sees Global 'Ambition Gap'" Bloomberg
News, January 30, 2012; www.bloomberg.com/video/85189
956-sandberg-sees-global-ambition-gap-for-women.html.

Page 13   **"It was, all in all, a benevolent version":** Gail Collins,
*When Everything Changed: The Amazing Journey of American
Women from 1960 to the Present* (New York: Little, Brown
and Company, 2009), 105.

CHAPTER 2 "A NEWSMAGAZINE TRADITION"

Page 15 **Classified ads were still segregated by gender:** "*Pittsburgh Press v. Pittsburgh Commission on Human Relations,*" http://aclu.procon.org/view.resource.php?resourceID=3124.

Page 16 **That infamous "tradition" began in 1923:** Robert T. Elson, *Time Inc.: The Intimate History of a Publishing Enterprise, 1923–1941* (New York: Atheneum, 1968), 72.

Page 24 **Liz later told him:** Osborn Elliott, *The World of Oz: An Inside Report on Big-Time Journalism by the Former Editor of* Newsweek (New York: Viking Press, 1980), 143.

Page 24 **Returning to the office at night:** Gwenda Blair, "The Heart of the Matter," *Manhattan Inc.,* October 1984, 73.

Page 31 **In 1965, Karen was sent out:** "Divorced. Alan Jay Lerner," *Time,* December 23, 1974.

CHAPTER 3 THE "HOT BOOK"

Unless otherwise noted, information about Osborn Elliott comes from his memoir, *The World of Oz: An Inside Report on Big-Time Journalism by the Former Editor of* Newsweek (New York: Viking Press, 1980).

Page 34 **"Ozzy baby, I know where the smart money is":** Elliott, *The World of Oz,* 3.

Page 35 **To get Phil Graham interested:** Ben Bradlee, *A Good Life: Newspapering and Other Adventures* (New York: Simon & Schuster, 1995), 224.

Page 36 **"Visually they are a nightmare":** *Newsweek,* February 24, 1964; Charles Kaiser, "A Magazine That Mattered," *Radar* online, May 6, 2010; www.hillmanfoundation.org/blog /newsweek-sale.

Page 36 **"With Kermit, we had a Jewish intellectual":** Alex Kuczynski, "Kermit Lansner, 78, Former *Newsweek* Editor," *New York Times,* May 22, 2000.

Page 39 **"No doubt the war":** Elliott, *The World of Oz,* 101.

Page 42 **Describing the weekly routine:** Carole Wicker, "Limousine to Nowhere . . . If You're a Girl at a News Magazine," *Cosmopolitan.*

Page 43   **"The dialogue was eighth grade":** Robin Reisig, "Is Journalism an Air-Brushed Profession?" *Village Voice,* May 16, 1974, 24.

Page 46   **Nation researcher Kate Coleman:** Kate Coleman, "Turning on Newsweek," *Scanlan's Monthly,* June 1970, 44.

CHAPTER 4 RING LEADERS

Page 52   **The famous "click!":** Jane O'Reilly, "The Housewife's Moment of Truth," *Ms.,* December 1971.

Page 54   **At that time, the Marshall:** "History 1960–1991," Marshall Scholarships; www.marshallscholarship.org/about/history/1960–1991.

Page 54   **the Rhodes wasn't extended to women:** "Second Class Citizens? How Women Became Rhodes Scholars," Rhodes Project; http://therhodesproject.wordpress.com.

Page 60   **In the fall of 1969, Judy Gingold:** Daisy Hernandez, "A Genteel Nostalgia, Going Out of Business," *New York Times,* February 23, 2003.

Page 62   **She was a "red-diaper baby":** Patricia Lynden, "Red Diaper Baby," *New York Woman,* August 1988.

CHAPTER 5 "YOU GOTTA TAKE OFF YOUR WHITE GLOVES, LADIES"

Page 77   **In October 1964 Otto Friedrich:** Otto Friedrich, "There Are 00 Trees in Russia: The Function of Facts in Newsmagazines," *Harper's,* October 1964, 59–65.

Page 79   **Fay wrote a scathing letter:** Fay Willey, "Letter to the Editor," *Harper's,* December 1964, 4.

Page 81   **The great-granddaughter of a slave:** Joan Steinau Lester in Conversation with Eleanor Holmes Norton, *Fire in My Soul: The Life of Eleanor Holmes Norton* (New York: Atria, 2003). Unless noted, biographical information about Eleanor Holmes Norton is based on *Fire in My Soul.*

Page 85   **The provision protecting women:** Gail Collins, *When Everything Changed: The Amazing Journey of American Women from 1960 to the Present* (New York: Little, Brown, and Company, 2009), 76. Feminist Jo Freeman argues that "sex" was not added to scuttle the bill. "How 'Sex' Got into Title VII," www.jofreeman.com/lawandpolicy/titlevii .htm.

Page 86   **"Congressman Smith would joyfully disembowel":** Don Oberdorfer, "'Judge' Smith Moves with Deliberate Drag," *New York Times Magazine,* November 12, 1964.

CHAPTER 6 ROUND ONE

Page 94   **At one point Vice President Spiro Agnew:** Spiro Agnew, "Speech to Alabama Chamber of Commerce," *American History Online,* Facts on File Inc., November 20, 1969.

Page 95   **"I idolized her":** Helen Dudar, *The Attentive Eye: Selected Journalism,* ed. Peter Goldman (Bloomington, IN: Xlibris Corporation, 2002).

Page 98   **Lucy was insulted:** Susan Donaldson James, "Newsweek Still Wages Gender War, 40 Years Later," *ABCNews.com,* March 23, 2010.

Page 101   **"My idea of a cold-sweat nightmare":** Brownmiller, *In Our Time,* 145.

Page 103   **As she wrote in her remarkably candid, Pulitzer Prize –winning autobiography:** Graham, *Personal History,* 340, 418.

Page 104   **Kay replied that she encouraged her employees:** "Kay in Miami," *Women's Wear Daily,* March 24, 1970.

Page 107   **Carrying hand-lettered signs:** "'Liberation' Talk of the Town," *New Yorker,* September 5, 1970, 28.

Page 108   **Describing the event on the ABC evening news:** Susan Jeanne Douglas, *Where the Girls Are: Growing Up Female with the Mass Media* (New York: Three Rivers Press, 1994) 163.

Page 109   **In a *New York Times* story about the agreement:** "*Newsweek* Agrees to Speed Promotion of Women," *New York Times,* August 27, 1970.

CHAPTER 7 MAD MEN: THE BOYS FIGHT BACK

Page 116   **When Katharine Graham suggested:** Graham, *Personal History,* 424.

Page 117   **Hef's memo as to why he didn't like:** Carrie Pitzulo, *Bachelors and Bunnies: The Sexual Politics of Playboy* (Chicago: University of Chicago Press, 2011), 142.

CHAPTER 9 "JOE—SURRENDER"

Page 140   **The *Post* women ended up filing:** Chalmers M. Roberts, *The Washington Post: The First 100 Years* (New York: Houghton Mifflin, 1977), 429.

Page 141   **"It was shortly after [the Metro Seven settlement]":** Dorothy Gilliam oral history, *Washington Press Club Foundation,* 1992–1993; http://beta.wpcf.org/oralhistory/gill4 .html.

Page 141   **Her close friend at the *Post*:** Graham, *Personal History,* 421.

Page 156   **The case had gotten so poisonous:** Robertson, *Girls in the Balcony,* 203, 205.

Page 159   **On October 4, 1974, fifteen women filed:** *Media Report to Women,* ed. Dr. Donna Allen, December 1, 1974.

CHAPTER 10 THE BARRICADES FELL

Page 162   **Its "statement of purpose" declared:** "The National Black Feminist Organization's Statement of Purpose, 1973," University of Michigan–Dearborn; www-personal.umd .umich.edu/~ppennock/doc-BlackFeminist.htm.

Page 163   **The largest employer of women, the Bell System:** Crista DeLuzio, ed., *Women's Rights: People and Perspectives* (Westport, CT: Greenwood Publishing Group, 2009), 197.

Page 163   **In 1971, a feminist attorney named Ruth Bader Ginsburg:** Ruth Bader Ginsburg, "Breaking New Ground— *Reed v. Reed,* 404 US 71 (1971)," Supreme Court Historical Society; www.supremecourthistory.org/learning-center /womens-rights/breaking-new-ground.

Page 164   **However, President Richard Nixon vetoed it:** Abby J. Cohen, "A Brief History of Federal Financing for Child Care in the United States," *Future of Children Journal* 6, no. 2 (Summer/Fall 1996): 32; http://futureofchildren.org /futureofchildren/publications/docs/06_02_01.pdf.

Page 164   **By the end of 1971, stories on the new women's move-
                ment:** Ruth Rosen, *The World Split Open: How the Modern
                Women's Movement Changed America* (New York: Penguin
                Books, 2006), 302.

Page 164   **Distrusting the coverage of the women's movement:** Pa-
                tricia Bradley, *Mass Media and the Shaping of American
                Feminism, 1963–1975* (Jackson: University Press of
                Mississippi, 2003), 49.

Page 164   **Beginning in 1968, publications calling for social
                change:** Martha Allen, "Multi-Issue Women's Periodicals:
                The Pioneers," Women's Institute for Freedom of the Press;
                www.wifp.org/womensmediach3.html.

Page 164   **In all, more than five hundred feminist periodicals:**
                Kathryn T. Flannery, *Feminist Literacies, 1968–75* (Cham-
                paign: University of Illinois Press, 2005), 23.

Page 165   **That same year, NOW filed a petition:** "Broadcasting
                Cases," National Women and Media Collection, Donna
                Allen (1920–1999) Papers, 1920–1992 (C3795), State His-
                torical Society of Missouri, University of Missouri, Columbia;
                http://shs.umsystem.edu/manuscripts/invent/3795.html
                #broa

Page 165   **In February 1973, fifty women at NBC:** "City Rights
                Unit Finds NBC Sexism," *New York Times,* January 24,
                1975.

Page 165   **The case would be settled in 1975 for $2 million:** Arnold
                H. Lubash, "$2 Million NBC Pact Is Set as a Settlement
                with Women of Staff," *New York Times,* February 17,
                1977.

Page 166   **In March 1970, a reporter for the British newsmagazine:**
                Lilla Lyon, "The March of *Time*'s Women," *New York Mag-
                azine,* February 22, 1971.

CHAPTER 11 PASSING THE TORCH

Page 193   **"A merger has created":** "Daily Beast, *Newsweek* to
                Merge," *Morning Edition,* National Public Radio, Novem-
                ber 12, 2010.

EPILOGUE: WHERE THEY ARE NOW
Much of the information on Liz Peer came from Gwenda Blair, "The Heart of the Matter," *Manhattan Inc.*, October 1984, 73.

BIBLIOGRAPHY

Bradlee, Ben. *A Good Life: Newspapering and Other Adventures.* New York: Simon & Schuster, 1995.

Bradley, Patricia. *Mass Media and the Shaping of American Feminism, 1963–1975.* Jackson: University Press of Mississippi, 2003.

Brownmiller, Susan. *In Our Time: Memoir of a Revolution.* New York: Dial Press, 1999.

Carter, Betsy. *Nothing to Fall Back On: The Life and Times of a Perpetual Optimist.* New York: Hyperion, 2002.

Chamberlain, Mariam K. *Women in Academe: Progress and Prospects.* New York: Russell Sage Foundation, 1988.

Chambers, Deborah, Linda Steiner, and Carole Fleming. *Women and Journalism.* London and New York: Routledge, 2004.

Collins, Gail. *When Everything Changed: The Amazing Journey of American Women from 1960 to the Present.* New York: Little, Brown and Company, 2009.

DeLuzio, Crista, ed. *Women's Rights: People and Perspectives.* Westport, CT: Greenwood Publishing Group, 2009.

Douglas, Susan Jeanne. *Where the Girls Are: Growing up Female with the Mass Media.* New York: Three Rivers Press, 1995.

Dudar, Helen. *The Attentive Eye: Selected Journalism.* Edited by Peter Goldman. Bloomington, IN: Xlibris Corporation, 2002.

Echols, Alice. *Daring to Be Bad: Radical Feminism in America, 1967–1975.* Minneapolis: University of Minnesota Press, 1989.

Elliott, Osborn. *The World of Oz: An Inside Report on Big-Time Journalism by the Former Editor of Newsweek.* New York: Viking Press, 1980.

Elson, Robert T. *Time Inc.: The Intimate History of a Publishing Enterprise, 1923–1941.* New York: Atheneum, 1968.

Ephron, Nora. *I Remember Nothing and Other Reflections*. New York: Alfred A. Knopf, 2010.

Flannery, Kathryn T. *Feminist Literacies, 1968–75*. Champaign: University of Illinois Press, 2005.

Friedan, Betty. *The Feminine Mystique*. New York: W.W. Norton and Co., 1963.

Fels, Anna. *Necessary Dreams: Ambition in Women's Changing Lives*. New York: Pantheon Books, 2004.

Graham, Katharine. *Personal History*. New York: Alfred A. Knopf, 1997.

Kosner, Edward. *It's News to Me: The Making and Unmaking of an Editor*. New York: Thunder's Mouth Press, 2006.

Lester, Joan Steinau, in conversation with Eleanor Holmes Norton. *Fire in My Soul: The Life of Eleanor Holmes Norton*. New York: Atria, 2003.

Pitzulo, Carrie. *Bachelors and Bunnies: The Sexual Politics of Playboy*. Chicago: University of Chicago Press, 2011.

Redstockings of the Women's Liberation Movement. *Feminist Revolution, an Abridged Edition with Additional Writings*. Edited by Kathie Sarachild. New York: Random House, 1975, 1978.

Roberts, Chalmers M. *The Washington Post: The First 100 Years*. Boston: Houghton Mifflin Company, 1977.

Robertson, Nan. *The Girls in the Balcony: Women, Men, and the* New York Times. New York: Random House, 1992.

Rosen, Ruth. *The World Split Open: How the Modern Women's Movement Changed America*, rev. ed. New York: Penguin Books, 2006.

Trillin, Calvin. *Floater*. New Haven, CT, and New York: Ticknor & Fields. 1980.

A READER'S GUIDE TO
THE GOOD GIRLS REVOLT

We are providing the following supplementary materials—the 2010 *Newsweek* article discussed in the prologue, a Q & A with author Lynn Povich, and questions for discussion—to enhance your reading of *The Good Girls Revolt* and provide a jumping-off point for reading group discussions. For more information about PublicAffairs books, visit us at publicaffairsbooks.com, at facebook.com/PublicAffairs, or follow @public_affairs on twitter.

***

In the prologue to The Good Girls Revolt, *Lynn Povich introduces Jessica Bennett, Jesse Ellison, and Sarah Ball, three young women working at* Newsweek *in 2009, who unexpectedly found themselves struggling against gender discrimination. After Jessica, Jesse, and Sarah learn about the landmark gender discrimination lawsuit that Lynn and her colleagues filed against the magazine in 1970, they become "determined to write a piece for* Newsweek *questioning how much had actually changed for women at the magazine, in the media, and in the workplace in general" (p. xvii). Here is the piece they wrote, which* Newsweek *published in March of 2010.*

ARE WE THERE YET?

In 1970, 46 women filed a landmark gender-discrimination case.
Their employer was Newsweek. Forty years later, their contemporary
counterparts question how much has actually changed.

By Jessica Bennett, Jesse Ellison, and Sarah Ball

They were an archetype: independent, determined young graduates of Seven Sisters colleges, fresh-faced, new to the big city,
full of aspiration. Privately, they burned with the kind of ambition
that New York encourages so well. Yet they were told in job interviews that women could never get to the top, or even the middle.
They accepted positions anyway—sorting mail, collecting newspaper
clippings, delivering coffee. Clad in short skirts and dark-rimmed
glasses, they'd click around in heels, currying favor with the all-male
management, smiling softly when the bosses called them "dollies."
That's just the way the world worked then. Though each quietly believed she'd be the one to break through, ambition, in any real sense,
wasn't something a woman could talk about out loud. But by 1969,
as the women's movement gathered force around them, the dollies
got restless. They began meeting in secret, whispering in the ladies'
room or huddling around a colleague's desk. To talk freely they'd
head to the Women's Exchange, a 19th-century relic where they
could chat discreetly on their lunch break. At first there were just
three, then nine, then ultimately 46—women who would become
the first group of media professionals to sue for employment discrimination based on gender under Title VII of the Civil Rights Act.
Their employer was *Newsweek* magazine.

Until six months ago, when sex-and gender-discrimination
scandals hit ESPN, David Letterman's *Late Show*, and the *New
York Post*, the three of us—all young *Newsweek* writers—knew virtually nothing of these women's struggle. Over time, it seemed,
their story had faded from the collective conversation. Eventually
we got our hands on a worn copy of *In Our Time*, a memoir written

by a former *Newsweek* researcher, Susan Brownmiller, which had a chapter on the uprising. With a crumpled Post-it marking the page, we passed it around, mesmerized by descriptions that showed just how much has changed, and how much hasn't.

Forty years after *Newsweek*'s women rose up, there's no denying our cohort of young women is unlike even the half-generation before us. We are post–Title IX women, taught that the fight for equality was history; that we could do, or be, anything. The three of us were valedictorians and state-champion athletes; we got scholarships and were the first to raise our hands in class. As young professionals, we cheered the third female Supreme Court justice and, nearly, the first female president. We've watched as women became the majority of American workers, prompting a Maria Shriver–backed survey on gender, released late last year, to proclaim that "the battle of the sexes is over."

The problem is, for women like us, the victory dance feels premature. Youthful impatience? Maybe. But consider this: U.S. Department of Education data show that a year out of school, despite having earned higher college GPAs in every subject, young women will take home, on average across all professions, just 80 percent of what their male colleagues do. Even at the top end, female M.B.A.s make $4,600 less per year in their first job out of business school, according to a new Catalyst study. Motherhood has long been the explanation for the persistent pay gap, yet a decade out of college, full-time working women who *haven't* had children still make 77 cents on the male dollar. As women increasingly become the breadwinners in this recession, bringing home 23 percent less bacon hurts families more deeply than ever before. "The last decade was supposed to be the 'promised one,' and it turns out it wasn't," says James Turley, the CEO of Ernst & Young, a funder of the recent M.B.A. study. "This is a wake-up call."

In countless small ways, each of us has felt frustrated over the years, as if something was amiss. But as products of a system in which we learned that the fight for equality had been won, we didn't identify those feelings as gender-related. It seemed like a cop-out, a weakness, to suggest that the problem was anybody's fault but our own. It sounds naive—we know—especially since our own boss Ann McDaniel climbed the ranks to become *Newsweek*'s managing director, overseeing all aspects of the company. Compared with the *Newsweek* dollies, what did we have to complain about? "If we judge by what we see in the media, it looks like women have it made," says author Susan Douglas. "And if women have it made, why would you be so ungrateful to point to something and call it sexism?"

Yet the more we talked to our friends and colleagues, the more we heard the same stories of disillusionment, regardless of profession. No one would dare say today that "women don't write here," as the *Newsweek* women were told 40 years ago. But men wrote all but six of *Newsweek*'s 49 cover stories last year—and two of those used the headline "The Thinking Man." In 1970, 25 percent of *Newsweek*'s editorial masthead was female; today that number is 39 percent. Better? Yes. But it's hardly equality. (Overall, 49 percent of the entire company, the business and editorial sides, is female.) "Contemporary young women enter the workplace full of enthusiasm, only to see their hopes dashed," says historian Barbara J. Berg. "Because for the first time they're slammed up against gender bias."

We should add that we are proud to work at *Newsweek*. (Really, boss, we are!) We write about our magazine not because we feel it's worse here, but because *Newsweek* was once ground zero for a movement that was supposed to break at least one glass ceiling. Just as our predecessors' 1970 case didn't happen in a vacuum, *Newsweek* today is neither unique nor unusual. Female bylines at major magazines are still outnumbered by seven to one; women are just 3 percent of Fortune 500 CEOs and less than a quarter of law partners and politicians. That imbalance even applies to the Web, where the founder of a popular copywriting Web site, Men With Pens, revealed late last year that "he" was actually a she. "I assumed if I chose a male name [I'd] be viewed as somebody who runs a company, not a mom sitting at home with a child hanging off her leg," the woman says. It worked: her business doubled once she joined the boys' club.

We know what you're thinking: we're young and entitled, whiny and humorless—to use a single, dirty word, feminists! But just as the first black president hasn't wiped out racism, a female at the top of a company doesn't eradicate sexism. In fact, those contradictory signs of progress—high-profile successes that mask persistent inequality—are precisely the problem. Douglas describes those mixed messages as "enlightened sexism": the idea that because of all the gains women have made, biases that once would have been deemed sexist now get brushed off. Young women, consequently, are left in a bind: they worry they'll never be taken as seriously as the guys, yet when they're given the opportunity to run the show, they balk. A recent Girl Scouts study revealed that young women avoid leadership roles for fear they'll be labeled "bossy"; another survey found they are four times less likely than men to negotiate a first salary. As it turns out, that's for good reason: a Harvard study found that women who demand higher starting salaries are perceived as "less nice," and thus less likely to be hired. "This generation has had it ingrained in them that they must thrive within a 'yes, but' framework: Yes, be a go-getter, but don't come on too strong. Yes, accomplish, but don't brag about it," says Rachel Simmons, author of *The Curse of the Good Girl.* "The result is that young women hold themselves back, saying, 'I shouldn't say this, ask for this, do this—it will make me unlikable, a bitch, or an outcast.'"

Somewhere along the road to equality, young women like us lost their voices. So when we marched into the workforce and the fog of subtle gender discrimination, it was baffling and alien. Without a movement behind us, we had neither the language to describe it nor the confidence to call it what it was. "It's so much easier when you're the generation that gets to fight against [specific] laws than it is to deal with these more complicated issues," says Gail Collins, the *New York Times* columnist. In a highly sexualized, post-PC world, navigating gender roles at work is more confusing than ever. The sad truth is that when we do see women rise to the top, we wonder: was it purely their abilities, or did it have something to do with their looks? If a man takes an interest in our work, we can't help but think about the male superior who advised "using our sexuality" to get ahead, or the manager who winkingly asked one of us, apropos of nothing, to "bake me cookies." One young colleague recalls being teased about the older male boss who lingered near her desk. "What am I supposed to do with that? Assume that's the explanation for any accomplishments? Assume my work isn't valuable?" she asks. "It gets in your head, which is the most insidious part."

Recognizing that sexism still exists despite its subtlety is one of the challenges of the new generation—though it doesn't hold a candle to what the dollies of 1970 pulled off. When they filed their legal complaint, the bottom tiers of the *Newsweek* masthead were filled almost exclusively by women. "It was a nice place—especially if you were a man," says Nora Ephron, a *Newsweek* "mail girl" in 1962. The women reported on the murder of a colleague, the State Department, and the 1968 campaign. But when it came to writing, they were forced to hand over their reporting to their male colleagues. "It was a very hopeless time," remembers Brownmiller. "After a while you really did start to lose your confidence. You started to think, 'Writing is what the men do.'"

Over dinner one night, a young researcher poured out her frustration to a lawyer friend, who ordered her to call the Equal Employment Opportunity Commission. She did, and slowly her colleagues signed on to a class-action suit. They found a fiery young lawyer—now D.C. Congresswoman Eleanor Holmes Norton—and they waited, nervously, until the time was right. "We were very staid, ladylike, not guerrilla-theater types," says Pat Lynden, one of the group's early organizers, who wrote cover stories for *The Atlantic Monthly* and *The New York Times Magazine* even while she wasn't allowed to write for *Newsweek*. "But eventually we just couldn't take it anymore."

A year later, as the national women's movement gathered steam, *Newsweek*'s all-male management decided to put feminism on their cover. Oblivious to the rebellion brewing at home, they looked past the legions of *Newsweek* women and went outside the building for a writer—to the wife of one of their top brass, whom they would ultimately describe, in an editor's note, as "a top-flight journalist who is also a woman." It was the final straw. The night before the issue hit newsstands, the *Newsweek* women sent a memo announcing a press conference. They pooled their money to fly a colleague to Washington to present a copy to Katharine Graham, the magazine's owner, who later asked, "Which side am I supposed to be on?" Then on Monday, March 16, 1970, the *Newsweek* women did what journalists do best: they took their story public. Crowded into a makeshift conference room at the ACLU, *Newsweek*'s "news hens" (as a local tabloid called them) held up a copy of their magazine, whose bright yellow cover told their own story: "Women in Revolt." Two days later the women of *The Ladies' Home Journal* would stage their own sit-in; others were soon to follow.

It was a moment of hope, one that set the stage for a wave of progress that continued rapidly through the 1990s. Twenty years after the *Newsweek* dollies rose up, mothers were entering the workforce in unprecedented numbers, women's organizations such as NOW saw surges in membership, and expanded affirmative-action programs ensured that girls had equal access to education. "Girl power" became the new female mantra, and young women's empowerment groups sprang up at YWCAs. By 2000, when the female employment rate peaked, many women thought the job was done.

In the years since, there has been what Douglas describes as "a subtle, insidious backlash." In the face of 9/11, two wars, and now the Great Recession, gender equality—and stereotyping—became a secondary concern. Feminism was no longer a label to be worn with pride; Britney Spears and Paris Hilton now dominated airwaves. But the changes were more than cultural. The Global Gender Gap

Index—a ranking of women's educational, health, political, and financial standing by the World Economic Forum—found that from 2006 to 2009 the United States had fallen from 23rd to 31st, behind Cuba and just above Namibia. Companies may have incorporated policies aimed at helping women, but they haven't helped as much as you'd think. "The U.S. always scores abysmally in terms of work-life balance," says the WEF's Kevin Steinberg. "But even here, [women] still rank 'masculine or patriarchal corporate culture' as the highest impediment to success." Exhibit A: the four most common female professions today are secretary, registered nurse, teacher, and cashier—low-paying, "pink collar" jobs that employ 43 percent of all women. Swap "domestic help" for nurse and you'd be looking at the top female jobs from 1960, back when want ads were segregated by gender.

The women of *Newsweek* thought, or hoped, they'd begun to solve these problems four decades ago. Yet here we are. "It's sad," says Lynden, now 72. "Because we fought for all that." There's no denying that we're enjoying many of the spoils of those women's victories. We are no longer huddled in secret; we're reporting for a national magazine, and we're the ones doing the writing. We have a president whose first act in office was to sign a law that promises equal pay for equal work. Yet the fact that such a law is necessary makes the point: equality is still a myth. "We've got the entire weight of human history behind us, making us feel like we're kind of lucky to have jobs," says writer Ariel Levy. "And I think it takes a lot of fearlessness to think, 'F—k it, go ahead and yell at me, I'm going to fight for what I deserve.'" We've come a long way, baby. But there's still a long way to go.

With Sam Register and Tony Skaggs

A CONVERSATION WITH LYNN POVICH

What inspired you to write The Good Girls Revolt—*and what worried you about writing it?*

I'm at the age when one looks back more than one looks forward. I realized that the *Newsweek* lawsuit had been one of the most influential events in my life—and no one knew about it. The history of our lawsuit had been lost and our legacy as the first women in the media to sue for gender discrimination had been forgotten. I wanted to tell the story of these brave women who opened the doors for so many female journalists—and many other women—so that at least my children, if not the next generation, would know.

However, I worried that no one would be interested in a lawsuit that happened forty years ago—important as it was. There has been great progress for women and people don't think about filing lawsuits as we did in the "protest decades" of the Sixties and Seventies. That was then—this is now. So I was blessed when I got a call in 2010 from three young women working at *Newsweek* who were experiencing similar obstacles in the workplace as we had forty years earlier. They had just found out about our lawsuit and were eager to hear about it. I realized our story still resonated and had relevance to young women in the workplace today.

How hard was it to interview people forty years after the event and did anyone object?

I wouldn't advise doing it! Some people have excellent memories but most of us are very selective in what we remember. Although I had the legal papers from the lawsuit, there wasn't any other original material so I had to report most of the book and reconstruct the story from interviews. The problems arose when someone's "clear" memory conflicted with another's "clear" memory. At those times I tried to triangulate and call others to see what they thought. And when I couldn't figure out which story was truly accurate, I resorted to saying, "As so-and-so remembered it."

Almost all of the women I interviewed were happy to talk because, like me, they wanted the story to get out. Only one woman, who gave me a long and very helpful interview, asked me not to quote her, so I didn't. But I knew a lot of her story from my own experience and others did too, so she is well represented in the book and is an important character.

What did you learn in writing the book?

There were stories women told me that truly shocked and dismayed me. The researcher who was not only stalked by her senior editor, which I did know, but who was told that if she didn't marry him she would have to leave, which I didn't know. Trish Reilly's story of turning down two promotions, panicking, and leaving *Newsweek*. And the story of Oz Elliott calling Fay Willey—twice—the night before we were going to sign our lawsuit to ask her to stop it and suggest that if we filed it, it would contribute to the Nixon administration's war on the "Eastern establishment elitist press."

I also learned a lot from the young women in the book who were working at *Newsweek* in 2010. It was interesting to me that when they came upon obstacles at work they didn't identify it as a gender issue. Like us forty years earlier, they thought it was them—they just weren't good enough. That surprised me because this generation was raised in the era of Girl Power. They were also told that you can be anything, you can do anything, the sex wars are over and there's a level playing field, which may be true for girls in school—but not so much in the work world. So learning about our story and meeting us changed their lives, too, and brought me in touch with this next generation of working women.

What surprised you about the responses to the book—positive and negative?

I figured that women who lived through the sixties and seventies would respond positively to the book because we all have these stories—and they have. Many are reading *The Good Girls Revolt* in their book clubs and giving it to their daughters so that they will know what the times were like for women and what their mothers went through.

What surprised me was how positively young women have responded to the book. I've been asked to speak to many colleges and universities, to people who have no idea of what women were up against back then. And they are fascinated. One reason is they can't believe how bad it was! It's like reading about the middle ages—people actually said that? But they are also interested in the personal struggles we went through because they are going through them, too—struggles about ambition, career, family issues, and managing it all—and, of course, sexism, which still exists even on campus.

I haven't heard too many negative responses. When I have it's from people who think women have succeeded and there isn't much gender discrimination anymore. If anything, they say we have to worry about the men.

What do you think about the current public discussion on women in the workplace today, the issues raised by Yahoo CEO Marissa Mayer and Facebook COO Sheryl Sandberg?

I give Sheryl Sandberg a lot of credit. When I was editor-in-chief of *Working Woman* magazine, I interviewed a lot of female CEOs and almost none of them wanted to be called a female CEO nor did they want to talk about women's issues. So I applaud her putting herself on the line for feminism and raising these issues. She restarted an important conversation and look, we're still talking about it.

Sheryl Sandberg's book, *Lean In*, has a lot of research and advice about gender bias in the workplace. Her book is about getting women into leadership positions so she focused a lot of the book on how women hold themselves back as well as the institutional barriers. And she raises very interesting points about women—especially younger women—not pushing themselves forward, not taking on riskier assignments, holding themselves back because they're considering having a family. And many younger women are grateful for her advice. One more thing: Sheryl Sandberg talks about an "ambition gap"—that women have to be more ambitious at work and men more ambitious at home. I think what she really means is that women have a "confidence gap"—still—and that's what I find fascinating.

As for Marissa Mayer, like all women at the top, everyone is looking at her and she's got big problems at Yahoo. So I understand that her priority is to make Yahoo successful. She felt she had to have everyone in the office to do that so she cancelled Yahoo's flexible hours policy. I think there are more reasonable ways to get people into the office without penalizing everyone and I don't think that is the way the workplace is evolving. All the research says that flexible hours increase productivity, health, and morale.

What happened to the three young women who were working at Newsweek *in 2010, Jessica Bennett, Sarah Ball, and Jesse Ellison?*
They all are doing very well in journalism but not at *Newsweek*. Sarah Ball is the deputy editor of Vanityfair.com. Jessica Bennett is a freelance journalist and editor-at-large for Sheryl Sandberg's "Lean In" foundation, which aims to increase the number of women in leadership positions. Jesse Ellison is now doing freelance journalism. Sadly, in December 2012, *Newsweek* printed its last magazine edition and is now available only in digital form.

QUESTIONS FOR THOUGHT AND DISCUSSION

1. What motivated the *Newsweek* women to sue their bosses? Do you think they should have aired their complaints to management first? Would you have joined the group? Do you think your mother would have joined? Your daughter?

2. What did you think about the choice *Newsweek*'s black researchers made not to participate in the suit?

3. What was the impact of the women's movement on the *Newsweek* women? How was feminism portrayed through the leading characters in *Good Girls Revolt*: the researchers, Liz Peer, Fay Willey, Eleanor Holmes Norton, Katharine Graham, and Lynn Povich herself?

4. How did the legal styles of Eleanor Holmes Norton and Harriet Rabb differ and why?

5. Why was the lawsuit ultimately so effective? What were the factors that contributed to the *Newsweek* women's success? And why do you think their case was largely forgotten over the years?

6. How do the *Newsweek* women change over the course of the narrative? What did you think about the women who couldn't make the transition to being "liberated" professional working women?

7. In the interview with Lynn Povich included in this reading guide, she makes a distinction between an "ambition gap" and a "confidence gap" inhibiting women in the work world. Do you agree? What, if anything, do you think inhibits you?

8. Have you had an insight or experience that ended up changing you, the way Lynn's and her colleagues' recognition that the "rules of work" were unjust changed them?

9. What do you think about the attitudes of the young women working at *Newsweek* in 2010? What do you think has changed and hasn't changed for women in the workplace today compared to forty years ago?

10. In telling the story of the first and the second rounds of the lawsuit, Povich draws a distinction between legal change and cultural change; between "official policy" and how things actually happen on the ground. What stories in the book illuminate that distinction? Have you recognized or experienced similar "disconnects" and discrepancies in your own life, or see them in the world around you?

11. If you saw something illegal or immoral happening in your workplace today, what would you do about it?

INDEX

Abbott, Leandra Hennemann,
  76
ABC, 108, 165, 194, 211
Abortion rights, 107, 163
Abramson, Jill, 193
Abzug, Bella, 107, 162
African Americans. *See* Black
  Americans
Agnew, Spiro, 94–95
Agrest, Susan, 6
Alexander, Shana, 145
*All Those Mornings. . . . At the
  Post* (Povich), 221
Ambition gap, 12, 199
American Civil Liberties
  Union (ACLU), 2, 81,
  84, 97, 108, 119
Associated Press, 9, 193
AT&T, 163
Atlantic (magazine), 62, 64,
  164, 202
Axthelm, Pete, 40, 44, 114

Back pay, 154, 155, 157
Ball, Sarah, 189, 190, 196,
  198, 199
Baltimore Sun (newspaper), 9,
  210

Barbi, Olga, 3, 74, 105, 145
Beatty, Warren, 184
Beauvoir, Simone de, 141
Beebe, Frederick "Fritz," 10
Benchley, Peter, 29
Bender, Marilyn, 157
Bennett, Jessica, 189, 190,
  192, 195, 196–197, 198,
  199–200
Bernstein, Lester, 99, 101,
  113, 120
Birth control pill, 12–13, 43
Black Americans
  in Congress, 162
  coverage of, 37
  as editors, 140–141, 188,
    193–194
  feminist movement and
    women as, 76, 84–85
  media-related lawsuit
    involving, 140, 148
  no attempt by, at *Newsweek*,
    to organize, 170–171
  quotas and discrimination
    against, issue of, 106–107
  recruiting women as, for the
    lawsuit, 76
  as reporters, 121, 140, 170

Black Americans *(continued)*
  as researchers, 216
  signatories on the lawsuit
    and, 87
  in writing positions, 105,
    119, 170
Blair, Gwenda, 208
Blocker, Joel, 22, 113–114,
  117–118, 123, 169
Blumenfeld, Helaine, 171
Boeth, Dick, 39, 47, 114, 134,
  135–137, 182
Bonventre, Pete, 44, 186
Borchgrave, Arnaud de, 23
Borgeson, Roger, 108
Boylan, Betsy Wade. *See*
  Wade, Betsy
Brackman, Jake, 88
Bradlee, Ben, 34, 35, 139,
  140
Braudy, Susan, 117–118, 123
Brazaitis, Tom, 213
Breach-of-contract suit, 133
Bright, Barbara, 117, 123
Brown, Helen Gurley, 7
Brown, Tina, 192–193
Brown v. Board of Education,
  67
Browning, Dominique,
  187–188
Brownmiller, Susan, 7, 8, 10,
  29, 98, 100–101, 115
Broyles, Bill, 208
Brynner, Rock, 211
Buckley, Kevin, 43, 88
BusinessWeek (magazine), 116,
  183, 184, 214, 220

Califano, Joseph A. "Joe," Jr.,
  148–152, 153, 157, 216–
  217
Camp, Holly, 5, 97
Camper, Diane, 76, 210–211
Carroll, Connie, 153
Carroll, Kathleen, 193
Carter, Betsy, 40, 44, 45, 115,
  172, 204
Carter, Jimmy, 181, 213, 215,
  216
Carter, John Mack, 7–8
CBS News, 169, 194, 206, 219
Center for the Study of
  Women, UCLA, 202
Child care, issue of, 107, 113,
  163–164, 194, 198
Chisholm, Shirley, 84, 162
Christopher, Bob, 76–77, 120,
  179
City University of New York
  (CUNY) Graduate School
  of Journalism, 220, 221
Civil Rights Act, 9, 29, 56, 85,
  86
Clark, Matt, 211–212
Classified ads, segregation of,
  15–16, 59
Clay, Margaret Montagno. *See*
  Montagno, Margaret
Clay, Pete, 203
Cleveland Plain Dealer
  (newspaper), 194
"Click!" moment, 52–53, 56,
  195
Clift, Brooks, 213
Clift, Eleanor Roeloffs,
  121–122, 181, 213–214

Coleman, Elisabeth "Lala," 46,
    73–74, 93, 121, 211
Coleman, Kate, 46–47
Collins, Gail, 13, 159–160
Columbia Journalism School,
    170, 183, 218
Columbia Law School, 124,
    129, 153, 156, 216
Comprehensive Child
    Development Act,
    163–164
Congress on Racial Equality
    (CORE), 83
Congress to Unite Women,
    69, 117
Consciousness-raising, 51–52,
    53, 141–142, 177, 203,
    212
Cook, Bill, 100
Cook, Joan, 157
Cooper, George, 129, 130
Cooper, Rich, 148, 152, 153
Cosmopolitan (magazine), 7, 42

Daily Beast (website), 193, 195
Daughters of Bilitis, 69
Davidson, Barbara, 123
Deming, Angus, 77
Deming, Madlyn Millimet. *See*
    Madlyn Millimet
Detroit News (newspaper), 9
Diamond, Ed, 46–47, 100, 118
Dirksen, Everett, 86
Dudar, Helen, 5, 87, 95–97,
    171
Duhau, Jacqueline, 23
Edmonson, Madeleine, 87, 108

Education Amendments Act,
    161
*Elizabeth Boylan v. The New
    York Times Company*, 156
Elliott, Osborn "Oz," 6–7, 10,
    15, 17, 23–24, 31, 33–39,
    41, 55, 90, 93–95, 97,
    98, 101–103, 105, 108,
    109, 111, 120, 142,
    145–147, 150, 151, 152,
    153, 169, 172, 176, 195,
    203, 216, 218–219
Ellison, Jesse, 189, 190, 195,
    196–197, 197–198, 199
Employment Rights Project,
    153, 216
Ephron, Nora, 18, 28–29,
    30–31, 42, 95, 115, 116
Equal Employment
    Opportunity Commission
    (EEOC), 1, 5, 56, 61, 69,
    97, 130, 133, 140, 144,
    153, 159, 163, 165, 215
Equal Pay Act, 9
Equal Rights Amendment, 163
Essence (magazine), 121

Facebook, 12, 199
Famous Writers School,
    134–135, 146
Federal Communications
    Commission (FCC), 165
Felker, Clay, 141, 146, 147
Fels, Anna, 11, 198, 199
Finberg, Alan, 148
Fire in My Soul (Lester), 82
Firestone, Shulamith, 8

Footlick, Jerry, 113–114
Fortune (magazine), 9, 123, 166–167
Fourteenth Amendment, 83, 163
Fraker, Susan, 170
Francke, Linda Bird, 147–148, 208, 209
Freeman, David, 202
Friedan, Betty, 69, 107–108, 162, 202
Friedrich, Otto, 77–79

Gander, Rod, 55, 74, 88, 93, 102, 106, 108, 114, 119, 122, 130–131, 132, 146
Gannett, 193
Gay rights, 4, 10, 69
Gelber, Alexis, 188
Gelman, David, 185
Gerry, Val, 104
Gilliam, Dorothy, 140–141
Gingold, Judy, 87, 98
  background of, 53–55
  beginnings as ring leader, 57, 60
  consciousness-raising of, 51, 52
  follow-up on, 201–202
  as lawsuit ring leader, 5, 61, 64, 69, 70
  path to the "click!" moment for, 55–57
  recruiting women for the lawsuit, 71–72, 73, 77, 79
  respect for editors felt by, 89–90

signing first settlement agreement, 108
writing tryouts and, 168
Ginsburg, Ruth Bader, 163
Glamour (magazine), 118
Global Report on the Status of Women in the News Media (2011), 194
Glueck, Grace, 157
Golden, Soma, 184
Goldman, Peter, 5, 20, 30, 37–38, 40, 47, 90, 95, 99, 100, 114, 134–135
Goldstein, Matthew, 220
Goldstein, Rita, 76–77
Good Housekeeping (magazine), 8
Goodman, Ellen, 28–29, 31, 219
Gore, Allen, 64, 204
Gosnell, Mariana, 89, 108, 150, 152, 153, 168, 211, 212
Graham, Don, 188
Graham, Katharine "Kay," 3, 6, 10, 65, 89, 103, 104–105, 108–109, 116–117, 140, 141–144, 148, 150, 151, 152, 153–154, 169, 187, 189, 193, 216
Graham, Philip L., 34–35, 103
Greenfield, Meg, 141, 145, 159
Griffiths, Martha, 86
Gunderson, Karen, 31

Hadden, Brit, 16, 17
Hagerty, Shew, 46, 100, 118, 123
Hall, Trish, 159
Halston cover story, 169
Harman, Sidney, 192
Harper's (magazine), 77, 79
Hefner, Hugh, 117
Height, Dorothy, 84
Hershey, Lenore, 8
Hertzberg, Rick, 88
Higgenbotham, A. Leon, Jr., 83
Holmes, Coleman, 81
Holmes, Richard, 81
Howard, John Eager, 58
Howard, Lucy, 3, 5–6, 7, 13, 19, 20, 43, 46, 57, 60, 98, 135
  background of, 58–60
  follow-up on, 202–203
  as lawsuit ring leader, 61, 64
  promotion of, 167
  recruiting women for the lawsuit, 71, 72
  salary of, 88
  signing first settlement agreement, 108
Humphrey, Hubert, 60
Hylton, Liz, 142

Institute for the Study of Women and Men in Society, USC, 202
International Women's Media Foundation, 194, 220
Iselin, John Jay, 55, 60

Jefferson, Margo, 170–171
Jezebel (blog), 197–198
Johnson, Lyndon B., 35, 86, 148
Jones, Jim, 118–119
Jordan, Barbara, 162
Junck, Mary, 193

Kalins, Dorothy, 188
Kellogg, Mary Alice, 121
Kennedy, John F., 35, 36, 60
Kennedy (Onassis), Jacqueline, 177
Kennedy, Robert F., 26–27, 57, 60
Kessler, Gladys, 55–56
Kilgour, Alison, 87
King, Billie Jean, 161–162
King, Martin Luther, Jr., 57, 83
Kinoy, Arthur, 126, 127–128
Klein, Ed, 177–178
Kosner, Ed, 40, 64, 167, 168, 171, 172, 173, 175, 176, 177
Krisher, Bernie, 39
Kroll, Jack, 48–49, 112, 114, 147, 168–169, 170, 209
Kunstler, Bill, 126, 127, 128

Ladies' Home Journal (magazine), 7–8
Lansner, Kermit, 36, 99, 101, 102, 104, 108, 111, 116, 120
Lee Enterprises, 193
Lerner, Alan Jay, 31
Lester, Joan Steinau, 82, 83

Levin, Judy, 51, 52
Lichtenstein, Grace, 156, 158
Life (magazine), 9, 145, 164, 166–167
Lilith (magazine), 164
Lindsay, John, 61, 84, 105
Look (magazine), 164, 214
Los Angeles Times (newspaper), 202, 213
Lubenow, Jerry, 100
Luce, Henry, 16, 17, 20
Lynch, Vela, 81–82
Lynden, Pat, 5, 6, 11, 28, 40, 61–62, 95, 96, 98, 115, 167
  background of, 62–64
  follow-up on, 204–205
  as lawsuit ring leader, 70
  recruiting women for the lawsuit, 71, 77, 79
  salary of, 88
  signing first settlement agreement, 108
  writing tryouts and, 113–114, 123

Mad Men (television show), 43, 200
Malamud, Phyllis, 72–73, 88, 108, 130, 153, 182, 211–212
Manning, Gordon, 36
Martin, Dwight, 40, 69, 115, 130, 168, 172
Martore, Gracia, 193
McCabe, Inger, 218
McCall's (magazine), 8, 145

McCarthy, Eugene, 57, 60
McDaniel, Ann, 188–189, 190
McDonald, Karen, 99
McGraw-Hill, 214
McLaughlin Group, The (television show), 213
McLean, Edward B., 65
McLoughlin, Merrill "Mimi," 74–75, 100, 108, 130, 133, 153, 168, 182, 187, 205–206
Meacham, Jon, 190, 192
Metro Seven, 140–141
Meyer, Eugene, 34, 65
Michener, Charlie, 177
Miller, Mark, 190, 191
Millett, Kate, 107
Millimet, Madlyn, 77
Mink, Patsy, 162
Montagno, Margaret, 47, 57, 60, 80, 98, 115, 153
  complaint filed by, 144–145
  follow-up on, 203–204
  as lawsuit ring leader, 61, 64
  promotion of, 167–168
Ms. (magazine), 52, 117, 141, 165, 171
MSNBC.com (website), 220
Murray, Pauli, 83
Myth of Equality, The (blog), 197
"Myth of the Vaginal Orgasm, The" (Koedt), 164

National Association for the Advancement of Colored People (NAACP), 82, 83

National Black Feminist
Organization, 162–163
National Organization for
Women (NOW), 108, 165
National States' Rights Party,
84
National Women's Party, 86
National Women's Political
Caucus, 162
NBC, 3, 9–10, 52, 98,
165–166, 194, 220
*Necessary Dreams: Ambition in
Women's Changing Lives*
(Fels), 11
New Haven Journal-Courier
(newspaper), 159
New Haven Register
(newspaper), 9
New York City Commission
on Human Rights, 105,
119, 165, 167, 215
New York Daily News
(newspaper), 2, 118
New Yorker (magazine), 60,
88, 192
New York (magazine), 141,
146, 147
New York Post (newspaper), 5,
30, 95, 141
New York Radical Feminists,
8
New York Radical Women, 51
New York State Division of
Human Rights, 133, 144,
153, 166
New York Times Magazine, 62,
86, 113, 117, 164

New York Times (newspaper),
2, 19, 109, 116, 119,
170, 181, 184, 193, 210,
212
lawsuit involving, 9, 154,
155–159, 160, 216, 217
New York Woman (magazine),
63, 204
New York Women's Exchange,
60–61
Newsday (newspaper), 2, 9
Newspaper Guild, 89, 131,
133, 149, 167
Newsweek Inc., 111, 188
Newsweek lawsuit (first)
agreement reached in
settlement of, 106–109
breach-of-contract suit
following, 134
failure of
editors/management to
enforce the agreement
from, 111–124
finding suitable lawyer for,
80–81
as first media-related lawsuit,
1–2, 85, 201
fortieth anniversary of, 190,
191, 193, 196
influence on younger
generation of women,
195–197
initial responses to, 5,
98–99, 99–100
leaks exposing possible plans
for, 93–94
negotiations following

Newsweek lawsuit (first) *(continued)*
  announcement of, 102–103, 104, 105–106
  new lawyer hired for new negotiations following, 124, 129, 130–134
  organizing/recruiting for the, 71–92
  press conference announcing, 1, 2–3, 97–98
  ring leaders of the, 51–70
  round one of the, 93–109
  as a seminal case, 9, 216
  See also specific people involved in the lawsuit
Newsweek lawsuit (second)
  barricades that fell after, 167–179
  filing of, 144–145
  gearing up for, 139, 144
  negotiations and events during, 148–152
  progress in decades following, 181–189
  response of Oz Elliott and management to, 145–148, 218
  settlement of, 152–153
  See also specific people involved in the lawsuit
Newsweek (magazine)
  beginning of, 17
  caste system at, 42, 96, 99
  comparison to *Time* magazine, 17–18, 19–21, 31, 36, 37, 78, 99

  controversial story on women in the workplace, 189–192, 195, 196–198
  cover stories on the feminist movement, 1, 4, 5, 87, 95–97, 164, 182, 190, 197
  coverage of women and women's issues, change in, 182–183
  flirting and office flings at, 43–44, 45–50
  government criticism of, 94–95
  growth of, 35
  ownership of, 3, 34–35, 77, 192
  parts dividing, sections in, 25–26, 27–28, 40–41
  sexual harassment at, 47–49
  Sixties culture in, 39–40
  spoof of the writing style of, 135–137
  subtle gender discrimination still at, 191–192
  top editors of, 36
  weekly routine at, 41–42
  writing style of, 114–115
  See also specific staff members
Nineteenth Amendment, 107
Nixon administration, 94, 97, 127, 128, 164
No More Fun and Games (journal), 164
Norton, Eleanor Holmes, 9, 119, 124, 134
  approach of, 129–130
  background of, 81–84

follow-up on, 215–216
hired as lawsuit lawyer, 87
Katharine Graham's attitude
    towards, 142–143
meeting with Oz Elliott and
    Kermit Lansner, 102
and negotiations following
    lawsuit announcement,
    104, 105–106, 106–107
reasons for taking on the
    lawsuit, 84–87
recommending legal action,
    89–92
signing first settlement
    agreement, 108
statement read by, at press
    conference, 2–3
at the "Women's Strike for
    Equality" event, 107
Notes from the First Year (New
    York Radical Women),
    164

Onassis, Jacqueline Kennedy,
    177
O'Reilly, Jane, 52–53
Orth, Maureen, 44, 146–147,
    148
Our Bodies, Ourselves (Boston
    Women's Health Book
    Collective), 165

Parker, Maynard, 39, 188
Parks, Rosa, 83
Peer, Liz, 4–5, 23–24, 25, 43,
    100, 114, 151, 171–172,
    177–178, 181, 207–209
Personal History (Graham), 103

Peyser, Marc, 189, 191
Pilpel, Harriet, 80
Plan B (morning-after pill), 198
Playboy (magazine), 117
Pleshette, Mary, 3, 6, 48, 72,
    75, 89, 108, 112, 115,
    123, 176, 209–210
Porter, Bruce, 73
Povich, David, 152
Povich, Ethyl Friedman, 66, 67
Povich, Lynn
    background of, 21–23,
        24–25, 65–69
    breaking the editorial
        barrier, 173–179
    in the decades following
        second lawsuit, 183–187
    follow-up on, 219–222
    as lawsuit ring leader, 152,
        179
    leave of absence, 172
    recruiting women for the
        lawsuit, 71–72, 73
    relationship between
        Katharine Graham and,
        143, 144
    on signing first settlement
        agreement, 109
    signing second settlement
        agreement, 153
Povich, Shirley, 24, 65, 66, 67,
    68, 143–144, 221
Pressman, Gabe, 3, 98

Quindlen, Anna, 158–159
Quinn, Jane Bryant, 10–11,
    28–29, 29–30, 45, 115,
    214–215

Rabb, Bruce, 127, 128, 129
Rabb, Harriet Schaffer
  background of, 125–129
  follow-up on, 216–217
  on her other media-related
    discrimination suits,
    154–157
  hired as lawsuit lawyer for
    new negotiations, 124,
    129, 130–134
  Joe Califano's negotiations
    with, in second lawsuit,
    148–150
  payment of, and signing
    second settlement
    agreement, 153
  reflections back on the
    second lawsuit, 154
Racial bias/discrimination,
  140, 148, 210
Racial discrimination lawsuits,
  67, 82, 140–141, 148
Racial segregation, 67, 82, 83
Radcliffe, 29, 31, 59, 74, 94,
  115
Ragsdale, Noel, 131
Reader's Digest (magazine),
  lawsuit involving, 9,
  154–155, 216
Redstockings, 52, 69
Reilly, Trish, 31, 43, 75–76,
  121–123, 146, 168–169,
  206–207
Reproductive rights, 107, 163,
  198
Riggs, Bobby, 162
Robertson, Nan, 157

Robinson, Janet, 193
Rockefeller University, 217
Roe v. Wade, 163
Ross, Ruth, 121
Ruby, Mike, 115, 187, 206

Saarinen, Aline, 116
Salembier, Valerie, 145–146
Salmans, Sandra, 132
Sandberg, Sheryl, 12, 199
Sarachild, Kathie Amatniek,
  51–52
Saturday Review (magazine),
  164, 220
Schiff, Dorothy, 141
Schroeder, Pat, 162
Sciolino, Elaine, 181
Scott, Ann, 123
Second Sex, The (Beauvoir), 141
Seligmann, Jeanie, 130, 211,
  212
Sex discrimination lawsuits,
  media-related
  additional, 9–10, 140,
    154–160, 165–167, 216,
    217
  first of, 1–2, 85, 201
  future opportunities created
    from, 160
  go-to lawyer for, 216
  See also Newsweek lawsuit
    (first); Newsweek lawsuit
    (second)
Sex discrimination lawsuits,
  other, proliferation of, 163
Sexism in the workplace today,
  189–200

Sex-segregated job ads, 15–16, 59

Sexual harassment, 47–49, 165

Shalala, Donna, 217

Shanahan, Eileen, 157

Sheils, Mimi. *See* McLoughlin, Merrill "Mimi"

Shepard, Steve, 114, 183–186, 219, 220–221

Simmons, Debra Adams, 193

Smith, Howard, 86

Smith, Howard K., 108

Smith, Margaret Chase, 86

Smith, Rick, 187, 188

Smith, Sunde, 6, 121

Sokolov, Ray, 88, 116, 122

Sovern, Michael, 156

Sports Illustrated (magazine), 9, 167

Spurlock, Karla, 87

Stadtman, Nancy, 131, 172

Steinem, Gloria, 107, 141–142, 143, 162, 171, 182

Steuart, Betsy, 52

Student Nonviolent Coordinating Committee, 83, 127

Students for a Democratic Society, 127

Suffragettes, 108

Sulzberger, Arthur Ochs "Punch," Sr., 156

Swann, Annalyn, 187

Terrell, Mary Church, 82

Thomas, Rich, 94

Time Inc., 9, 166–167

Time (magazine), 16–17, 34, 42, 77, 115, 116, 164, 187, 194

comparison to *Newsweek* magazine, 17–18, 19–21, 31, 36, 37, 78, 99

lawsuit involving, 9, 166–167

Title IX, 161

Title VII, 56, 61, 85–86, 129, 130

Tompkins, Grant, 102, 131, 132

Tumblr (website), 195

US Congress, 161, 162, 163, 215

US News & World Report (magazine), 187, 206

US Supreme Court, 16, 67, 82, 83, 84, 163, 210

USA Today (newspaper), 193

Vanity Fair (magazine), 192

Vanityfair.com (website), 198

Vassar College, 21–22

Vietnam War, 12, 36–37, 38–39, 151, 183

Village Voice (newspaper), 72, 146

Vincent Astor Foundation, 34

Voice of the Women's Liberation Movement (newsletter), 164

Voting rights, 107, 126

Wade, Betsy, 156, 157–158

Wage gap, 10, 177, 191

Wall Street Journal (newspaper), 88, 202

Wallendas, 36, 42, 76, 90, 104, 118, 150, 187, 188, 196

Walters, Barbara, 52, 171

Washington Post Company, 3, 103, 148, 188, 192

Washington Post (newspaper), 3, 34–35, 65, 94–95, 103, 145, 193, 214, 221

discrimination at, 139–142

lawsuit involving, 9, 140, 148, 217

Watergate, 143, 167, 183, 210

Waters, Harry, 26–27, 41, 49–50, 69, 100, 114, 175

Watson, Russ, 147–148, 172

Weatherman Underground, 7, 127

Werthman, Ruth, 87

Weymouth, Katharine, 193

When Everything Changed (Collins), 13

Whitaker, Mark, 188

Whitmore, Jane, 121

Wicker, Carole, 42

Willey, Fay, 28, 77, 79–80, 90, 93–95, 97, 108, 121, 205

Willis, Jack, 72, 176, 209

Willis, Mary Pleshette. *See* Pleshette, Mary

Women's Media Group, 7

Women's Wear Daily (newspaper), 103, 104

Woodward, Ken, 175–176

Working Woman (magazine), 220

World of Oz, The (Elliott), 24

Wright, Marian (Edelman), 83

Writer training program, 131, 134–135, 146, 153

Wulf, Mel, 108, 119

Yee, Min, 100

Young, Jeffrey, 25, 44–45, 172, 173–174, 176, 183

Zimmerman, Diane, 118

Zimmerman, Paul, 41–42, 170

Zorn, Franny Heller, 18–19

Lynn Povich is an award-winning journalist who has spent more than forty years in the news business. She began her career at *Newsweek* as a secretary. In 1970, she was one of forty-six women who sued *Newsweek* for sex discrimination. Five years later, Povich was appointed the first woman senior editor in the magazine's history. Povich left *Newsweek* in 1991 to become editor-in-chief of *Working Woman* magazine, the only national business magazine for women. She joined MSNBC.com in 1996 to help launch the twenty-four-hour news and information cable/Internet venture, overseeing the web content of NBC News as well as MSNBC cable.

Povich has received numerous honors, including a 1976 Matrix Award from Women in Communications for Exceptional Achievement in Magazines. In 2005, she edited a book on her father, famed *Washington Post* sports columnist Shirley Povich, called *All Those Mornings . . . At the Post*. A native of Washington, D.C., Povich graduated from Vassar College, where she was executive-in-residence in 1996. She serves on the advisory boards of the International Women's Media Foundation and the Women's Rights Division of Human Rights Watch. She is married to Stephen B. Shepard, former editor-in-chief of *Business Week* and founding dean of the Graduate School of Journalism of the City University of New York. They have two children.

PublicAffairs is a publishing house founded in 1997. It is a tribute to the standards, values, and flair of three persons who have served as mentors to countless reporters, writers, editors, and book people of all kinds, including me.

I. F. STONE, proprietor of *I. F. Stone's Weekly*, combined a commitment to the First Amendment with entrepreneurial zeal and reporting skill and became one of the great independent journalists in American history. At the age of eighty, Izzy published *The Trial of Socrates*, which was a national bestseller. He wrote the book after he taught himself ancient Greek.

BENJAMIN C. BRADLEE was for nearly thirty years the charismatic editorial leader of *The Washington Post*. It was Ben who gave the *Post* the range and courage to pursue such historic issues as Watergate. He supported his reporters with a tenacity that made them fearless and it is no accident that so many became authors of influential, best-selling books.

ROBERT L. BERNSTEIN, the chief executive of Random House for more than a quarter century, guided one of the nation's premier publishing houses. Bob was personally responsible for many books of political dissent and argument that challenged tyranny around the globe. He is also the founder and longtime chair of Human Rights Watch, one of the most respected human rights organizations in the world.

·　　·　　·

For fifty years, the banner of Public Affairs Press was carried by its owner Morris B. Schnapper, who published Gandhi, Nasser, Toynbee, Truman, and about 1,500 other authors. In 1983, Schnapper was described by *The Washington Post* as "a redoubtable gadfly." His legacy will endure in the books to come.

Peter Osnos, *Founder and Editor-at-Large*